MAINSTREAM *SPORT*

LIONS OF WALES

A CELEBRATION OF WELSH RUGBY LEGENDS

PETER JACKSON

MAINSTREAM
PUBLISHING

EDINBURGH AND LONDON

First published in Great Britain in 1998 by
MAINSTREAM PUBLISHING COMPANY (EDINBURGH) LTD
7 Albany Street
Edinburgh EH1 3UG

This edition 1999

ISBN 1 84018 244 X

A catalogue record for this book is available from the British Library

Printed and bound in Finland by WSOY

To Anne for her support, the players for their
unfailing co-operation and the Lions for making
them legends in their spare time

The author wishes to acknowledge the following for their help in the preparation of this book:

Fran Cotton, for writing the foreword; Harry Bowcott, Jack Matthews and Bobby Windsor for providing ready access to their personal scrapbooks; David Rogers, Clive Lewis, Howard Evans, Siân Trenberth and Robert Cole for their photographs; Bill Campbell at Mainstream (it was his idea!) and Cathy Mineards for putting it all together against the clock.

Contents

	Prologue	9
	Foreword by Fran Cotton	13
1	Wine, Women and the Wild Rover	17
2	The Medical Student Who Fought Marciano	26
3	Blessed Bleddyn	39
4	The Man Money Couldn't Buy	51
5	Twinkle, Twinkle, Little Star	66
6	Chopping the Pine Tree	77
7	Mervyn Davies: The Full Case History	88
8	From the Slagheap to Everest	103
9	The King and his Abdication	115
10	Gareth the Great	127
11	Gentleman Gerald and a Twickenham Strike	137
12	The Grand Slam Lunch Bill	148
13	Drunk in Charge	161
14	Game, Set and Match	175
15	A Win Bonus from Robben Island	186
16	The Warrior Prince	197
	Appendix 1: The Test Lions of Wales	209
	Appendix 2: Lions Records	217

Prologue

Whenever Willie John McBride feels the need for a little inspiration, he casts his mind back to a New Zealand winter long ago and conducts an imaginary roll-call in suitably reverential tones: 'Edwards, John, Gibson, Dawes, Davies, Duckham, Bevan and J.P.R. Williams.'

Theirs was arguably the ultimate achievement in Lions history, a unique series victory over the All Blacks made possible by a set of backs who dared to succeed and did so beyond their wildest dreams despite playing behind a largely beaten pack. Against crushing odds, they had the collective wit and nerve to put British and Irish rugby at the summit of the world game. As Willie John, whose powers of endurance established longevity records as a Lion which look to be even more untouchable now than they did when he set them, says, 'I just love repeating the names of those backs. When will we see their like again?'

At the end of the tour the All Blacks paid them the supreme back-handed compliment, their players declining *en masse* to attend the Lions' farewell party despite an invitation extended to them by John Dawes in his capacity as captain.

It is hardly coincidence that of the eight backs to make full appearances throughout that four-match series, six came from Wales. The only other player to appear in a Test behind the scrum as a replacement, for Gareth Edwards in the first match at Dunedin, also came from Wales, Ray 'Chico' Hopkins.

It is an indisputable fact that Wales has provided the Lions with more Test players down the decades than England, Ireland and Scotland, the other countries who form the official organisers of the Lions, the Four

Home Unions. How strange, therefore, that the country responsible for supplying the most players should have had the least number of captains. Of the seventeen Lions tours, seven have been led by Irishmen, with England and Scotland accounting for four apiece. Wales have had two, a disproportionate number even allowing for the fact that at least one tour, New Zealand in 1977, was overloaded by at least three Welshmen too many.

Throughout the two most successful expeditions of all, to New Zealand in 1971 and South Africa three years later, Welsh players never failed to supply the largest representation from one country. In New Zealand, for instance, Welshmen constituted more than half the team for the first three Tests, the Lions starting with nine and finishing the tour with seven. Against the Springboks, they never contributed fewer than six per Test to the only unbeaten Lions series. No wonder they changed the jersey from blue to red!

And what players they were, too, each instantly recognisable to the British rugby public at large by an abbreviated form of identity, a single name, a nickname or nothing more than a set of initials. There was Gareth and Gerald, Benny, Merve the Swerve and The Duke, J.P.R., B.J. and J.J. In the '70s, they were to rugby union, albeit on a much smaller global scale, what Beckenbauer, Cruyff, Moore and Pele were to soccer.

Those who created the Golden Era of Welsh rugby also played an unwitting role in its subsequent demise. Their emergence as the prototype superstars of the game inspired a whole generation of English youngsters, among them three in particular who would repay the favour by demolishing the Arms Park jinx long before the demolition of the old stadium itself.

As a boy, Will Carling supported Wales because they were always the team to beat. Jeremy Guscott followed them in his formative years, acknowledging later how, even when Wales were behind in a Five Nations match at Cardiff with time running out, he knew they would always win, just as Liverpool always seemed to win at Anfield in those days. Guscott contends that legendary status can only be conferred on any player from the British Isles via the Lions, hence his acknowledgement that Wales have so many legends and England so few – although he, unquestionably, is one of them. Rob Andrew, then barely ten years old, made no secret of the fact that Bennett was the player he imagined himself to be in his 'moments of wildest fantasy', a fantasy based on watching the Welshman's mercurial opening gambit in the try of the century during the Barbarians–All Blacks classic in 1973.

Even as devout an Englishman as Brian Moore concedes, if somewhat grudgingly, that Wales of the '70s left a lasting impression. The international match he attended at Twickenham in February 1978 turned out to be Gareth Edwards's 50th. The budding English hooker remembers waving a flag in the enclosure and 'an irate, horrible Welshman grabbing it. I placed the rude Welshman in my memory and stored it up for later motivational use.'

Selecting the Lions of Wales was no easy task, given the wealth of talent from which to choose. The first task was knowing where to begin. There had been eight British tours to the outposts of the old Empire between 1888 and 1910 but none constituted a truly representative British Isles team in the accepted sense. The first such tour took place to South Africa in 1924, under the official, if long-winded, title of The British Isles Rugby Union Touring Team. Exactly when they became the Lions and precisely who coined the most enduring soubriquet in the game, nobody knows for sure, but the title had won sufficient approval from the Four Home Unions for James 'Bim' Baxter to wear a Lions lapel badge throughout his management of the 1930 tour of New Zealand and Australia, an epic spanning five months and thirty matches.

This book makes no claims, least of all to being a definitive account of the Lions of Wales. Mine is purely a subjective choice, from Harry Bowcott in the '30s, through the decades via Bleddyn Williams, Cliff Morgan, David Watkins and the '70s gang, to the present and Ieuan Evans, Scott Gibbs and Neil Jenkins, whose achievements have been widely documented and acclaimed in recent publications.

The result is nothing more, nothing less than an attempt to do justice to a group of extraordinary players. Some experienced tragedy as well as triumph, but they shared a common denominator: their deeds on the fields of glory.

Foreword by Fran Cotton

Fran Cotton was manager of the victorious 1997 Lions in South Africa and a major figure in three Lions tours as a player, first as a permanent member of the Test front row during the unbeaten series against the Springboks in 1974, then in New Zealand three years later, and again three years after that. A former England captain, he played 30 times for his country.

To be a British Lion is the pinnacle of any British or Irish rugby player's career. Like all young boys, as a youngster my imagination was fired up by the Lions legends of the past such as Bleddyn Williams, Cliff Morgan, Tony O'Reilly, Jeff Butterfield and Hughie McLeod, whose great deeds on Lions tours are part of our rugby folklore. For me to go on three Lions tours as a player, in 1974, 1977 and 1980, and to manage the 1997 tour was beyond my wildest dreams.

Lions tours were changed forever in 1971 when we won a Test series in New Zealand for the first time. Previously, only the 1955 tourists to South Africa had distinguished themselves by drawing the series instead of losing it, as had been the case in the past.

The turning point for the Lions coincided with the dominance in European rugby of one of the greatest Welsh teams of all time and the acceptance of coaching, which had been regarded with suspicion because of fears that it would stifle flair and instinct. How ironic it was that the Welsh team of the late '60s and early '70s was a cut above the rest because it was full of flair players whose individual brilliance could win a game on its own: J.P.R. Williams, Gerald Davies, John Dawes, John Bevan, Barry John and Gareth Edwards – a backline that any country in the world, even in the modern era, would kill for. Add to that arguably the finest coach these islands have ever produced in Carwyn James and a pack of forwards that won more than 40 per cent of possession and it is easy to see how the series was won in 1971 and the British Lions' reputation for playing expansive rugby enhanced.

The 1971 tour laid the foundation for success three years later in South Africa. It was my first Lions tour and I always say it was the easiest rugby I have ever played in the sense that, for once, you only had to do your own job and not worry about anyone else.

The forwards of '74, who developed into a superb unit, had one task: to deliver good ball to Gareth Edwards. Gareth was the greatest rugby player I ever played with. I never lost a game when he was in the same team and in '74 he was at his absolute peak. He tormented the opposition.

When Gareth finished with the ball, he had his half-back partner Phil Bennett to call on. The debate continues to rage in Wales as to whether Bennett or Barry John was the better fly-half. All I can say is that if Barry was better than the Bennett vintage of '74, he must have been superhuman. Benny was brilliant, particularly on the hard grounds of the high veldt. When Gareth and Phil were at half-back, you only ever went forward. How I envied the Welsh forwards throughout the '70s.

The Lions of '74 earned a reputation for having a hard, competitive edge, and none was more competitive than J.P.R. Whether in a Test match or at a training session, he only ever gave 100 per cent commitment. Whatever he did, tackling, counter-attacking, catching high balls and even joining the odd fracas, J.P.R. was awesome. Turning around to see him at full-back gave one an inner glow of confidence.

Just as competitive was J.J. Williams, who finished the series with a record number of tries. He was the consummate finisher whose pace, work rate and deft kicking skills made him a very dangerous opponent. He became a great mate during the '74 and '77 tours when he also became an honorary member of the front row union – an enormous honour for a winger.

The '74 forwards were a tough, battle-hardened group, many of whom had earned their spurs in '71. 'Mighty Mouse' McLauchlan, McBride, Brown, Slattery and Merve the Swerve were the hard core. Mervyn Davies was supreme in the Test pack and the pivotal triangle of Davies, Edwards and Bennett is the best the Lions have produced in their history.

I was a new boy in the Test pack along with my front-row colleague Bobby 'The Duke' Windsor. I think Bobby enjoyed the punch-ups more than the rugby and was forever talking to the opposition. I will never forget his classic line in the first Test of the series when Theo Sauerman, the Springbok loose-head prop, was complaining to the referee. It prompted the response: 'Oye! Shut up, puddin' face!' I almost burst out laughing.

The Lions having reigned supreme in '74, the expectations for the tour to New Zealand three years later were high. Seventeen of the players selected were Welsh, and Terry O'Connor, covering the tour for the *Daily Mail*, made the comment that even the itinerary was in Welsh! As often happens, ordinary players surrounded by great players appear better than they really are. To leave players like Mike Slemen and Jim Renwick at home was a mistake.

Phil Bennett was appointed captain and John Dawes coach. John was a disappointment as coach and became embroiled with the media as well as being obsessed with avoiding comparisons with the '71 team. In my view Phil needed the support of stronger management. The fact that he didn't get that resulted in him not enjoying the best of tours. Benny is a lovely man and an all-time great, and I enjoyed his captaincy.

The 1977 tour was a missed opportunity. The Lions had a superb forward unit and, on paper, an exciting backline. If Gareth had toured we would have won the series. Losing the series was the biggest disappointment of my rugby career.

That tour saw the career launch of one of Wales's and the Lions' greatest props, Graham Price. He was my most formidable opponent and, in combination with Peter Wheeler, formed the best front row I ever played in. Only one word comes to mind when thinking of Pricey and that word is respect.

By the time I was asked to manage the Lions tour of South Africa in 1997 there had been a massive shift in the playing power in Europe. England, and occasionally France, held sway, and this was reflected in the selection, with 20 members of the team from England. Even so, Wales made a telling contribution in the form of Scott Gibbs and Neil Jenkins.

Everyone asks me for my finest memory of the tour, expecting me to say Jerry Guscott's drop goal which won the series. They would be wrong, though, because my own personal delight was encapsulated in the moment during that second Test when Scott Gibbs came back on the angle towards the forwards and ran into the 20-stone Springbok prop Os du Randt, dumped him on his backside and carried on. That epitomised the commitment of the squad.

Neil Jenkins won us the series with his phenomenal goalkicking.

What a lovely man. I have the utmost respect for the way he has handled all the stick he has taken from the media in Wales, having to put up constantly with unfair comparisons with Bennett and John. 'Jenks' has just carried on doing what he does best, accumulating points. I still feel he is the answer for Wales at fly-half.

The British and Irish Lions has a proud history and Wales has made an immense contribution. The Lions is a special concept which needs to be maintained and developed. It was only in a Lions shirt that I ever felt totally confident that we could compete on equal terms with the southern hemisphere. Having witnessed the events of the summer of 1998, nothing has changed.

Happy reading.

Fran Cotton, 1998

1

Wine, Women and the Wild Rover

Harry Bowcott was only 22 when they made him captain of Wales. He was still only 22 when the very people behind his appointment made him the ex-captain of Wales. No sooner had they put him there than they gave him the elbow, their hollow words of congratulations over the captaincy still ringing in his ears.

Indecent was scarcely the word for their haste, but then the Welsh have tended to be ruthless in their disposal of losing captains, especially those who commit the cardinal sin of losing to England. They were never more ruthless than during that period between the wars when the master butcher's son from Cardiff began to make his mark on the rugby field.

The fact that Harry Bowcott approaches the millennium as the oldest international of the century at 91 puts him in a class all by himself, his nonagenarian status providing the only enduring link with the Lions of so long ago that they played in a navy strip. He made the tour in spite of the Welsh selectors, not because of them.

When they installed him as captain for the opening match of the 1930 season, against England at Cardiff Arms Park, young Bowcott would have been forgiven for thinking that a poisoned chalice had been raised to his lips. The Big Five's forbearance was such that their latest skipper did not need to overtax his brain power in order to appreciate the consequences of returning to the dressing-room with anything other than a win under his belt.

Selectorial patience with Welsh captains was such that for twenty-one consecutive internationals over the previous six years they had had a different captain for every one. By the time Bowcott found himself thrust into the hottest of hot seats, only one player, William Guy Morgan, defied the trend and actually led his country twice in a row. He had lasted for all of three matches before Bowcott took his bow.

One look at the fate of a myriad predecessors would have convinced him that what he had been handed was liable to be more a notice to quit than an elevation to the highest honour a thankful nation could bestow. No losing captain over the six previous years had lived to tell the tale, and quite a few winning ones hadn't either.

In season 1924–25, for instance, Wales played five internationals and had a different captain for every one: John Wetter (against New Zealand, lost 19–0), Tom Johnson (against England, lost 12–6), Stephen Morris (against Scotland, lost 24–14), Robert Cornish (against France, won 11–5), Walter Idris Jones (against Ireland, lost 19–3).

Plenty more came and went over the next three seasons before Bowcott joined the list. 'The captain was the first one to be kicked out,' he said. 'If you didn't win, you could forget about it for the next game. I knew that if Wales didn't beat England, I'd be for the high jump.'

The jump turned out to be savagely high. Bowcott, a classical centre, lost not only the job but his place in the team for the remainder of the championship. By the time the Lions finalised their list for the New Zealand tour, the former captain of Wales was still in the wilderness, and the selectors decided to leave him there.

'At the time I was considered the one certainty to go, but when the selection was announced my name wasn't there. I was so fed up that I went with the Cambridge team to France a few weeks before the Lions were due to leave. Then something happened. An Irish chap dropped out of the original party. Lo and behold, I was chosen. I'd have been quite happy to have said no. I asked my father, "Should I go?" He said, "Of course you must go."

'I got back from France on the Monday. My father gave me the £80 we all had to pay before departure because I didn't have a penny and I was off to London to join the Lions the following morning for a farewell dinner that night attended by the Duke of York. Excellent meal, as you can imagine. More courses and more wine than you get nowadays, and we all shook hands with the future King.

'There were the usual farewell speeches with the usual nonsense spoken. Most of us managed to find a nightclub of some kind. We were, after all, on the eve of a great adventure into the unknown.'

They set sail from Southampton on the MV *Rangitata*, and the Lions had never run such a tight ship. There were 30 of them, 29 players and an insurance broker from Merseyside who, as manager, would change the shape of New Zealand rugby in a way that no visiting player had done before or has done since. There were no coaches, no doctors, no physiotherapists, no dieticians, no psychologists, no goalkicking gurus and no management consultants. 'And no journalists! There would be no urgent messages flashing back to London saying that we'd been naughty boys. We had the place to ourselves.'

They were not exactly waiting with bated breath in the back streets of Derby, or anywhere else, for news about an event which hardly rated much more than the occasional mention. The British public were far too preoccupied with a new sporting phenomenon that summer, Don Bradman on the first of his three Australian cricket tours of England, to notice what was happening on the other side of the world.

The rugger lads were not exactly complaining at such isolated bliss. Back then nobody, least of all the rugby Establishment, had heard of the Lions, a soubriquet which had still to be coined, let alone pass into common usage for a team officially known by the prosaic title of The British Isles Rugby Union Touring Team.

There must have been good reasons why every player had to stump up £80 as insurance against a tour emergency as well as providing his own dinner suit, but such prerequisites did nothing to dilute the middle-class flavour of an expedition which demanded that the players present themselves for dinner each and every evening suitably attired in black tie.

'The RFU were more concerned about that than the other Unions. They were most anxious that we were seen to be real gentlemen. The menus were delightful, there was always plenty of food and, being young men, we didn't leave much on the table. There was no restriction on food and drink. We did pretty much as we wanted to.

'Nobody had any idea of flying round the world at that time because flying was still a thing of the future. We travelled first class and every player had his own berth for a voyage that lasted five weeks. We had the usual sports on deck. There was the mock court run by the players, but I suppose eating took up most of our time.'

Training, in the loosest sense of the word, was organised by an army officer, Tony Novis, the England wing from Blackheath who had been the oldest surviving Lion prior to his death late in 1997 at the age of 91. Novis was said to have approached training with military precision, starting at seven-thirty sharp each morning and putting the players through their paces for two hours.

Bowcott's recollections of training on ship suggest that it was a lot more genteel and that certainly nobody was in any danger of suffering from exhaustion. 'Nothing too hard. A gentle run round the deck for a quarter of an hour. All we did was keep our legs stretched. It wasn't severe. Don't forget we'd all just finished a long season.

'For a team of young men, there were times when it was a fairly dismal journey. There weren't very many other passengers on ship and the youngest woman on board must have been about 50. There were no young women on board. We had to make our own fun and I would have to say that it wasn't terribly exciting.'

The voyage wasn't exactly a bundle of laughs for one Welshman, Jack Bassett, the coalminer-cum-policeman from Penarth whose perform-ances would earn him lavish praise as a full-back, better even than the renowned George Nepia. 'Bassett was seasick as soon as he got on board,' Bowcott said. 'He didn't get out of his sick bed for ten days. It was entirely mental, if you ask me. Nobody else suffered.'

The social scene would improve appreciably as the tour progressed, but more of that later. The All Blacks soon discovered that in addition to some outstanding players, no Lion was to prove more formidable than their *chef de mission*, a 59-year-old director of a Cheshire insurance company who had been through the mill, propping for Birkenhead Park and England.

James Baxter, 'Bim' to his friends, was not a man to be trifled with. The 28th president of the RFU in season 1926–27, he had won three caps and a silver medal at the 1908 Olympic Games in the 12-metre yachting class. A past captain of both the Mersey Rowing Club and the Royal Liverpool Golf Club, he was decidedly not a member of the 'sweep-it-under-the-carpet' school of rugby administration.

Baxter had done more than play the game at the highest level. He refereed six international matches during the '20s and served as chairman of the Liverpool and District Referees' Society for 19 years. His reaction to what he witnessed in New Zealand, starting with the Wanganui team walking off at half-time for a ten-minute break, guaranteed he would go down in history as the only Englishman to give the All Blacks a collective red card.

Much to the delight, no doubt, of his team, 'Bim' spent a considerable amount of time during the 1930 tour campaigning against what he saw as the illegality of the New Zealand pack, a 2-3-2 formation which provided a two-man front row of specialist hookers and allowed for the detached wing forward to be deployed as an auxiliary scrum-half. They called him 'the Rover', and Baxter wasted no time in letting it be known that such a ploy contravened International Board laws.

The use of that most emotive word in the sporting dictionary, 'cheat', ensured that the row would blaze away from the start of the tour to the finish and beyond. The Lions' first exposure to the seven-man scrum and the Rover, during the opening match at Wanganui, provoked Baxter into firing the first volley, arguing that the tactic was 'contrary to the spirit of rugby football'.

In due course he took an increasingly tougher line, accusing the Rover, in the Test series none other than former All Black captain Cliff Porter, of being a cheat. After New Zealand had won the third Test in Auckland, the hosts could contain themselves no longer, Baxter's opposite number Ted McKenzie choosing the occasion to ignore protocol and give the British a piece of his mind over their persistent condemnation of the wing forward as 'the wolf of the game'.

'Once Mr Baxter called him a cheat,' McKenzie told his captive audience of players, officials and dignitaries in the dining-room of an Auckland hotel. 'I appreciate Mr Baxter's remarks, as they were made by a man so high in the game. And I feel I might reply by criticising certain aspects of the British side's play.'

He then accused them of deliberate obstruction and persistent jersey-pulling. The Lions' acting captain Carl Aarvold, who became His Honour Sir Carl Aarvold, Recorder of London, President of the Lawn Tennis Association and noted after-dinner speaker, tried to interrupt the invective. McKenzie slapped him down: 'I am speaking now, Mr Aarvold, not you.'

Having provoked the diplomatic incident, McKenzie ploughed on regardless, sinking deeper into his mire, as reported by the distinguished New Zealand commentator Winston McCarthy in his book *Haka! The All Blacks' Story*. 'I will not pretend our players are perfect,' McKenzie told the embarrassed assembly. 'They may also on occasions be guilty of lapses in this respect. But I will say that the British team is a fine enough side to win matches without resorting to obstruction and similar tactics which may, or may not, be intentional. But I must say that some of the instances of obstruction appeared to have been deliberately studied.'

And so it went on, right to the bitter end. After the Lions had been routed 22–8 in the final Test in Wellington, Baxter left his hosts in no doubt that the Lions might never darken their shores again because New Zealand were in danger of being outlawed. 'The rules under which we play are laid down by the International Board and, in our opinion, are good enough for the average young man to play under,' he said. 'We don't intend to alter them one jot. Those who don't want to play under them can stay outside.'

The Kiwis, adamant all along that they were not breaking any laws because there was no law at that time to say that a specific number of players constituted a set scrum, ultimately relented, abandoned the seven-man unit and fell into line with the rest of the world, a decision which, if nothing else, ensured that the Lions would, with one glorious exception, go on paying a heavy price once in a while.

The other, lesser controversy could have been avoided with a little gumption on the part of the organisers, the Four Home Unions Tours Committee, an august body of fine, upstanding men representing England, Ireland, Scotland and Wales. Incredibly, it somehow escaped the astute assembly of administrators that black and navy blue was always liable to result in a colour clash. Aware, as surely they must have been, that the All Blacks played in, er, black, the Lions sent their players off on the high seas, each one armed with four jerseys of exactly the same colour. No change strip there. A closer shade of blue to black it would have been hard to find.

'Even people who didn't know a thing about rugby knew that New Zealand played in black,' Bowcott said. 'It became a topic of discussion as soon as they saw the colour of our jerseys. Everywhere we went, they were telling us that we would have to change for the Test matches, but we couldn't change. We had no other jersey to change into.

'Nothing could have been more stupid, but it went on and on until after the first Test. We couldn't understand it. In the end they had to change and play in white jerseys. They weren't at all happy about it.'

The blunder at least paved the way for the birth of a team name which is revered the world over. Each navy jersey carried the motif of three lions, Baxter wore a silver lion lapel badge – and so the famous amalgam of four countries stumbled across a collective name which would give them a unique identity the world over.

On the field, Bowcott and the Swansea hooker Dai Parker established themselves as Test regulars throughout the series, which was more than could be said of the tour captain, Doug Prentice from Leicester. He played in one of the four matches, having the good grace to step down from the other three – unlike more than one of his post-war successors when struggling to justify their place as players.

No Lion, though, made as great an impact on New Zealand as Ivor Jones, the Llanelli back-row forward. They called him 'The King', and a few survivors of the oldest generation scattered around both islands still do. Jones, who devoted a lifetime to the service of Welsh rugby in many guises, including chairman of selectors and president, was almost a one-man team.

There wasn't a thing he couldn't do, including kicking goals, off the ground or out of hand. In another age, he would have been acclaimed as a superstar. He left his indelible mark on New Zealand all those years ago with the decisive act of the first Test at Dunedin, creating the try for Newport wing Jack Morley which gave the Lions a 6–3 win. Almost 70 years on, Bowcott remembers it as though he had witnessed it a few weeks ago.

'It was a very cold day. There were snow showers before the game and a blizzard during it. We changed at the hotel and it was entirely due to Ivor Jones, the king of the tour, that we got off to a winning start. He broke clear at our ten-yard line and went all the way downfield so that there was only George Nepia, the New Zealand full-back, left to stop him.

'He drew Nepia and slipped the ball to Jack Morley for him to get over in the corner. We'd beaten this wonderful team called the All Blacks, much to their disgust. We were delighted. We lost the next three, the third when we were down to fourteen men, but if it hadn't been for poor Sobey, I think we'd have seen them off over the four matches.'

Wilfred Sobey, of Old Millhillians and England, was the best scrum-half of his day. His Lions tour failed to survive the opening match, a severe knee injury forcing him to watch the rest of the tour. In an era when a replacement would take at least five weeks to arrive, the tourists had no alternative but to make do and mend. With the alternative scrum-half, the uncapped Howard Poole from Cardiff, struggling to fill Sobey's boots, the Lions had to improvise.

They converted Dr Paul Murray of Wanderers and Ireland from centre with such immediate success that he stayed there for the rest of the tour, ensuring a supply swift and accurate enough for Bowcott to use his 'spin kick', a technique which he perfected off either foot, 'undercutting' the ball in a way which guaranteed that it spun into touch without losing distance. 'I could land it on a sixpence with either foot,' he said.

When Murray cracked a collarbone during the second Test in Christchurch, who should step into the breach at scrum-half but the fearless Jones, his performance enhancing an already awesome reputation as the most complete British player ever seen in New Zealand. Yet Wales were never to pick him again.

Socially, the Lions swept all before them, whether it was skiing on Mount Cook, studying the geysers in Rotorua or going for broke on the golf course. As amateur sportsmen on the expedition of a lifetime, their existence was always going to be less than monastic, given the native reluctance to let them buy a solitary drink.

'We had a subsistence allowance of 21 shillings (£1.05) a week. Each week we were given chits of paper to that value, some for a shilling (5p), some for sixpence (2½p), and you could spend these at the hotel bar. Unless you were a fool, you didn't have to spend a penny.

'They worshipped us. Entertainment and hospitality were laid on for us and I can't ever remember having to buy a drink. After every match we'd have a dance. There were no bars in the dance hall and no bars outside because they'd all be shut. So we'd go to the tables which were heavily laden, knowing that a lot more liquor would be stored underneath.

'Wives would be chasing us and their husbands would be pleased if we looked after them. As soon as we returned to the hotel from playing the match, we'd get paged. There was one woman who followed me all over both islands with the permission of her old man. He thought it was an honour, and I never abused it. All the fun of the fair!

'We enjoyed ourselves at the right time. We were never denied alcohol but I don't recall any wild boozing. We had just one law before every game: in bed by ten. There was an obligation to carry out the management's wishes to beat these boys but, other than that, there were no restrictions.'

Regrettably, there were no restrictions, either, on New Zealand's tries during the last quarter of the last Test. They scored six, Porter, the rogue Rover, helping himself to two, although by then he was on borrowed time thanks to Mr Baxter's unflinching pursuit of law and order.

The Lions had lost the battle but Baxter would win the war. By 1932 the outraged Lions manager had convinced the custodians of the game, the International Board, to amend the hooking and scrummage offside laws in a way which left the All Blacks no alternative other than to fall into line, despite loud grumbles about the British having far too big a say in the administration of the global game.

The running row did nothing to dilute the popularity of the Lions. 'There were thousands on the quayside at Wellington when we left for Australia,' Bowcott said. 'We'd had a lot of fun before saying our farewells. We were disappointed at having to go.'

More than half a century elapsed before Bowcott was to return to the Land of the Long White Cloud. This time it was on an all-expenses-paid trip to appear on television in a *This Is Your Life* tribute to George Nepia, his renowned opponent from 55 years earlier. Nepia had been given the red-carpet treatment wherever he went in Wales during the Maori tour of 1982 which brought an emotive reunion with Ivor Jones at Stradey Park a few weeks before the old Llanelli warrior died at the age of 80.

By then Bowcott, once instantly recognised for the immaculate centre parting of his hair, had served the Welsh game in a variety of roles since finally making it back from the Lions tour in the October. He had been given a dinner in his honour by the Cardiff club, as well as a token of their appreciation, a pair of silver hairbrushes.

His status among the élite of British and Irish players now beyond dispute despite Wales deciding earlier in the year that he wasn't good enough for them, Bowcott forced the selectors to change their mind, albeit only briefly. They recalled him at outside-half and kept him there for the first two matches of the 1931 championship before reminding him that he still had no immunity from being on the receiving end of their more baffling decisions.

Before the Scotland match at Swansea, the selectors attempted to explain his absence by saying they had asked him to stand down, which gave it a euphemistic spin, if nothing else. Harry would hardly have volunteered to give up his place. The selectorial *raison d'être* in this case was to clear the decks for the introduction of the uncapped Swansea half-backs Ron Morris and Bryn Evans, on their home ground at St Helen's. Wales duly flopped and another piece of strategic planning had backfired.

If Bowcott anticipated an apology from the selectors in the form of his prompt reinstatement, he had another thing coming. The Big Five, for reasons best known to themselves, kept him waiting for so long that Harry, having long graduated from Cambridge with a degree in economics, began to wonder if they had written him off for good.

His return after two years turned out to be well worth the wait, the match coinciding with Wales winning at Twickenham for the first time, at the eleventh time of asking. Bowcott stayed for the next match in Belfast, where an Irish win finished him. This time there was no coming back, at least not as a player. Instead he became an influential figure at London Welsh, gained election to the Welsh Rugby Union in 1961 and duly became chairman of selectors, in charge of the Big Five whose long-departed predecessors had made him suffer more than his fair share of slings and arrows before the war.

A retired civil servant, his presidential season, 1974–75, brought the dazzling dawn of Wales's second golden era, and if recent performances have beggared belief, then the Grand Old Man of British rugby, watching every move from his home in the village of Wenvoe, can at least say he has truly seen it all.

2

The Medical Student Who
Fought Marciano

Between 1947 and 1955, Rocky Marciano bludgeoned every challenger into submission before deciding there was nobody worthwhile left to put away. When he retired as undefeated heavyweight champion of the world, he did so with a record which justified the claim made on his behalf: that he was 'the greatest slugger in boxing history'.

He won all 49 professional fights, 43 by knockout. The long procession of horizontal heavyweights in world-title contests began with Jersey Joe Walcott in Philadelphia in September 1952, and ended the same month three years later in New York with the legendary Archie Moore.

No challenger went the distance with the solitary exception of Ezzard Charles, and once he had demanded a return, Marciano duly knocked him out in eight rounds. The British champion Don Cockell stayed one round longer before being counted out – which was more than The Rock could manage against his previous British opponent.

Not even Marciano could stop a medical student from Bridgend who went on to play rugby for Wales and the Lions. When Jack Matthews climbed into the ring at RAF St Athan in March 1943, it was to box an American whose name, not unnaturally, meant nothing to him. The 19-year-old GI in the opposite corner had still to acquire the abbreviated, anglicised version of the real Italian thing, Rocco Marchegiano. The contest went the scheduled three rounds but ended without a winner being declared. 'That's the way it was, boxing just for the fun of it,'

Matthews said. 'There were no knockdowns and I was still there at the end of the three rounds.

'I didn't know whom I'd fought until years later, when it was confirmed that Marciano had been based at St Athan for a brief period. I'd been told before the fight that he was a useful boy who could punch a bit. He was a hard boy all right. I'd have been 14 stone then and he was a shade lighter, and that's about all I can remember. I was in the pub one night about 50 years later and this bloke came up to me and said, "I was there that night you fought Marciano." Talk about a small world.'

There is but a fleeting reference to Marciano's wartime service in the biography written by Everett Skehan: 'In March 1943, Rocky was drafted into the army. He was stationed in Wales for a while. Then his outfit was assigned to ferry supplies across the English Channel to Normandy. It was one of the least enjoyable periods of his life for, at least temporarily, his dreams of becoming a major league baseball player were sidetracked.'

It could have been worse. Marciano at least avoided any exposure to the Matthews tackle which he executed with such bone-crushing ferocity that one such hit during the Lions' 1950 Test series in New Zealand resulted in the All Black centre Ron Elvidge breaking his sternum. As a doctor, he was never slow when it came to adding a few extra patients to his list.

'What people generally don't realise about tackling an opponent is the importance of accelerating into the tackle,' he said. 'You've got to do that otherwise you won't be able to hit a 16-stone opponent and knock him back. They don't seem to do that very often these days. I can't say that I was ever hurt in a tackle but there were times when I didn't feel anything.'

Playing for Wales against Australia in 1947, Matthews made the first tackle of the match, and not only could he not feel anything for the remaining 79 minutes and 40-odd seconds, he also had not the foggiest notion what he had been doing that afternoon. He could not remember playing in the match, let alone anything about it.

'I could remember Trevor Allan, the Australian captain, catching the ball from the kick-off and me hitting him. After that, I didn't remember anything until the next day. Bleddyn Williams, who played with me in the centre, told me later that he couldn't understand why I kept asking him "What's the score?" every two or three minutes.

'Late that night, I said to my wife, "I've got to be up early in the morning. We're playing the Wallabies." She said, "Don't be so stupid. You played them this afternoon." And all I could say was, "Did we . . . ?"'

As a schoolboy, Matthews had worked hard at acquiring the raw power which enabled him to cut a swathe through international rugby. The apprentice blockbuster seldom missed an opportunity to work on his endurance by seeking the most physically demanding work available during the summer months.

'As a kid, I used to go lumbering with navvies around Margam way, where we'd chop down trees with axes. No electric saws in those days. At half past six most mornings, I'd be running up and down the sandhills not far from my home in Bridgend.

'I had a big, heavy sandbag in the loft of my home. I spent a lot of time tackling that bag, hitting it as hard as I could, developing my technique and learning how to time the hit. I kept hitting that bag until I felt as though I knew how to tackle properly. It stood me in good stead when I was put to the test in the years to come.'

He came so far so soon that in 1939 he went within a whisker of winning his Wales cap while an 18-year-old sixth-former at Bridgend Grammar School. Halfway through the final Welsh trial during that last season before the outbreak of the Second World War, Matthews found himself pressed into action for the last 40 minutes against some illustrious opponents.

Typically, he made his presence felt. 'It was a wet day and there was Wilf Wooller and company lined up against me, including Arthur Rees, then an established international. I hadn't been on for very long when I handed him off. During a stoppage in the game, I felt this big hand on my shoulder and I looked round. It was Arthur. "Boy," he said "With a hand-off like that, you're going to be a great player."'

They gave Matthews a purple cap, the last one ever given for a final trial. The cherished red one was finally his in 1947, seven years after the youngster had been chosen alongside Wooller for Wales against England in a non-cap match at Gloucester in 1940. The war took such a savage chunk out of his rugby life that he was deprived the opportunity of at least 28 internationals, 11 more than he actually gained in post-war competition.

His wartime service brought him into contact with the legendary Battle of Britain pilot Douglas Bader. 'I met Bader at Oxford and got to know him very well. I used to meet him every two years at Twickenham for a drink and a chat. Mind you, he was an awkward old so-and-so, but I got on well with him. He played scrum-half for Harlequins and he would probably have played for England if it hadn't been for the accident that nearly killed him.'

When he disembarked in Wellington with the Lions in 1950,

Matthews discovered that his image had preceeded him. New Zealanders being shrewd judges of who was who and what was what, their newspapers were not guilty of overstating his case. 'Matthews,' they wrote, 'has a reputation as a deadly tackler.'

One of three fully qualified doctors on the tour in addition to four medical students, Matthews would appear to have excelled on the dance floor as well as the rugby field. In one of his earlier speeches during the tour, the manager, Surgeon-Captain A.L. 'Ginger' Osborne, a Royal Navy dentist, made one major revelation: 'When it comes to ballroom dancing, all the boys are pretty hot.'

There was nothing dour about the 1950 tourists. When they kicked off against a combined team at Trafalgar Park, Nelson, the Lions let everyone know they were delighted to be there. As the local paper observed, 'Members of the British Isles team were singing lustily when they arrived at the park by coach. They were met at the gates by a pipe band and led to the dressing-room. The British team made a colourful picture in its bright uniform, scarlet jersey with the badge of the four Home Unions, white shorts and blue stockings with green tassles.'

They were given a welcome wherever they went and whatever the time, even on the quayside at half past six in the morning, as was the case in Nelson. The ubiquitous musicians, this time playing under the banner of the Nelson Citizens' Band, were on hand to accompany them to their hotels.

The very notion of the hosts being unable to house the Lions under one roof would be unacceptable by modern standards but in rural New Zealand almost half a century ago they took it in their considerable stride. 'The one unfortunate feature of their arrival was that because of a conference of the Plymouth Brethren, not all the players could be accommodated at the one hotel,' the local paper reported. 'However, a small group which went to the second hotel took the break without a murmur. It was at this hotel that Jimmy McCarthy, the Irish back-row forward, made Nelson history with his first breakfast. Having called for a glass of water, "not too warm and not too cold", he then requested three raw eggs. Before the astounded waitress, he broke these into the water and, with a flip and a gulp, put them down the hatch.'

The Lions may have lost the series but Matthews had made a shuddering impact on New Zealand long before the end of a very long tour. Those who had acclaimed him on arrival for his 'deadly' tackling were soon moved to upgrade the description to that of 'iron man'. By then the Cardiff doctor had made a mockery of the theory that he was over the top and a fair way down the wrong side of the hill.

'In the first match it looked as though the British comments that he had passed his best were well-founded,' the *Wellington Evening Post* told its readers at the end of May. 'However, at each subsequent appearance he proved that even if he were an "old dog", he still had plenty of life in him.'

At no time did the old dog make more of an impact than when he captained the Lions at Gisborne against Combined Districts, a team representing the Poverty Bay, East Coast and Bay of Plenty unions. The match happened to coincide with his 30th birthday and Matthews could hardly have given himself a more rewarding present. The tourists scored five tries and the skipper had at least a hand in virtually every one, as verified by the *Gisborne Herald*'s description of a one-sided match which the Lions won 27–3: 'Outstanding in the British side was the centre, Matthews, captain for the day. In addition to scoring two tries, he made openings for most of the others by strong runs which carved holes in the Combined team's defence.'

Matthews captained the Lions again when they opened the Australian leg of their odyssey in Canberra. Once they had survived a stormy passage across the Tasman Sea, the remaining matches turned out to be relatively plain sailing.

'The Tasman can be rough at the best of times but the day we crossed from New Zealand it was really rough. It was so bad that when we tried to have breakfast, most of the players kept sliding away from the table. They'd get up, then the ship would lurch and they'd slide away again! In the end the only people who managed to hold on and eat their breakfast were all Welshmen: Bleddyn, Cliff Davies, Rex Willis and myself.'

Of the 29 matches, Matthews appeared in 20. Only Roy John played more, but Jack knew he was beginning to run out of steam. He played for Wales throughout the Five Nations the following year, ending up captaining his country for the only time against France in Paris in place of an injured John Gwilliam. It turned out to be Matthews's last international, but not before the Welsh selectors hastened his retirement by an extraordinary episode the following season. It ended with the so-called Big Five making themselves look very small by holding a selection meeting in the toilets at Twickenham! They therefore found themselves bogged down before a ball had been kicked, with their heavyweight Lion the unsuspecting victim of a selectorial volte-face.

Wales began their first post-war Grand Slam season against England at Billy Williams's old cabbage patch on 19 January 1952. Matthews, dropped from the team, had planned to spend that Saturday playing for Cardiff at Bath when the phone rang at his home very late on the Friday night.

'I was called at midnight by the Welsh Rugby Union to be told, "You're playing at Twickenham tomorrow. Bleddyn [Williams] has cried off so you'd better get up here as soon as you can in the morning." I said, "Hang on a minute. This is silly. You've got Alun Thomas there as the reserve, and if Bleddyn's dropped out, then surely Alun should play instead?" Again I was told to get to Twickenham because I was playing. When I inquired as to where exactly I was to go, I was told, "See the man on the gate." See the man on the gate! At Twickenham on the day of an England–Wales game? With 60,000 people milling around?

'Anyway, next morning I got up early and caught the eight o'clock train from Cardiff to Paddington. All the rugby journalists were there going to the big match and they were very surprised to see me. "You're on the wrong train," they said. "Aren't you playing at Bath today?"

'I quickly explained what had happened, because I had a more important question for them: "Do you know where the Welsh team are meeting for lunch?" They told me they were meeting at The Winning Post, a restaurant just down the road from Twickenham. I got a taxi there from Paddington – and eventually I got my fare back from the Union, which was fairly amazing.

'When I got there, Enoch Rees, chairman of the Big Five, said, "You are playing." I said, "You've got Alun Thomas here as reserve. Why's he not playing?"

'"Well," says Enoch, "the Big Five have decided you are playing."

'So when we got to the dressing-room, I got changed. A quarter of an hour before kick-off, the Big Five came into the dressing-room and went into the toilet. I didn't have a clue what was going on but they called John Gwilliam in as captain a few minutes later. He came out to tell me I wasn't playing after all.

'You can imagine how I felt. I'd been called up at short notice and told I was playing, and there I was, ten minutes before kick-off, being told to get changed again because I wasn't playing. I went straight in to see the selectors and I gave it to them straight. I said, "Gentlemen, two things. I should never have been asked to come here in the first place. But, secondly, after dragging me up here and telling me I was definitely playing, I should have played because I'm all changed and ready. Never pick me for Wales again." They never did. I changed back into my clothes, went to watch the match from behind the goalposts and that was that.'

Two tries from Ken Jones proved too much for England, and when the Welsh season ended in a Grand Slam climax, two penalties from the youngest Lion in captivity made all the difference in the 9–5 win over

France in one of the last internationals to be held at St Helen's, Swansea. They were the last goals Lewis Jones would kick for his country. Before the end of the year he had gone north, his meteoric union career over at the age of twenty-one after eight caps, two at full-back, three on the left wing and three at centre. Leeds, having failed in their bid for Bleddyn Williams a few years earlier, had got their Welshman at last for what was then the princely sum of £6,000. For what he achieved in rugby league, Jones would have been a good buy at twice the price.

A real all-rounder, he played first-class cricket at Lord's and had the opportunity to become a professional footballer with Swansea Town. Every Saturday, Jones would turn out at full-back for the Gowerton County school 1st XV in the morning, then at centre-forward for Gorseinon Thistles in the afternoon. Ten goals in one match were more than enough to persuade Swansea that Lewis Jones would be better off hitting them under the crossbar than over it.

'They offered me £15 to sign as an apprentice, which would have meant rubbing shoulders with the likes of such great players as Trevor Ford and Ivor Allchurch, then both on the books at the Vetch. My father told me that I would have to make a choice, that I couldn't go on playing both and expect to do justice to myself. So I sat down and based my decision on which sport I thought I would be better at.'

Once he had opted for rugby, there was no holding him back. A schoolboy international at 16, he played in a team captained by an outside-half who would become a legendary Lion in his own right, Carwyn James. He took the rest in his stride with dazzling speed: his debut in first-class rugby, with Neath, at 17; for Wales at 18; for the Lions at 19. He achieved it all long before completing his two years' national service in the Royal Navy.

Stationed at Devonport, Jones wasted no time in leaving an indelible mark on naval rugby. Against the Army during the RFU's annual inter-services tournament, he landed what was described in some quarters as the longest penalty goal ever seen at Twickenham. The 'wonder goal', struck from the touchline on the halfway line, sailed high between the posts with an astonishing amount of room to spare. So much room, in fact, that the goal was measured by no less a judge than Vivian Jenkins, the Welsh Lion in attendance in his professional capacity as rugby correspondent of the *Sunday Times*. He calculated that the ball travelled almost 80 yards from the point of contact to the spot where it landed.

'What a life I had in the Navy, mainly rugby and cricket 12 months of the year. I trained every Tuesday and Thursday and played rugby every Saturday. Then in the summer this commander used to pick me up in his British racing green Lagonda and we'd go off to play cricket. Wonderful!'

It was on the cricket field, playing for a United Services XI at Plymouth, that S/A (Stores Accountant) Jones learnt that he was required on the other side of the world – and, what's more, required in such a hurry that he would become the first Lion to make the journey by aeroplane. They were in such a hurry to inform him that the 12th man was dispatched to give him the word.

'I was fielding in the covers when this lad came running out to say I was wanted on the phone. It was Mr Haigh-Smith, a famous Barbarian and one of the top officials of the time. He asked if I'd like to join the Lions in New Zealand because it looked as though George Norton, the Irish full-back, would miss the rest of the tour because of injury. I was so taken aback that I think I said something like, "Can you give me time to think?" You don't get a request like that every week, straight out of the blue. Then, when I'd just about taken it all in, I said, "Oh, okay then! When do you want me to go?"'

Given time to finish off his cricket match, Jones took off seven days later. While the rest of the party had taken five weeks to reach New Zealand, the Welsh teenager made it in less than four days – which was particularly appropriate for someone who had shot to the top in next to no time.

Jones had ample reason to feel nervous about climbing into an aeroplane. Three months earlier, the Llandow air disaster had claimed the lives of 80 Welsh supporters returning from their team's win over Ireland in Belfast. Jones had played in that match. Fortunately, the Welsh Rugby Union had stuck to the old-fashioned travel arrangements and sent their team by boat.

'I don't think I've ever been as nervous as I was when I got on the Boeing Stratocruiser at London Airport, as it was called at the time. I'd never been in a plane before and here I was going to places I'd never heard of. We touched down at Shannon in Ireland, then Gander in Newfoundland and on to New York. We changed planes there and I got on a Super Constellation for the next part of the trip. We stopped at Chicago and San Francisco, stayed overnight and changed planes again. Then it was down through the Pacific, three or four more stops, including Honolulu, and I arrived in Auckland after three and a half days. That was unbelievable in those days, but the last time I made the trip it took me less than 24 hours.'

Far from being overawed at mixing with the best of British and Irish,

Jones was never going to take long to graduate from the supporting cast and establish himself as a Test Lion. In a matter of weeks, he graduated from tour new boy to share the top billing with three of the best players in the game.

An advertisement in the *Auckland Star* for the final Test at Eden Park extolled the virtues of four players. It read: 'Jack Kyle: can you remember one better? Bleddyn Williams, a centre with the hallmark of class. Jack Matthews, whose magnificent defence is matched by his grand attack, and Lewis Jones, the 19-year-old British star who seems destined to become the world's greatest full-back. What a goalkicker!'

Far from being intimidated by such an introduction, Jones responded in a way which made the words in the advertisement sound all too prophetic. He made his Test debut at the end of the series against the All Blacks and then did something against Australia which no Lion had done before or has done since. He went through the card, scoring in every possible way: one try, two conversions, two penalty goals and one drop goal, ensuring the Lions a decisive 19–6 win over the Wallabies in Brisbane. There was nothing, it seemed, that the sailor from the village of Gorseinon couldn't do.

'I had a fairy-tale year in 1950, real *Roy of the Rovers* stuff. At the start of the year, Frank Trott was such an institution as full-back for Wales that the Big Five used to start picking the team by writing his name down. He was such a fixture that they never thought about picking anyone else. So when Frank retired, they didn't know what the hell to do.

'They'd heard that I was playing, well, sort of all right for Devonport Services, so they decided to give me a trial. I hadn't played at full-back since I was in the Welsh Secondary Schools team. I'd never played there in senior rugby and there I was being invited to play in a Welsh trial at Cardiff.

'The upshot of all that was that I didn't do anything. Looking back, I suppose it's fair to say that while I didn't do anything, that meant I didn't do anything wrong either. Lo and behold, a few days later a letter came, saying, "You have been selected to play for Wales against England at Twickenham on 21 January 1950, kick-off 2.30 p.m. Make sure you are at the ground at least two hours beforehand so you can meet the rest of the team. Shirt, shorts and stockings will be provided. The shorts and stockings must be returned at the end of the match. Make sure your boots have been polished and that the laces are white." How times have changed!'

Just as one cricket match coincided with news of Jones's selection as a Lion, so another cricket match, at no less a place than Lord's itself, brought him into initial contact with Kenneth Dalby, team manager of Leeds rugby league club. They met in the Long Room, during the occasion of the Royal Navy's annual match against the Army on 25–26 July 1951.

Jones, 11 not out when the Navy declared their first innings at 249–6, bowled 11 overs, finishing with 0–31 as a fully fledged England Test player. Signalman Brian Close made an unbeaten 134. At the end of the first day's play Jones was introduced to Dalby, and while their conversation touched only briefly on the subject of rugby football, the young Welshman began to realise that rugby league was not at all as it had been portrayed in the union heartland of South Wales. Dalby's correction of various misconceptions was to pay a spectacular dividend.

Success with Wales and the Lions made Jones an obvious target. One early attempt by an ambitious northern club to separate him from the Navy drew a heated response from the Senior Service. Jones feared the worst when he was summoned one morning before the Commanding Officer at Devonport, Captain R.W. Marshall.

'My heart sank when he said, "Look here, Jones. I've had a couple of fellows here looking for you. They say they're from a rugby league club. So I had them escorted out and turfed overboard! For your own good, you know, my boy. All right. You may go now."'

By the time Leeds made their move, there was never any danger of the Navy making them walk the plank. Jones, his national service done, returned to civvy street to discover that it wasn't only the union Establishment which took such a superior view of the 13-a-side professional code. Too many officials at too many clubs were only too quick to do their level best to make anyone going north feel like a social outcast, an attitude which merely served to perpetuate the hypocrisy of the supposedly amateur game.

They were quick to give Jones the cold shoulder. Within weeks of signing for Leeds, he returned to South Wales to marry Maureen Williams, a marriage which, considering the groom's status, ought to have been one of the social events of the rugby year. It was more than coincidence that only one of his Welsh international colleagues, Cliff Morgan, attended the wedding.

'I admired Cliff in many ways but I really admired him for that. He was the only player to turn up. He put his head on the block in doing so because even by talking to a rugby league player in those days you could get yourself into trouble. I've got to hand it to Cliff, because he never gave a thought for the consequences.

'I don't know why but there seemed to be a bit of a social stigma about going to league as far as the people in union were concerned. Once you'd gone north, it was made fairly clear that you wouldn't be made welcome at any of the clubhouses back in Wales. I never went back to any of the grounds. It was that bad.

'I can't say that I was ever turned away because I never went back. I always avoided any risk of causing anyone any embarrassment by deliberately staying away. Whenever I went back home, I never went to see a single match in Wales because I'd heard so many stories about league players being kicked out. I never even went back to Stradey, where I'd been playing for Llanelli up until I left for Leeds. Once I'd gone, I don't think I spoke to one of the players I'd played with in the Welsh team for years and years, with the notable exception of Cliffy.'

The iron curtain between the codes, removed at a stroke the moment union took the sham out of amateurism and declared the sport open in August 1995, generated a cold war which sounds even more preposterous now than it was then. 'You can't believe how black a picture everyone in union painted of league. There was no communication between the two codes, no televised matches and the union people were never slow to show their contempt for anybody who would want to turn professional. Playing for money? You don't do that, old boy.

'Well, I did, and I never doubted that I'd made the right decision. Anyone thinking I went with the best wishes of the Welsh Rugby Union must be joking. They thought I was a traitor. I didn't exactly give Llanelli notice because it was all top secret, so there was no time to say, "Goodbye, chaps."'

Jones had been driving a dumper truck at Carmarthen Bay power station when Leeds made their offer. Joining a club which prided itself on its reputation as the Arsenal of rugby league and being paid into the bargain meant that there was always going to be a vacancy for a dumper truck driver.

'Six thousand pounds to sign on was a hell of a lot of cash. I think it took me all of a year to spend it! Leeds contacted my father as the go-between. When he told me they were going to pay a signing-on fee of £6,000, he gave me two words of advice: "Take it." I took it and I have never had the slightest regret.

'I knew what I was leaving behind. I'd had three lovely years which gave me everything I could have wanted from rugby union. A Grand Slam with Wales and a tour of New Zealand and Australia with the Lions. There was nothing else left for me to do.'

His knowledge of the northern code was such that Leeds gave him a book which their new signing tried to concentrate on reading amid all the excitement of the rail journey taking him to a new life. The book was entitled *The Rugby League Instruction Manual.*

Not to put too fine a point on it, Jones was, in his own words, 'a complete flop'. He missed so many tackles and dropped so many passes that he began to wonder whether he would finish up as the most expensive failure in rugby league history. In the end Leeds had no option but to drop him for the second half of the season at Headingley. It was to be the making of Lewis Jones, the league legend.

Given four months to learn the new game at reserve level and watch the first team from the stand, Jones reappeared 12 months after his arrival, his employers convinced that this time he really was ready to be unleashed as a league centre in all his majesty. Shredding defences with the speed and subtlety of his running and blasting teams with the metronomic accuracy of his goalkicking, Jones scored sixty points in three matches.

The following month he made his debut for the distinctly low-key Welsh League team against France in Marseilles along with George Parsons, the policeman who had been ejected from the train when he was last chosen by Wales for a match in France. This time he made it across the Channel without anyone questioning his right to be there.

The next year, 1954, Jones was back in Australia with another Great Britain rugby team, his selection making him the first double Lion. Another young Welshman went with him despite the fact that he had played only a handful of matches for Wigan since leaving his native Cardiff, but then Billy Boston never was one to hang about.

A few years earlier Jones had extended his boundaries to include a season in Minor Counties' cricket with Cornwall, because he had lived on the Cornish side of the Tamar during his naval days. Wisden dutifully records his efforts: 8 innings, 165 runs, highest score 78, average 20.62.

By the time he retired from British rugby in 1964, Jones's career had assumed record-breaking proportions. Like all the best records, they have stood the test of time. His 1,244 goals in 12 years at Headingley, his 2,920 points and his 13 goals in a single match, against Blackpool Borough in August 1957, are all club figures which still stand today, untouched down the decades.

Jones went to Australia from Leeds, coaching the Sydney club Wentworthville for nine years and putting a new string to his bow to good use as a schoolteacher specialising in mathematics, a skill no doubt acquired in keeping track of all those goals. He taught on his return to

Leeds in 1973 and lives there today in contented retirement at the age of 67. Having given all his rugby souvenirs for display at the Gorseinon club, his prize possession now is a pair of Stanley Matthews football boots which the man himself gave him back in the '50s.

While Jones never had any qualms about going north, the other Matthews, Jack, his minder during the 1950 Lions tour, never had any qualms about staying in union. When Dewsbury made a direct approach before the war, Matthews's father sent them back whence they came with 'a flea in their ear'. His rugby days over, Matthews stayed in sport as a medical adviser to the Welsh area council of the British Boxing Board of Control, officiating at fights involving such famous figures as Tommy Farr, Joe Erskine, Dick Richardson, Brian London, Willie Pastrano and Henry Cooper.

Jack was on duty on that riotous night of the Richardson–London fight at Porthcawl which ended up with a bigger fight outside the ring than the one inside it. He was also there for Richardson's staggering battle against Cooper for the British title when Cooper, all but down and out, somehow stopped his opponent before the referee, Ike Powell, could stop Henry because of blood pouring from a gash in his forehead. Matthews put eight stitches into the wound and the rest, as they say, is history.

Having rejoined the Lions as medical officer for their tour of South Africa in 1980, the man who fought Marciano pulls no punches in his condemnation of recent Welsh efforts at international level. 'The performances of the Welsh team make me feel like not watching, and I never thought I'd ever feel like that. It's tragic. The money they're being paid is ridiculous. They're supposed to be fit from full-time training. We were just as fit in my day training twice a week.'

Jack Matthews still lives in Cardiff, still going strong at 78. Strong enough, at least, to make anyone think twice about trying to tackle him . . .

3

Blessed Bleddyn

In 1947 it would have been possible to buy a four-bedroomed detached property, park a Rolls-Royce in the drive and still have enough change left from £6,000 to go on a round-the-world cruise.

At a time when petrol cost five pence a gallon and the average weekly wage for a skilled worker barely amounted to a fiver, £6,000 was more than most people in a country ravaged by the Second World War could reasonably expect to save in their working lives.

When a bottle of whisky cost fractionally more than £1 and a family saloon car £500, £6,000 really was a king's ransom – and £6,000 was what Leeds rugby league club was offering a young airman then adjusting to life in civvy street after four and a half years' wartime service.

He came from Taff's Well, a little place not known to have been on the Luftwaffe's hit list – which was just as well, because, quite apart from anything else, it housed the nearest thing to the mythical Welsh fly-half factory. Except that the one at 11 Moy Road, the home of eight brothers, diversified to such an extent that there were scrum-halfs and centres as well as back-row forwards.

Leeds, rebuilding like everyone else from the rubble of war, dispatched their manager, one Edward Waring, to South Wales on a money-no-object mission, imploring him that he return to Yorkshire with the best rugby union centre money could buy. League clubs had made a killing in Cardiff, never more so than with their capture of two then relatively unknown union players whose names today are spoken of in reverential tones, Billy Boston and Gus Risman.

Neither cost a fortune, but what the young Eddie Waring had to offer was proof that his club, at least, were prepared to pay the earth for the finished article. The sum involved bore some resemblance to what the top Football League clubs of the time were paying on the transfer market for the best players of the day. Soccer's transfer record then stood at £12,500, coincidentally set by another Welshman from a large footballing family in Merthyr Tydfil, Bryn Jones, who had been sold by Wolverhampton Wanderers to Arsenal. Bleddyn Williams was being offered something approaching half as much, and all he had to do was sign on the dotted line.

The modern equivalent, calculated on the £15 million Newcastle paid Blackburn for Alan Shearer, would be for a Guscott, a Gibbs or a Horan being offered £7.5 million. Great players though they all are, the idea, of course, is preposterous, even compared with the often preposterous finances of a union game careering towards the next millennium as if there were no tomorrow.

Attitudes towards professionalism were very different half a century ago. Snobbery bred by the yawning class divide between union, the 15-man amateur code, and league, its 13-a-side professional alternative, was such that there was, indeed, a social stigma attached by the union Establishment to any player going north in exchange for some filthy lucre.

Bleddyn Williams knew all about it despite the fact that he came from the same working-class background as all those lads whose clubs in the north of England broke away from the RFU when the English Union refused to sanction 'broken-time' payments as a means of compensating players for losing their Saturday shift, hence the Great Schism of 1896.

Fifty years on, young Williams found himself faced with the decision of his life: to take the money and run, or to stay put and carry on playing strictly for the love of the game. His eldest brother, Gwyn, had already gone north, to Wigan, and the same club had, not surprisingly, tested young Bleddyn's reluctance to cut the umbilical union cord.

'Harry Platt, the Wigan manager, had asked me about turning professional in 1944 and followed that up by offering me £5,000,' Williams said.

'I said, "I can't do anything because of the war, but I'll tell you what I'll do, Harry. If I contemplate going to league at any stage in the future, I'll give you at Wigan first refusal."

'He said, "Is that a promise?" And I said it was. After the war Harry approached me again. I said, "Look, I don't think there's any chance I'll ever turn professional, but my promise holds good."'

It was shortly afterwards that Eddie Waring came a-knocking on his door, anxious to prove that every man has his price. The sheer size of the offer made Williams, newly married at the time, think long and hard about whether he could go on resisting such vast sums of money.

A man of principle, his first action, had he decided in the affirmative, would not have been to rush Mr Waring's cheque into his bank account but to phone Harry Platt and offer himself to Wigan as promised. They would have been more than anxious to up their original offer and match the one made by Leeds – not that theirs was confined to cash.

'I nearly went,' Williams said. 'As well as £6,000 in my hand there was the promise of a decent job because I'd had a reasonable education. In the end I turned it down. When Harry got to hear of the Leeds approach, he was back on the phone. I said, "Harry, I'm not going, but if I had decided to go, I'd have been straight on to you, as I promised."

'The money was tempting, but the truth is I never wanted to go. There were two reasons why I stayed. Firstly, I loved rugby union, and secondly, I'd had a scholarship to Rydal School in North Wales and I felt that somewhere along the line I'd be letting them down if I cashed it all in to play rugby league.'

Harry Platt kept it all under his hat, Bleddyn never said a word and a tight-lipped Eddie Waring returned whence he came to find more success as the 'up-and-under' voice commentating on rugby league than he had had poaching centres from Wales. The Union dealt with those poor innocents on the receiving end of such offers in such draconian fashion that anyone even suspected of talking to a rugby league club was immediately declared *persona non grata*.

Williams was among those who watched in disbelief when the Welsh Rugby Union ordered one of the Welsh team off the train taking the party to the Five Nations match against France in Paris. It was a good job that no informer had told the Gestapo-like Welsh Union of Williams's meeting with Leeds, or their star centre would have been ordered off the train before it pulled out of Cardiff General.

When it stopped at Newport for the Monmouthshire contingent to board, one of them, George Parsons, had no sooner got on than he was being thrown back off again, as the train pulled out of the station. If anyone tried to do that now there would be a public outcry, but back then a man could be thrown out of the team on the spur of the moment and banned from the game for life on the merest suspicion of having been approached by the devil incarnate, rugby league.

That not even the most devoted union player could stop a league club approaching him in a democratic society was presumably something which simply did not occur to the hanging judges of the Welsh Rugby Union. The secretary, Captain Walter Rees, was clearly out of the Joseph Stalin school of rugby administration.

Parsons thus became the first, and last, player to be sent off *en route* to a Five Nations championship because of an offer he may, or may not, have had. 'On that basis the entire Welsh team had probably been professionalised,' Williams said. 'Everyone had been approached at some stage or other. What they did to George was an absolute disgrace.

'As far as I could understand, it was based on nothing more than that he was alleged to have been seen talking to a rugby league scout. As soon as George got on the train he was sent for by Walter Rees, and he was then fairly promptly ordered off the train. We only took one reserve, so we proceeded to Paris with the bare minimum 15 players – and 32 committeemen.

'I was on the train that day. None of us was privy to the conversation which took place in the carriage where the selectors were sitting, and it wasn't until later that we found out about George being sent off. George was in the police and there was a suggestion that someone in higher authority, an inspector or superintendent who didn't like George getting so much time off to play rugby, had let it be known that he'd had an approach from rugby league.

'They would never get away with it today but, on the strength of that, he was banned from playing rugby union for the rest of his life. It seems hard to believe now, but that's how it was back then. A word in the wrong ear at the wrong time and you were liable to be finished for good.'

Parsons, given no choice but to pursue a career in league whether he had been planning one or not, had been excommunicated with such indecent haste that he left minus the cap he had won earlier that season. It took the Welsh Rugby Union 34 years before its collective conscience finally pricked and some attempt was made to address the injustice of the Parsons affair by presenting him with the cap which had been denied him all those years before. At 67, he thus became the oldest new-cap of all time.

Others suffered too, like Alban Davies, Cardiff's pre-war full-back at a time when the young Williams was learning to master the craft which would make him the finest attacking centre three-quarter in the world. Davies, a coalminer from Cross Keys, had been chosen to play in one of the most prestigious fixtures of the calendar, for Major Stanley's XV against Oxford University.

Williams tells the story of what happened next. 'Alwyn was asked for his expenses. He put them in and said, "Look, I've lost a day's pay from work to come here." They reported him to the RFU at Twickenham and he was then banned from the game. So, all of a sudden, he had no choice but to go north.'

The rules were so absurd that Williams might unwittingly have infringed his amateur status by appearing in a couple of harmless wartime matches playing with and against Gus Risman, a Welsh centre who would surely have been a giant centre of the union game had he not left his native Barry at the age of 17 to play for pay in a league career which took him to the pinnacle of the game as captain of Great Britain.

Risman, whose son Bev played stand-off for England during the early '60s, played opposite Williams for the Army's union team against the RAF, and the pair then appeared together for the Welsh Services team. Williams, far from worrying about what the union Establishment would have regarded as 'contamination' with a professional, considered it a privilege. 'Gus was a magnificent rugby player,' he said. 'It was an amazing thing for me to play alongside him.' If the Union had dared to treat Williams in the same high-handed fashion as the hapless George Parsons, had they caught a whisper of Eddie Waring's visit from Leeds, it would surely have made them a laughing stock. By the late '40s when more than 40,000 often turned up at the Arms Park for Cardiff club matches, Bleddyn was, quite literally, the centre of attraction.

Often players of any sport fall into two broad categories: those with natural talent but not the application to make the most of it, and those with the application but no talent. Williams was a classic example of someone who had both. The third of eight rugby-playing brothers, he was eight years old when he began working at his game in the fields at the back of the family's modest working-class home in Taff's Well.

'One of my earliest rugby memories is of watching Cardiff play Taff's Well and seeing the way their full-back, Tommy Stone, side-stepped in counter-attacking from his own 25. I couldn't believe the way he did it, the ease with which he beat opponents. So I went home, tried it myself and found I could do it, too. That was the greatest thing that ever happened to me in terms of my development as a rugby player.

'Then I worked to try and perfect the technique. I tried it against my brothers and found that I could beat them. When they weren't around, I'd put sticks in the field and side-step them. The real art of the side-step is to do it in such a way that makes your opponent do something, either by sending him in the wrong direction or by throwing him off balance just enough for you to get past.

'Gerald Davies had a natural side-step, Phil Bennett didn't. Mine was natural, and people used to say to me, "You won't get past me." I was never a betting man but I'd say, "I can beat you every time." Sometimes they'd be so concerned about the side-step that all I had to do was run straight.'

The young Williams proved a good listener, too. One lesson which he was to remember for the rest of his rugby days came during his formative years at Rydal, the public school in North Wales where he gained a scholarship with a little help from a distinguished Rydal old boy, former Glamorgan cricket captain and Wales centre Wilf Wooller.

At 14 Williams was engaged in regular 1st XV school competition against 17- and 18-year-olds. 'During this particular match, the headmaster, the Reverend A.J. Costain, was prowling up and down the touchline, as he invariably did. Towards the end, I scored a try by beating four men, and I really thought I was the cat's whiskers.

'When I came off the field at the end, the headmaster put his arm around me. "Now then, young Williams," he said. "That was a great try. You beat four opponents – but if you had passed to your wing, he would not have had to beat anyone." And what he said stayed with me for the rest of my life.

'I'd always realised that the ball could do more than any individual and that the timing of the pass was everything. I organised my game with that in mind, which is why so many wings playing outside me scored so many tries.'

For someone whose primary function was to create the space for others to apply the scoring finish, Williams managed an astounding number of tries, 175 in 252 matches for Cardiff, 7 more in 22 matches for Wales and 11 in 17 appearances for the Lions during their tour of New Zealand and Australia in 1950, the first of the post-war era. And to think he achieved all that despite having a large chunk taken out of his sporting life by the Second World War, a fate which also befell his formidable partner in midfield for Cardiff and Wales, the thunderous Jack Matthews. Instead of starting his career in senior rugby as he ought to have done on turning eighteen in 1941, Williams had to wait five years. He, at least, survived the hostilities, unlike many of his generation.

A newly trained pilot in the RAF, Williams had been due to attend an advanced course as a fighter pilot. Instead the Arnhem disaster in 1944 resulted in his deployment as a glider pilot for the subsequent battle for the Rhine. Once the paratroopers had cleared the landing zone, he flew in under instructions to land as close as possible to the designated headquarters, a disused farm.

It was hardly the ideal way to prepare for a big rugby match the following weekend. Great Britain were playing the Dominions at

Leicester, and Williams had been asked to play. His prospects of making it, decidedly gloomy given his precarious state in enemy territory, promptly took a marked turn for the worse.

'I lived in a slit trench for a week because the American airborne division had landed on the wrong zone. Luckily I had my parachute with me, which at least meant I could keep warm at night. My commanding officer was Colonel Hugh Bartlett, then captain of Sussex County Cricket Club.

'On the Friday morning, he said to me, "What about this game you're supposed to be playing in at Leicester tomorrow?"

'"Yes, sir, and a fat chance I've got, by the look of things."

'"Well, pack your bags, Williams, and be ready to move out."

'"I haven't got any bags to pack."'

The next thing he knew, he was on the way from the Rhine to Welford Road. 'I was driven across the Rhine, then by jeep to Eindhoven in Holland, from where I was flown to Brize Norton, the RAF base in Oxfordshire. I had time to see my young wife, who had got a message which made it seem as though I'd been lost in action. I picked up my kit and the next morning I went across country and got to Leicester on time. Amazing, but true.'

The end of the war left him free at last to assume his place on the international stage denied him for so long. With so much catching up to do on and off the field, Williams wasted no time furthering the pursuit of excellence with Cardiff and Wales as well as tackling his new job as an executive with the Steel Company of Wales.

When the next Lions tour finally came round, most people had forgotten that they ever existed. There had been no such tour for 12 years, not since Sammy Walker had taken his Lions to South Africa before the war, and there had been no tour of New Zealand for 20 years. No wonder, therefore, that when they set sail from Liverpool the Lions knew that, if nothing else, they would be assured the friendliest of welcomes, something which could not be said of subsequent tours to the Antipodes.

When the SS *Ceramic* pulled down the Mersey and out towards the high seas, Williams was only too relieved to be among the passengers. For most of that season he had been reduced to passenger status by an accident during the final Welsh trial. He damaged his knee so badly that he spent the next three months in plaster and had still not played when the Lions finalised their party.

They insisted that he prove his fitness or spend the summer at home. Therefore on the day Wales beat France to win the Grand Slam,

Williams went to Bath to do as the Lions had asked and prove his readiness for the tour in a Cardiff team featuring a new boy at outside-half by the name of Cliff Morgan. Naturally enough, Williams assumed that every other injured Lion or potential Lion had been ordered to take a similar test.

'When I joined up with the rest of the party in London, I found out that Doug Smith [the Scotland wing who went on to manage the 1971 Lions] had arrived with a broken arm. I thought it a bit odd that I'd been asked to prove my fitness and then someone else turned up with a pretty serious injury. As it turned out, Smith only played three matches on the whole tour.'

It took the 1993 Lions barely 24 hours to reach New Zealand. In 1950 it took them five weeks on a voyage via the Panama Canal. Lions tours have also now shrunk to a matter of weeks. When Bleddyn and company made their journey, it took them more than six months, from early April to late October.

In South Africa in 1997, the Lions were accompanied by enough journalists, radio reporters and television crews to form their own media circus, more than 50 strong. When they set sail down the Mersey in 1950, however, the media party numbered one, starting and finishing with Dai Gent, rugby correspondent of *The Times*. Not even he lasted the distance, sailing home at the end of the New Zealand adventure and skipping the Australian leg of the longest tour.

Every Lion was instructed to bring his own dinner suit and, if his wardrobe did not extend that far, to buy one. The dinner suit was *de rigueur* every night throughout the voyage, and heaven help any player who expected the Lions to foot the bill. The clothing arrangements tended to be so hit and miss that they were scarcely the best-dressed team ever to set foot in New Zealand.

'We were only given two ties and a blazer badge,' Williams said. 'We had to buy our blazers from the same shop in Edinburgh. When they arrived they were not exactly what you'd call tailored to measure. They fitted wherever they touched. I don't know who gave them my measurements, but mine was miles too big. Most of us had to get them adjusted during the tour.'

Williams, his status acknowledged by his appointment as vice-captain to the Irish hooker, Karl Mullen, a Dublin gynaecologist, wondered whether the Lions would prove more than sartorially challenged. The omission of certain players puzzled him, and he was all the more puzzled when he found out that some had been deliberately left at home because they were considered 'too rough'. For a Test series against the All Blacks?

'Some excellent players were non-starters, like Douglas Elliot, the great Scottish wing forward. His father died just before the tour and Douglas couldn't make it because he had to run the family farm. But others were missing who should have been there, like the Welsh flanker Ray Cale, from Pontypool.

'But they wouldn't take Ray because they felt he was too rough, and they very nearly didn't take Jack Matthews, the great Welsh centre, for the same crazy reason. Both were hard players, just the type we would need in New Zealand and Australia. At least common sense prevailed as far as Jack was concerned, but we couldn't believe Ray had been left at home.'

As vice-captain, Williams ran the backs and Mullen the forwards. On ship it was left to the two physical training instructors in the party, John Robbins and Ken Jones, to keep the rest in some sort of shape. Back then a coach was something which had rather a lot of seats in it for the purpose of transporting people from A to B, and while training was primitive by today's standards, nobody complained.

All that mattered was how they played for 80 minutes twice a week when they got there, not how they prepared for it. 'By today's standards, our training would have been dismissed as nonsense. We'd go out and hold a runaround. People like Jack Kyle and Billy Cleaver always believed that once round the field was enough for them. It wasn't that they were shirking anything. It was just that they were superb rugby players.

'We scrummaged, we had line-outs and general things, but we only trained once a day, usually for a couple of hours in the morning. We did a lot of our training at schools all over New Zealand. We'd train, have lunch and then talk to the school. From start to finish we were very conscious that we were there as ambassadors of the British Isles.

'We went everywhere by boat and train and we saw more of the country than any other team. The modern Lions teams don't meet the people the way we did, and they are all the poorer for missing that because it was such a great experience. They hadn't had a touring team in New Zealand since the Springboks in 1937 and the support for us was quite remarkable. We drew the crowds not just because we were the British Lions but because of the quality of our rugby.'

The Lions drew the first of the four Tests in Dunedin, then lost the other three when they might easily have won the last two instead of losing both by three points. Williams, deputising for the injured Mullen, captained the Lions in two Tests and at least had the satisfaction of inspiring a try which his old friend and foe, former All Black captain and coach Fred Allen, still talks about to this day.

'We had a scrum virtually on our own line and I made the decision to run it. The idea was that the ball would come from Kyle to me and that I'd have room to beat my opposite number and send Ken Jones clear on the wing. That was the plan and it worked like a charm, except that I had nothing to do with it whatsoever!

'When the ball came out, Lewis Jones came into the line from full-back, took the pass from Kyle and went straight through the middle. When he got up to Bob Scott, the New Zealand full-back, it was a simple job of passing on to Ken Jones, who scored under the posts. The crowd erupted. They'd never seen a try like it.

'Being made captain at the eleventh hour didn't affect the way we played. Generally the forwards knew what to do and the backs liked to play it off the cuff. We always felt we had the beating of them behind the scrum, but our forwards as a unit were not strong enough physically.

'Dai Davies was a magnificent hooker, and each time he came in for Mullen the change was too late for Dai to get his name in the programme. Roy John was a tower of strength in the line-out but despite his performances we didn't get enough ball. We could have done with Bill Tamplin, the Cardiff prop, but the selectors thought he was over the hill, although he wasn't, as his performance against the Springboks the following year proved.'

The Lions' most notable setback outside the Tests occurred in Dunedin, where Otago swept them aside with a dynamic rucking game, a phenomenon which left such an impression on the tourists that Williams took it upon himself to send the Welsh Rugby Union a report on the subject when he returned home.

'We had never seen any rucking like it in our lives. We tried to incorporate it into our game but we had no chance of developing something in three or four weeks which the Otago people had been working on for three or four years.

'We tried telling the WRU what a great development this would be for our game. All they needed to do was find the right coach, get the forwards organised and they would be home and dry. They took not a blind bit of notice of what we said.'

Subsequent events ensured that they would go on paying not a blind bit of notice, and Williams had a fair bit to do with the subsequent events in question. As a fitting climax to his career, he captained club and country to epic victories over New Zealand within the space of a few weeks in 1953, something no Welsh team has achieved in almost half a century since, with the glorious exceptions of Newport in 1963 and Llanelli in 1972.

Cardiff's 8–3 win over the All Blacks assumed such historic significance that the players have held an annual reunion to commemorate a victory achieved so long ago that, at the last count, only nine of the team had survived the passage of time. Far from a fluke, the match went almost exactly the way Cardiff planned it.

'Cliff Morgan, Rex Willis and myself made a point of watching the All Blacks in the two games before they played us. We reckoned if we got 40 per cent of the ball we'd beat them. They were stronger in the line-out so we used full line-outs on our throw to tie in their back row and leave us man-for-man behind the scrum. It worked like a charm, and we scored two cracking early tries and held on at the end when our hooker, Geoff Beckenham, won a strike against the head in a scrum on our own line.'

Three weeks later, Wales were celebrating an even more famous victory over the same opponents. In five matches as captain of Wales, Williams had won them all and not even the All Blacks could spoil his record. 'I thought New Zealand lost it that day rather than Wales winning it. They made the big mistake of failing to exploit their numerical advantage when our centre, Gareth Griffiths, was off the field for 20 minutes because of a dislocated collarbone. With the score level at 8–8, we were never going to settle for a draw and the Welsh pack somehow found the will for one last supreme effort.

'I'd torn my knee ligaments so I was a virtual passenger, and when Clem Thomas found himself in possession he knew there wasn't much point passing to me. Instead he cross-kicked for Ken Jones on the wing. As luck would have it, the ball bounced beautifully for Ken to score and win the match. It was a win-or-bust move, because if the bounce had gone against us, there is no doubt that Ron Jardine, the New Zealand full-back, would have scored at the other end.'

Nobody could imagine then how terrible a price the Kiwis would make Wales pay over the years for that match. Williams witnessed all the subsequent events unfold from the press-box at the Arms Park in his role as rugby writer for the *Sunday People*. He has felt the sense of humiliation like everyone else, but the incident which angered him more than any other robbed Wales of a rare win, in November 1978.

Wales led 12–10 when a late line-out resulted in Roger Quittenton awarding the penalty which Brian McKechnie goaled to get his team out of gaol. Williams is adamant that the English referee was 'fooled' by the antics of the All Blacks' second-row pair Andy Haden and Frank Oliver, and that New Zealand cheated their way to victory.

While Quittenton has always maintained that he penalised the Welsh lock Geoff Wheel for obstruction at the front of the line-out, Graham Mourie, New Zealand's captain that day, confessed in his autobiography some years later that Oliver and Haden had hatched a plan to deceive the referee. One of them would hurl himself out of the line-out as if he had been barged by an opponent, which is what happened.

'That saddened me greatly,' Williams said. 'I could hardly believe that they went to those lengths to con the referee. There was no question that Quittenton was fooled by it. I'm sure the All Blacks cheated that day and that's a general feeling in New Zealand as well. I know a lot of people there were quite appalled by it. There's no doubt in my opinion that Wales deserved to win that match.'

Bleddyn Williams, never one to break the spirit of the game, came from a generation to whom cheating was anathema. Still hale and hearty at 75, he surely deserves to be back in Welsh rugby on a formal basis as their next president.

4

The Man Money Couldn't Buy

By the time Cliff Morgan made his first break and entered the human race one April morning in 1930, the single most important decision of his life had already been taken. A few months before his son's birth in the mining village of Trebanog, Clifford Morgan senior had been offered an apparently glamorous alternative to the Rhondda Valley and the grime of life in a coalmine.

The new job promised him sweat of a different sort, on the ground rather than beneath it, as a professional footballer with Tottenham Hotspur. His wife, Edna May, effectively blocked the move, just as she would block her son's departure to Wigan some 20 years later when they covered the breakfast table in £5,000 worth of white £5 notes.

Morgan refused Spurs and went on playing centre-half for Trebanog Rovers in the Ely Valley League as though nothing had happened. In deciding that the grass was greener in the Rhondda, even if much of it was in the process of being buried beneath slag heaps, Mrs Morgan had ensured that her little treasure would be brought up in such a way that ultimately the country would acclaim him as a national treasure which no number of fivers could buy.

Others from the outside-half factory may have played more matches and kicked more goals, but none of them can match the wonderful journey which catapulted Morgan from 159 Top Trebanog Road, Trebanog, Porth, to a position of such pre-eminence at the BBC that he became even more influential as a major player in global television sport than he had been on the fields of glory – which is saying something.

Nor did he restrict his sphere of influence to the tramlines of sport.

In 1981, the collier's son from the Rhondda was responsible, as head of outside broadcasts, for televising the biggest live event in the Corporation's history, the wedding of Prince Charles and Lady Diana Spencer, a seven-hour extravaganza watched by more than 500 million people all over the world.

Few rugby men had the charisma to become household names during a post-war period when the sport was nowhere near as popular as it is today. Morgan's charisma was such that he found himself as much a household name as a television executive of rare versatility, achieving greater status more than a quarter of a century after hanging up his boots than he had enjoyed as the archetypal Welsh fly-half.

The toes began twinkling from the moment he could first remember darting off into a shaft of space and playing makeshift football in the schoolyard at Tonyrefail primary. 'I began to get a feel for the game from my mother's knee. My father was a damned good player and he encouraged me to play football. We'd play with a tennis ball, kicking it against a wall and beating a man. I had that nervous awareness from an early age about what you had to do to beat an opponent. I suppose those little delicacies came from my father.'

His initiation into a different kind of football took place at Tonyrefail Grammar School, where he had the good fortune to come under the wing of a games master, Ned Gribble, whom he affectionately refers to as 'a gale of humanity, a teacher who taught us how to play with love and feeling in your heart. He cared about young people and he cared about style.'

He cared about it so much that after Morgan displeased him in one match against Maestag Grammar School by dropping a goal when Gribble believed he should have scored a try, the teacher showed his disapproval by dropping his protégé for three matches. He had begun as hooker, moved to the wing and eventually arrived at outside-half via centre. Years later, when Morgan asked why he had been shunted out to the wing before being allowed to occupy his true position, Gribble told him, 'So you'd know how bloody awful it was to play on the wing when the fly-half never lets the ball out.'

Gribble, sensing that his pupil had a rare talent, gave him invaluable instruction in how to protect himself, something which Morgan adopted to such effect that despite making a monkey out of a whole battalion of back-row forwards he survived such dangers with only one bad break, a fractured leg in Dublin – and even then he didn't know he'd broken it until after the match.

'I loved Ned's philosophy. He showed me how to turn my body in such a way that the hardest parts, like your elbows, are towards the opposition so you don't get hurt. The first thing you had to learn in big-time football was how to protect yourself, because they came in bloody hard. That's why Richard Sharp [England's distinguished fly-half of the '60s] suffered a broken jaw in South Africa.'

One teacher, less than thrilled at the young fellow's academic progress, passed a caustic judgement in one school report: 'Not very good in class. His biggest assets are his buttocks.'

At 18, when Cardiff considered Morgan ready to be exposed to the big boys, there were plenty waiting to knock his block off – figuratively speaking, of course. Cardiff rang Tonyrefail Grammar to say he was required for a match the following night and, typically, the only problem he had was gaining entry to the Arms Park, past an officious steward.

'Billy Cleaver, the Welsh international, was doubtful, so down I went with my father's old bag in which he'd carried his kit all those years before. When I got to the ground, the chap on the door, who'd probably been there for a hundred years, said, "You can't come in here. The schoolboy entrance is over there. Other side of the ground." Anyway, Billy Cleaver turned up and played.'

Morgan's bow at Porthcawl the following week gave him an introduction to the Cardiff greats and some who would be great, among them a wing from Tiger Bay by the name of Billy Boston who played in the same 2nd XV, the Rags, alongside several international players, including Des O'Brien of Ireland, then selling Guinness in South Wales.

When Morgan made his debut for Wales at the age of 20, against Ireland at the Arms Park, who should be waiting to greet him in the opposition back row but O'Brien, in his last match before succeeding Karl Mullen as the Irish captain. O'Brien sent his Cardiff colleague a telegram: 'Congratulations Cliff, bach. Is your life insured . . . ?'

Wales, victims the previous month of what was then arguably the most surprising result in a century of Five Nations matches when Scotland, the perennial wooden-spoon winners, blitzed a team packed with 11 Lions, made Glyn Davies carry the can and chose Morgan. When they announced the team late that Monday afternoon, he was on a bus going home, unaware of his selection.

'The team came out on the six o'clock news when I was going home from college in Cardiff. I'd nodded off. I'd been up since seven that morning for lectures, but there was never any danger of missing the stop because there was a bump in the road between Tonyrefail and Trebanog which never failed to wake me up. Then it'd be up the hill to my stop.

'Suddenly I was aware that there was a mass of people and flags and streamers. Somehow they'd put them all up in the hour or so between hearing the news on the radio and my arriving home. Everyone was cheering and shouting. The bus driver got out of his seat and came and shook my hand. Those experiences have never left me and never will.'

The Rhondda had not been as excited about one of their own entering the international arena since Tommy Farr had gone across the Atlantic for his unforgettable shot at Joe Louis and the world heavyweight title, a fight which everyone, including the seven-year-old Cliffy, listened to in the early hours of the morning.

An intimidating telegram from O'Brien suggested that young Morgan was about to face a few Irishmen with the potential to inflict even more damage than Louis, considering that in the heat of a ferocious physical contest like international rugby few bothered with the niceties of the Queensberry rules. Morgan received O'Brien's oblique reference to his future well-being at a time when the newcomer was checking and rechecking his invitation from the Welsh Rugby Union which he remembered as being written on 'something like lavatory paper'.

> Dear Sir,
> Ireland v. Wales, 10 March 1951
> You have been selected to play in the above match, for which the instructions are:
> *Friday 9 March:*
> 4.00 p.m. – Report at Cardiff Arms Park with your kit for practice.
> *Saturday 10 March:*
> 12.30 p.m. – Report to Queen's Hotel, Cardiff, for lunch.
> 2.40 p.m. – The team will be photographed.
> 3.00 p.m. – The match.
> 6.00 p.m. – Dinner at Queen's Hotel.
> Please let me know by return of post whether you can attend. You are to wear the white-topped stockings issued for the Scotland match. Please do not forget them, as stockings have become very scarce.

Despite Ireland scoring the only try, through the incomparable Jackie Kyle, a penalty goal from Ben Edwards, a Newport lock playing in his first and last international, saved Wales.

A day when their new number ten announced himself on the grand stage as if to the manor born ended with Morgan being given an immediate insight into the Welsh Rugby Union's tight-fisted approach to the subject of match expenses. Eric Evans, the Union's secretary, gave

Morgan a harder time with his than the Irish back row had given him that afternoon. There was no superstar treatment in those days. Morgan used to consider himself lucky if he got a seat on the bus taking him down to Cardiff on the morning of the match, which was more than he managed before his debut against Ireland: 'The bus was packed so I stood for the whole journey.'

After the match, the team changed, walked along Westgate Street to the Queen's Hotel for an early supper and caught the last bus home, a red Rhondda double-decker, along with the supporters. Wales had a new hero, and while he may have gone blasting off the launch pad that afternoon *en route* to the stratosphere, he still needed the fare. Almost 60,000 people had watched his every move that afternoon, and yet before the Welsh Rugby Union would pay him a bean, they asked him to identify himself. 'We walked up the first flight of stairs in the hotel and Eric was sitting there with his card table and a black exercise book. When I got to the front of the queue, he said, "Name!"

'"Morgan, Mr Evans."

'"Expenses?"

'"Five shillings, sir. Two return fares, Trebanog to Cardiff."

'With that, he flicked through his black exercise book and slammed it shut. "You liar and cheat! Two and four pence return, Trebanog to Cardiff. That's four shillings and eight pence."

'He gave me half a crown, a two-shilling piece and two pennies, and I've still got them in a scrapbook under my bed. When I got home at midnight that night off the last bus, my parents were waiting to talk to me about the match. I told them the story about the expenses. My dad said, "Duw! What a clown. What nonsense." My mother said, "Wait a minute. Mr Evans was quite right, wasn't he? It was two and four return. That's four and eight. He was quite right." Nothing like a mother for honesty and integrity!'

When Wales won the Grand Slam the following year, their first for more than 40 years, Morgan's father was at Lansdowne Road to see his son create a spectacular try for Ken Jones. And thereby hangs a tale. 'Dad got so excited jumping up and down that his false front teeth shot out and landed about 12 rows in front of him. He never found them.'

Tony O'Reilly, Morgan's fellow Lion and lifetime friend who became president of the Heinz baked bean empire as well as ex-President Bush's tennis partner, added a sequel to the story after listening to the Welshman's blow-by-blow account of his father's flying gnashers. 'Be Jaysus, Morgan,' said O'Reilly. 'Sure I know a man down in Tipperary who's still wearing them!'

The Grand Slam Welsh were suddenly in demand, not least from rugby league clubs. On the very weekend that Leeds signed Lewis Jones, Wigan made their big play for Morgan, the chairman and vice-chairman arriving outside 159 Top Trebanog Road one Sunday morning amid a rustling of curtains which could have been heard for miles. The subsequent rustling of £5 notes was rather more discreet.

'We'd played Llanelli the day before and I was in bed when they knocked on the door at nine o'clock in the morning. My mother came up and said, "There are some gentlemen here from Wigan to see you." I said, "Mam, I can't see them because if I talk to them I become professionalised. I'm not allowed to do this."

'"Well, you can't leave them on the front doorstep."

'She took them in. Normally on a Sunday my mother always brought two eggs, bread, butter and jam and a cup of tea up to my room on a little tray which I'd made at school. The principal reason for this was that I had to be up by half past ten for chapel. This Sunday morning was an exception.

'When I got downstairs, they were in the kitchen having bacon, egg and black pudding. My mother could never be rude to anyone. She had no idea what professionalism meant and then they put the money on the table. There was a lot of it, £5,000 in white fivers. I'd never seen a white fiver before. On top of that, there was a cheque for £2,500 post-dated for six months' time.

'My mother believed in the security of village life. The house, clean clothes, chapel and love were the most important things. That's why she stopped me going to Oxford University. My mother was the gaffer. If she said, "Don't touch that," nobody touched it. She was the boss.'

While the Wigan deputation went north empty-handed, the 22-year-old resumed his studies at Cardiff University in botany, zoology and chemistry. The offers kept coming ('every week there was something') and Morgan kept knocking them back. He confesses now, in hindsight, to more than a twinge of regret that he didn't take the plunge.

'I now regret that I didn't go, in a sense. I never proved that I could have played rugby league. Lewis Jones, David Watkins and Jonathan Davies all proved they could play both games. I have two regrets in my life: that I never played for the Lions in New Zealand and that I never played rugby league.'

Had he chosen to ignore his mother's wishes, Morgan would still have had to contend with a pre-war international of firm right-wing beliefs, Wilf Wooller, who regarded rugby league with about the same contempt as he did the Communist party. 'He said, "What do you want to do with your life? Do you want to enjoy your game and play rugby for Wales, or do you want to be told when you're going to play? I think you'll make a better living sticking as you are."'

When it came to witch hunts against players rumoured to have been in any kind of contact with the devil incarnate in their flat caps and V-necked jerseys, Wales were more active than the rest. Morgan thought their attitude was 'daft' and proved that he, at least, couldn't have cared less about being accused of guilt by association, hence his appearance as the only Welsh player at Lewis Jones's wedding a few weeks after he had turned professional.

Perhaps it was just as well that the bigots on the WRU were oblivious to the fact that his father had taken him to see the 1947 rugby league Challenge Cup final at Wembley, Bradford Northern against Leeds. 'We went up by train from Cardiff, £3 return. What I saw was unbelievable. I love rugby league, always have.

'That's why I'd go out to dinner with anyone from rugby league any time and never give it a second thought. That's the beauty of being independent, and staying in union gave me the independence to say to Cardiff every so often, "I'm not training on Wednesday night. Choir practice. We're doing Elijah."' It sounds incredible but Morgan's independence and his passion for music dictated that he spent the Friday night before one international performing on a different stage. 'I was playing Mozart and Grieg in the orchestra, or singing in a concert, and nobody said a word. They didn't want to see you on Friday night because we all stayed at home. The game mattered, of course it did, but it didn't matter that much.'

A second tenor in the Porth and District Choral Society, Morgan used his innate musical ear to ensure that throughout South Africa during the summer of 1955 the Lions raised their entertainment value to new heights, on the field as well as off it. Not for nothing does Morgan call it 'the best time of my life'.

He went to Dublin in 1954 to manage a company manufacturing wire ropes, joined Bective Rangers and met a red-headed Aer Lingus stewardess, Nuala Martin. They were engaged before the Lions tour began and married the following December on the weekend when the groom happened to be in Dublin, captaining a combined England–Wales team against Scotland–Ireland to mark the opening of a new stand at Lansdowne Road.

'It was the best time of my rugby life because you could play as you wanted to play. There was no coach, nobody to tell us what to do in terms of detailed strategy. We didn't have any schemes but we did have

Jeff Butterfield, the England centre, and he drilled one thing into us – that we had to be fit. He'd say to me, "Cliffy, these buggers will run at us all day long until they drop, unless we make them turn. So stick the bloody thing up in the sky and make sure they turn, because they can't think on the turn." He was absolutely right. We had to do something different, whether it came from a careless little Welshman, a stout Englishman, a sturdy Scot or a wild Irishman. And that's why the Lions tour was a success. We did something different.

'We weren't politically aware the way they are today so that wasn't an issue. We had the perfect blend of players: Angus Cameron, Butterfield, Gareth Griffiths, Davies, Cecil Pedlow, O'Reilly, a terrific front row of W.O. Williams, Bryn Meredith and Courtenay Meredith, the mighty Rhys Williams in the second row, Russell Robins and the Scot Jimmy Greenwood. And then there was Clem [Thomas]. I can hear him now: "Bloody hell, I'll kick their b******* if they come near you, Cliffy." And then there was the rich Thomas laugh: "Ho, ho, ho, ho."

'O'Reilly was 18 but even then he was 30 years ahead of us all mentally. The Irish, like the Welsh, enjoy two things in life: success and failure. When I went round Ireland as I used to in my job, people used to complain about O'Reilly, that he couldn't tackle and that he didn't have any guts. During that Lions tour I saw him carry two enormous Springboks on his back and score a try. I saw him fall on the ball and get kicked to pieces for his trouble. Even today, almost 50 years on, he's still the record try-scorer for the Lions. What I remember most about that tour was how we took all the knocks, the bad decisions, the mistakes by officials, and nobody ever argued about a single incident.'

How the crowds loved them. Throughout what remains the only drawn series in the Lions' history, they smashed box-office records wherever they played, the four Tests drawing aggregate crowds of almost 250,000. An estimated 105,000 witnessed the first, at Ellis Park, where the Lions held on for a famous win, 23–22. They would have lost by a point had Jack van der Schyff landed a last-minute conversion, at a time when O'Reilly claimed to have been in direct communication with the Vatican! If the miss effectively ended van der Schyff's Springbok career, then the Lions could always claim that five tries to four meant justice had been done.

Tom van Vollenhoven, destined to set records at St Helen's which still stand today (almost 400 tries in 11 years ending in 1968), won the second Test in Cape Town with a scorching hat-trick before the Lions bounced back to win the third at Pretoria, 9–6. They won it, what's more, with a team containing eight Welshmen under a different captain,

Morgan leading the team in the temporary absence of the Irish lock Robin Thompson. He was back at the helm in Port Elizabeth three weeks later for the final act in a momentous series. Another van Vollenhoven try eased the 'Boks home with 14 points to spare, so squaring a series which overflowed with tries, 24 in all, 14–10 in South Africa's favour. The Lions departed as they had arrived, singing their heads off.

Morgan, the pianist-cum-musical director, had gone out of his way at the party's pre-tour base in Eastbourne to ensure they were in good voice. 'We went down to the piano room every night. We learnt English, Irish, Scottish and Welsh songs and we sang until we were word perfect.' As someone who never had any problem looking further than his nose, Morgan persuaded and cajoled the rest into learning an Afrikaans song as well, 'Sarie Marrais'. He did not need any public relations spin doctor to advise him of the importance of such a gesture, and having that up their sleeves made the Lions an instant hit.

As winning Lions performances go, the one they gave upon arrival at Jan Smuts Airport, Johannesburg, demands a place on the high list, if only for sheer spontaneity. 'We'd gone via Rome, Cairo and Livingstone in what was then Rhodesia. We'd been up and down all the way and when we landed in South Africa we were five and a half hours late. It must have been the middle of the night but there were thousands of people at the airport waiting to welcome us. I said to a few of the others, "We can't just walk off." So we stopped at the bottom of the steps leading off the plane and sang 'Sarie Marrais'. They all joined in, and the *Rand Daily Mail* said we were the greatest team ever to visit South Africa. We hadn't played a game!'

Morgan captained Wales throughout the 1956 championship, when three wins out of four were enough to capture the Five Nations title outright. By 1958 he was being lined up to captain the Lions in New Zealand the following year, and when word reached the selectors that their man was planning an early retirement, no less a figure than Wavell Wakefield, later the ennobled Lord Wakefield of Kendal, wrote Morgan a letter pleading with him to change his mind and lead the Lions.

'"Wakers" said to me, "You cannot retire. You must take the Lions to New Zealand." I used to see him often. I don't think it was as important to us then as it is now. It got to the point where I couldn't afford to go on playing. We were living in a flat in Cardiff. We didn't have any money. I suppose I could have gone and run into debt, as we had to later because of my illness. It took me 20 years to pay it all back. Rugby was important but it was not *the* most important thing in my life.'

'There was nobody then to say, "Here's £10,000, off you go," because the sport, then as now, was not important enough to the majority of the Great British public. These days players need money to pay the mortgage and buy a car. When I played for Wales, none of us had a mortgage. We certainly couldn't spell it, and I didn't have a car until I was 25. I was sad to retire because I was playing the best rugby of my life, but I had to retire. I had to face up to my responsibilities.'

It was the ultimate paradox. The man money couldn't buy had none to call his own. And so, after the home match against France, Morgan called it a day, less than a fortnight before his 28th birthday. The French, obliging to the very end, sent him on his way with a pair of cracked ribs, something which was hardly designed to make the wincing stand-off reconsider his decision. It was time to forge a career, if only someone would give him a nudge in the right direction. That someone turned out to be Hywell Davies, the head of BBC Wales.

'I came out of the after-match dinner feeling sick and holding my ribs when I bumped into Hywell Davies at the top of the stairs outside the dining-room. Everyone knew that the only rugby I had left to play was with the Barbarians in South Africa. Hywell said to me, and I'll never forget his words, "When you come back from South Africa and get those ribs fixed, I'd like you to come and see me. I might have something of interest . . ."'

Morgan launched his new career later that year, joining the BBC in Cardiff as sports organiser for Wales. His was not the most auspicious of starts. 'I did my first TV broadcast from a paint shop because that was the only "studio" available. There were only two chairs and they were both occupied by the guests, so I did the interview sitting on a bag of cement in the middle of the floor.'

Morgan the Organ took it all in his stride with a natural ease. If anything, his new career would prove to be even more meteoric than the old one. Four years after beginning to learn the ropes, Morgan had created such an impression that he went straight from regional television into one of the top network jobs in London, as editor of *Grandstand*.

On those rare occasions when he paused to catch his breath, Morgan could always recall the prophetic nature of Wilf Wooller's words all those years before when he counselled against a move to rugby league. 'Wilf was right. Nobody could have had a richer life than me, being paid to do something I'd have done for nothing. I loved it. I loved broadcasting and showing off and I had the best job in Great Britain for twelve and a half years, head of television sport and outside broadcasts. A rare privilege. I've been a rugby professional all my life in a sense. Everything

I've done in life has been because of rugby. I was picked up in Wales because of rugby. I did my first broadcast because of rugby.'

Every time Morgan had appeared on television as a rugby player, the fee, usually two guineas, had gone straight into the Welsh Rugby Union's bank account. The price he paid to protect his amateur status was nothing compared with the one he paid for his frenetic lifestyle as a television personality in demand all over the country. It almost cost him his life.

Having conquered sport at the highest television level with *Grandstand*, Morgan switched channels and branched out into current affairs as editor of ITV's prestigious investigative programme *This Week*, his three-year stewardship spanning the Aberfan disaster in October 1966. Those who scoffed at a rugby player dabbling in the world of politics scoffed no more once they had finished spluttering on their cornflakes after Morgan delivered what was truly a world exclusive.

When Ian Smith declared unilateral independence for what was then Rhodesia in the late '60s, the world wanted to interview him. Morgan beat them all to it, his network of rugby contacts opening doors which led him directly into the prime minister's office in Salisbury. 'Dai Williams was a third-generation Rhodesian whose grandfather had gone out from Wales with a pick and a shovel. I'd been sending Dai a Christmas card over the years not knowing what he did for a living. As luck would have it, he was the head of the government department directly responsible for Smith's day-to-day schedule. After I'd called Dai, he rang back to say he knew a Cliff Morgan and I said, "Yes, that's me." And he said, "Good God, boy! You must come out straight away." We did and I met Smith.'

The BBC, suddenly aware of what they had lost, redoubled their efforts to bring him back into the fold. Shortly after his return, the BBC launched a quiz programme which was to become so popular that it is still running today, *A Question of Sport*. As captains they chose the mercurial Welshman and Henry Cooper, whose guests for the inaugural edition in 1969 included George Best, Tom Finney and the late Lillian Board.

In his role as a freelance broadcaster, Morgan had gone to West Germany to commentate on the Army Cup final near Cologne. He began to feel unwell after the match. 'The room was spinning around and I had difficulty focusing on the people around me. I thought I'd better go to bed so I made my excuses and left.

'I woke up the next morning and I couldn't move. I couldn't feel one side of my face. Then I fell out of bed and the next thing I knew I'd woken up in hospital with all sorts of tubes sticking out of my nose and arms. I'd had a stroke. I was 41 and I'd never had anything wrong with me in my life until then.

'I'd been doing too many daft things. Showing off, really. Someone would say, "Come to Swansea and do this." So I'd go to Swansea and do it, and the next morning I'd have to be in London for an appointment at nine-thirty. I'd drive back through the night and then the next night I'd be in Scunthorpe because someone had asked me to do something there. I couldn't say no to anyone. That was my trouble.'

A classic case, therefore, of burning the candle at both ends, an observation which Morgan gladly grasped as a cue for a 'lovely' poem by the American Edna St Vincent Millay:

> My candle burns at both its ends
> It will not last the night.
> But, ah! my foes, and ah! my friends
> It gives a lovely light!

The overnight trips extended far beyond Swansea and Scunthorpe. When the Australians invited him to present their annual sports-writing awards, the indefatigable Clifford jumped on a plane to Sydney. He was there and back in four days and thought nothing of it, unaware that such a remorseless schedule would one day take its toll.

'And there I was, lying in hospital, knowing that my life was hanging by a thread. I was terribly conscious of my mortality, that it would only take something to go click and I would be gone. I'll never forget waking up in hospital the first time and seeing this beautiful woman beside my bed. She was a nun. Whenever I woke, she was always at the bedside.

'I noticed that each time I woke up I was nearer the window at one end of the ward. I wondered why and then I realised the beds were being moved up towards the window because they had moved those out who had died during the night. I was being moved nearer and nearer to that window. I thought, "Hello, what's happening here?"

'But there was no way I could feel sorry for myself, not when I looked around and realised that some of the poor devils in the same hospital would never get better, that some of them would never, ever walk or talk again. Nuala arrived and after about ten days Air Commodore Larry Lamb, the international referee, fixed for me to be transferred to a posher, RAF hospital. And there I shared a room with a German who had been a prisoner of war in Bridgend, of all places. Every day he shaved me and took me to the lavatory. Unbelievable!

'I was in a wheelchair for three months, then a rehabilitation centre, walking round on calipers. The stroke had left me with slurred speech and a twisted mouth, which was the cause of the slurring. The left side of my body was paralysed, including half my tonsils and half my tongue. Only one side was working and so every day I had to try to make the vowel sounds, ah-ee-ey-oh-uh and so on, until the constant practice forced the muscles in my mouth to function properly.

'I had to learn to walk again and in all the recovery took 11 months. And do you know a funny thing? You won't believe this, but I am glad that it happened because it changed me in many ways, all of them for the better. Most of all, it stopped me being arrogant and self-centred.

'The doctor said, "No smoking, no drinking." I smoked 30 a day but was never a big drinker so that wasn't a problem, although I do love a shandy when I finish in the gym, three days a week. I cut out the fags a couple of months ago and when I went back to work I worked harder than I did before.

'A stroke can happen to anyone at any time but I've never wasted energy worrying whether it will happen to me again. I didn't want to let anyone down and, most of all, that meant my family. We had nothing. In that position you have to work and you said yes to people when they offered you work because you knew you had to survive.

'There'd never been any money in rugby and I never thought about it because I was having such a good time. We had no money and two children at private school. I sold the car and in the end Nuala had to sell her engagement ring so we could pay the more urgent bills.

'Jack Solomons, the boxing promoter, sent me a cheque for £2,000 with a nice little note saying, "You'll be needing this." I kept the cheque in a drawer at home and it was eight months out of date when I sent it back to Jack, thanking him for his kindness and telling him, "I'll never forget you. I have started walking again today."'

Richard Burton, the actor and rugby fanatic who made the odd appearance in the back row for Aberavon, not far from his native Pontrhydyfen, also wrote to Morgan, offering him any of the various houses he and his then wife Elizabeth Taylor had dotted around the world. The letter concluded, 'Should you require anything as mundane as money, you only have to ask.'

No matter how parlous his financial side, Morgan was never one to let it stand in the way of principle. In October 1969, for instance, he abandoned a lucrative arrangement with the *News of the World* as their rugby correspondent in protest at the paper's serialisation of the scandalous Christine Keeler memoirs. A lesser man would have shrugged his shoulders and carried blithely on with the excuse that it was nothing to do with him.

Cliff, then presenting the children's television programme *Hobby Horse*, saw it very differently. 'I am the last person to moralise,' he said at the time. 'But I simply felt I could not write for the sports page and read on the front page something I did not agree with.'

His indomitable will drove him through overwhelming odds and back to work 11 months later. It would have been difficult enough had he specialised in the printed word, but for Morgan the broadcaster to reappear as if he had never been away took courage of a rare kind. The voice which many feared would be silenced from the airwaves sounded as good as new

Typically, he reintroduced himself not at any old rugby match but at the one which produced what was arguably the try of the century, the one a startled Phil Bennett started in front of his own posts and Gareth Edwards finished for the Barbarians against the All Blacks at the Arms Park in January 1973. Morgan's commentary, awe and admiration rolled into one, makes the most replayed piece of videotape in the history of the game sound all the better.

His career took him ever upwards until he reached the top as head of outside broadcasts for BBC Television, a post he held for 11 years. Granted such an overview of the sporting spectrum, he was one rugby union man who would never fall into the trap of overestimating the value of the sport. For all his love of the game, Morgan is impeccably qualified to assess precisely where it stands in the affections of the great British public.

'The maximum audience for an England–Wales match at Twickenham on *Grandstand* used to be five million. On the same night, Cambridge United against Manchester City in the FA Cup on *Match of the Day* would attract thirteen and a half million. Football has always been the most important sport in Great Britain.'

Reverting to freelance mode, his *Sport on Four* programme became compulsory listening every Saturday morning for some 11 years until the mandarins at Broadcasting House pulled the plug, inexplicably, on the morning of the 1998 Grand National.

True to form, Morgan took his leave without any palaver and only the faintest hint that he would not be back in the same place at the same time the following Saturday. 'Thanks very much to you all for listening,' he said. 'May your weekend be a happy and profitable one.'

While careful to avoid falling into the trap of 'it ain't what it was in my day', Morgan does not like all he sees as sport hurtles on into the next millennium. 'There's too much sport today. Give a kid too many sweets and he gets sick. It's a bit like that now. Too many people getting too much for too little.

'I don't envy rugby players being paid. What I do resent are the big fees being paid in any sport to those who can't play. I wouldn't have cared tuppence how much Gareth Edwards earned, or Barry John, or Phil Bennett, or David Duckham and so on. I read that one current Welsh player has a five-year contract worth £2 million. That's more money than you would pay six prime ministers put together. I just hope that one day the money dries up, because rugby could then pay international players a fixed amount at the end of each season.'

At 68 Morgan still has much to keep him occupied, as well as watching his daughter Catherine's 12-year-old son Jack playing mini-rugby at London Welsh, celebrating his 43rd wedding anniversary with Nuala and following his son Nick's career as an orthopaedic surgeon. And every so often, his mind will drift back to Trebanog where it all began.

So what if his father had decided to join Tottenham Hotspur and Clifford Isaac had been born in London? 'I tell you what would have happened. I'd have played football for the Arsenal and cricket for Middlesex, just like my hero Denis Compton!'

He probably would, too. And poor old Wales would never have known what it had missed.

5

Twinkle, Twinkle, Little Star

When they pushed the Salford rugby league contract under his nose over lunch at the Royal Hop Pole Hotel in Tewkesbury, David Watkins suddenly found it difficult to put pen to paper. So difficult, in fact, that the document had to be presented for his signature on five occasions over a period of two hours.

Each time he would take the pen out of his breast pocket, reach forward and then lean back, as if he could not quite bring himself to cut the umbilical cord and cross the iron curtain then separating union from league. Once a few minor alterations had been made to the small print, Salford finally got their man at the sixth time of asking.

With a trembling hand, Watkins went the whole hog and completed what was then, on 19 October 1967, the most expensive cross-code transfer. At a stroke, the Welsh Lion from the Gwent valleys had made himself richer by £11,000 plus a guaranteed £1,000 a year for each of the five years of his contract: £16,000, a staggering sum of money at a time when £5,000 could buy him the house of his dreams.

Had he known exactly what he was letting himself in for, Watkins might have been better off signing for Jack Solomons and demanding that the big-fight promoter add another nought to the sum. Over the next year or so, a whole battalion of heavyweight sluggers, none of them particularly fussy about adhering to the Queensberry rules, would be queuing up to take a swing at him. The way they saw it, a fancy Dan from South Wales had come into their patch to take their money and he would have to be taught a lesson.

Being a shrewd sort of bloke, Watkins knew he would be given a rough ride, that the record fee would make him fair game for every hard case north of Birmingham. It turned out to be much, much rougher than he imagined. The on-field assaults were of such systematic violence that the brutality almost drove Watkins out of the game. 'Brutal is the only word to sum up the punishment I took in the first couple of years. Rugby league at that time was probably the most brutal sport in the world apart from boxing.

'After the 1969 Challenge Cup final at Wembley, when I had a pretty appalling match, I said to Jane, my wife, "I don't know whether we should go home. I can't take much more of this." I'd broken my nose four times, had a double fracture of the jaw and broken my ribs, all in off-the-ball incidents.'

One of the worst happened, appropriately enough, on Boxing Day, in a local derby against Leigh. 'One of their players was a real head-banger whose sole aim was to maim me. I'd passed the ball long before this guy smashed me with his forearm and broke my nose. I got up and for the first time in my life I complained to the ref, Joe Manley, one of the most senior officials in the game. I just said, "Crikey, you must have seen that." He just said, "Look, son. You've been paid enough to look after yourself." In other words, they couldn't, or wouldn't, stop people hitting me.

'For the first two years in rugby league, there were times at several grounds where I was being threatened physically. It got so bad at times that I wondered whether I should go out and play. I don't mind admitting there were times when I was scared to go out. I'd played against some pretty rough customers in union, like the French and the All Blacks, but because I'd grown up in the game I knew where trouble lay and how to avoid it. In league it seemed as if nobody in the early days was prepared to help. It was a case of: "Bugger him. He's had all this money, he can look after himself."

'When I got to my lowest ebb, Jane urged me to hang in there and that it would all come good. She was right, but I had to change my attitude to make it work. Until then I'd never thought about striking an opponent. Whenever I was hit in union, there were people at Newport who would finish it off for me. Now I had to fend for myself, and so I learnt that if anyone hit me in league, I would get them sooner or later and pay them back.'

By then Watkins's arrival in the north of England had been greeted with a potent concoction of friendliness, curiosity and downright animosity. Not everyone in the Salford dressing-room was turning cartwheels at discovering that such a highly paid practitioner of the union code had landed in their midst. For every smiling face, there would be a hit-man lying in ambush, or so it seemed.

The first match, a Friday night affair against Oldham, passed off without any major incident, the only threat to life or limb coming from the enthusiasm of a crowd which had swollen to some three times more than the average, ensuring that, if nothing else, Salford were able to reclaim a small percentage of their investment. There was, as Watkins wryly observed, much interest in seeing 'why on earth Salford had paid 16 grand for a midget from South Wales'.

He had a lot of convincing to do. 'My own dressing-room wasn't too bad apart from one or two players, but at least they reckoned that if I was as good as some people thought I might be, then they'd be better off by winning a few more matches. Of the crowd that flocked in for that first game, one third were true Salford supporters, one third came to see how I would adapt and the other third came to see me fall on my face.'

The newcomer scored a try and dropped two goals and the first £20 win bonus rolled in, plus an extra £6 as man of the match. Even so, it did not take him long to become inured to the standard type of greeting from wags, wits and half-wits alike. 'It was stuff like, "You're a big girl's blouse, Watkins." If I missed a couple of tackles, someone was almost always bound to wait until there was a deathly silence in the match and then shout out, "Hey, Watkins. Next time hit him with your bloody wallet!"'

There was nothing funny about the first time someone gave him a severe going-over. It happened during a cup-tie at Featherstone, a tough Yorkshire mining village where once upon a time they used to stand at the pit head and whistle up a rugby team. Except for the accents, Watkins might have been back in his native Blaina – but there the similarities ended.

'Featherstone was a very small ground with the old hooped railings, and they were so close to the touchline that if you got tackled with any ferocity you were liable to go through the hoops and come out the other side feeling a bit like a potato that's gone through the chip-peeler. Everyone was breathing down your neck and the crowd that day was 7,500, more than the entire population of the village.

'They were baying before the game began and most of it was directed at me. 'Where's the midget? Can he walk on water? Can he heck.' Featherstone were very difficult to stop when they were going down the slope. Going uphill, as we were, in the first half meant we were in for a torrid game.

'They had a lot of big forwards, 18 and 19 stone, and they rolled them down the slope at me like big boulders. Even the scrum-half looked like a giant for someone playing in that position. Carl Dooler was a tough, uncompromising type of player who had been with the Great Britain squad on tour down under a couple of years before. When I tried to go round a scrum in the first three or four minutes of the match, Dooler stretched out an arm, grabbed me by the collar and threw me down with such ferocity that I must have bounced about four times. When I came to a stop, he stood over me and said, "Twinkle, twinkle now, little f****** star!"'

Twinkle he did, despite the intimidation, standing the test of time longer than most to earn a place right up there among the other Welsh goalkickers who left union to earn a place among the ten all-time highest scorers in league, legendary names like Gus Risman, Lewis Jones and Kel Coslett. In emulating Jones as a double Lion, Watkins achieved the distinction of becoming the first to captain his country at both codes whilst adding six Great Britain Tests to the six he had played for the Lions against New Zealand and Australia in 1966. What Dooler did to him at Featherstone the following season was nothing, in terms of an international incident, compared with what the All Black colossus Colin Meads had done to him during the final Test in Auckland.

The previous week Watkins had phoned his grandfather, Semi Bridgeman, at the British Legion club where he worked in Blaina, a mining village perched at the top of the Sirhowy Valley. It was hardly the sort of place to be inundated by calls from Newport, never mind New Zealand. The 24-year-old asked Mr Bridgeman to pass the astounding news on to his parents, then unconnected by telephone. He had done his level best to put one of the more remote corners of Monmouthshire on the map.

Yet only a few months earlier Watkins had been fretting as to whether he had done enough to clinch a place on the tour. Once those fears had been allayed, he then had to contend with the imposing presence of Mike Gibson for the right to a Test place at fly-half. They came from very different social strata, Watkins's working-class roots in stark contrast with Gibson's privileged upbringing in Belfast which enabled him to launch his long association with the Lions from Cambridge University.

While both played in all four Tests, Watkins at number ten and Gibson at centre, they were not exactly bosom pals. 'The first time Mike Gibson was picked at inside centre, he told me he had no doubt that he was a better stand-off half than me. I told him I didn't think he was. I told him I was faster, more elusive and that I played at a higher level of club rugby in South Wales than he did in Ireland.

'Roger Young, another lad from Belfast, was my half-back partner. I could meet him anywhere, any time as an old friend. If I met Mike Gibson tomorrow, I don't think he'd know who I was. On tour I got the impression he thought he was deserving of the better things in life. He was fairly aloof. He would never join the boys on a night out. Mike Gibson wouldn't do anything like that.

'As a room-mate, you never got much out of him. He was a tremendous player but he was a non-team man off the field. He was never one of the lads. That was a pity, because on a Lions tour you can make friends for life.'

It never occurred to the young Welshman that he would end up calling the shots as captain. That honour having been bestowed upon a Scottish army officer, Mike Campbell-Lamerton, there were ominously early signs that he would not be up to the job. Another Welshman from Gwent, the late Alun Pask, had been so widely touted for the captaincy – especially in South Wales, naturally enough – that his appointment had been considered in some quarters as little short of a formality. Campbell-Lamerton, after all, had failed the litmus test of any prospective captain, namely being good enough to command a first-team place on merit.

Sadly, the bungling over the captaincy set the tone for the whole tour, the 1966 Lions stumbling from one problem to another and the series of botches culminating in their whitewashing by the All Blacks. They were one down with three to play when Watkins found himself promoted to the biggest job of all. One Test had proved one too many for Campbell-Lamerton. 'I would rather die than suffer humiliation like that again,' he was quoted as saying after New Zealand had run away with the first Test at Dunedin 20–3. 'I would rather die.'

The selectors had still to deliver a verdict on the Watkins–Gibson fly-half rivalry when they called the Newport player aside during training. 'My first reaction was, "Oh s***. Does this mean I'm out of the Test side?" They told me that Mike Campbell-Lamerton was standing down and that they wanted me to captain the team. Mike said, "You are the life and soul of the team and the right man for the job."'

By then the Lions were being beaten up as well as beaten. Between the first and second Tests, Canterbury had, in Watkins's words, 'kicked seven kinds of hell out of us. They laid out Willie John McBride. They laid out Colin McFadyean. They laid out Gibson. They laid out just about everyone they could hit.'

It was bad enough to force Jim Telfer, the hard-as-nails Scot captaining the Lions that day, to do what rugby people rarely do at formal after-match occasions and give them a piece of his mind. 'We were all sitting down to dinner in what looked like an aircraft hangar,' Watkins said. 'There must have been about 350 people there, including all the bigwigs from the Union.

'Jim got up and went straight to the point. "Thanks for giving me the opportunity to speak," he said. "I would just like to say that New Zealand rugby contains thugs, cheats and liars." Apart from the journalists dashing off to beat their deadlines, you could have heard a pin drop. Jim's a very honest chap and he didn't mess about confusing that honesty with diplomacy. He was absolutely right in what he said, even though it meant we were stuck with the usual label of whingeing Poms.'

The violence escalated in the wake of Telfer's speech to such an extent that another X-certificate match, against Auckland, prompted calls for the tour to be abandoned. The Governor General felt it necessary to intervene in an attempt to save the whole tour from going down the plughole.

'Delme Thomas and a few other players decided they weren't going to take any more and they started smacking them back. As captain, I made it clear we had to stick up for ourselves. We'd had enough of the thuggery. If they hit us, we'd hit them back.'

One of the last blows caused a national outcry, in New Zealand as well as in Britain. The punch, delivered by the heavyweight Meads during the last Test, laid the comparatively flyweight Watkins out for the count. Meads packed enough power to cause serious damage, as another Welsh international, Jeff Young, discovered three years later at the expense of a broken jaw.

'Meads was one of the best players I ever played against. He was also the best referee I ever played against. He never stopped talking, always chivvying the ref about how he should handle the game, always complaining about a knock-on, a forward pass, an offside, whatever. He did it all the time.

'We were awarded a penalty. Meads didn't go back the compulsory ten yards for me to take it. I said something to him in the heat of the moment which was probably not that complimentary. The ref then intervened, Meads went back and I kicked for touch. As the ball spiralled into touch, he ran through and knocked me over. It didn't really hurt me but I got up to remonstrate with him. I probably called him a dirty b****** or something and he smacked me straight in the face. I went down and later had six stitches put in my mouth. As I came round, I heard several players, including Mike Gibson and Ken

Kennedy, screaming abuse at him and remonstrating that he should have been sent off.'

There was never any question of the New Zealand referee, Pat Murphy from North Auckland, giving New Zealand's most revered player his marching orders. Meads's bully-boy behaviour went unpunished and the Lions had to take it where they had taken a great deal else on that tour: on the chin. According to his victim, Meads, far from apologising for his action, defended it.

'The All Blacks had a habit of going round schools to talk about the Lions tour. When he went to Westlake Grammar School, where they had 600 pupils, Meads was asked why he had taken it upon himself to hit little Dai Watkins, 5ft 6in, 10½ stone wringing wet, when he was 6ft 3in and some 17 stone. Meads gave them a two-word answer: self defence!'

Ironically, when Meads *was* sent off, against Scotland at Murrayfield the following year, Watkins, who had just transferred to league, must have thought that justice had been done at last. While the Welshman is still waiting for an apology, he responded to Meads's dismissal in Edinburgh by sending him a letter of sympathy – which, considering the background, was a remarkably generous gesture.

'I wrote to him saying I didn't think he was a dirty player. I wished him well and hoped it would not have any adverse effect on his career. It didn't matter that he hadn't apologised to me. The way he saw it, rugby was a man's sport where if somebody remonstrated with you, you gave him a dig. If he'd done it these days, there's no doubt he would have been sent off.'

Meads did admit that the Lions had demanded that he be given an early bath. He also admitted that he had been abused by members of the public over the incident. 'The Lions were awarded a penalty and took a tap kick for a better angle for Watkins to kick to touch,' he wrote in his book, *Colin Meads: All Black*. 'I tried to smother the kick. My arms were above my head for the charge and David hit me in the stomach. My reaction was automatic, a reflex if you like. I back-handed him. He went down.

'The Lions screamed at me, especially the hooker, Ken Kennedy, who abused me violently, from a distance. Afterwards I was sorry I had done it. But if anyone belts me, I belt them back. It's something I'm never proud of, but in the same circumstances it would happen again. You are wrong because you hit a little guy, but when you react to that sort of provocation, you react urgently, without thought. The size of the man does not occur to you.

'He might as well have been a giant. I'd have reacted in the same way. David is such a nice little bloke and he put on such a nice little act. He recovered very quickly and was mighty sprightly immediately afterwards for a man who had been "knocked out" for a couple of minutes.

'For a couple of weeks I received abusive mail and telegrams. I wasn't proud of the incident and I felt sorry about it. The message I received from David after I had been sent off at Murrayfield was one of the nicest of all.'

The Lions' consistent failure resulting in their first whitewashing by the All Blacks in a four-Test series confirmed the popular view that the wrong captain had been chosen. Pask, the multi-purpose back-row forward who specialised in flummoxing opponents by running with the ball glued to one hand, had begun that year by scoring the try which beat England at Twickenham. A home win over Scotland set Wales up for a Triple Crown in Dublin, but their resultant failure was to cost their captain more than the mythical trophy. There is a theory, still unsubstantiated after all these years, that Pask talked himself out of the Lions job by antagonising the Establishment with a forthright interview before the Irish match, in which he tempted fate by saying that Wales would win. The Lions party was being chosen that weekend, and when Pask was confined to a place among the ranks, Watkins, for one, suspected he knew why.

'Pask blotted his copybook by criticising the Irish and saying we were going to win. He was too up-front for their liking and I'm convinced it cost him the Lions captaincy. It's human nature that if enough people tell the selectors to pick a certain player, they'll go and pick someone else.

'The Welsh were regarded as being pretty cocky in those days and there was a feeling among some that we were getting a bit too big for our boots. Paskie should have been captain but he took it well. He wasn't a better player than the other No. 8, Jim Telfer, but he was a better captain. They could have found room for both.'

At the end of a day which began with the IRA blowing Nelson off his famous pillar in O'Connell Street, they found room instead for Campbell-Lamerton, the Scottish captain who was always going to struggle for a Test place in the second row. 'Mike worked hard but Pask was a player of immense skill who made few mistakes and who was always prepared to help others out by telling them what and what not to do. Tactically, he could read a game.

'Mike's team talk was all about guts and glory, "up out of the trenches and at 'em". Pask would have been more analytical than that. The All

Blacks knew our backs were better than theirs but we were torn between using our backs and taking them on up front. They were so fearful we were going to run it that they intimidated us up front.

'The choice of captain surprised everyone. McBride and Brian Price were the probable Test locks. Mike was a nice guy but one had doubts at the outset as to whether he was good enough to go as a player, let alone as captain.'

And so it came to pass, Campbell-Lamerton returning for the third Test, only to be dropped again for the fourth. Pask, whose all-round skills enabled him to hold the fort for Wales on one occasion as an emergency full-back, retired the following year and kept in close touch with the game as an invaluable member of BBC Wales's production staff. He lost his life at the age of 58 in tragic circumstances, trying to rescue some belongings from a fire which engulfed his Gwent home in November 1995.

Watkins captained Wales when Pask played the last of his 26 internationals, against Ireland at the Arms Park in March 1967. By then he had discovered that leading the Lions carried no guarantee of any security with Wales. It did not take him long to realise that what the selectors told him they would do was always liable to turn out to be nothing of the sort.

A new number ten had appeared on the scene, and while Watkins may have been the undisputed *numero uno* for the best of British and Irish, he suddenly found himself second choice for Wales and out on his ear. Barry John took over for the first match of the 1966–67 season, against Australia. For his predecessor, it was a more wounding blow than the Meads punch.

'I came home from the longest Lions tour to be told I would captain Wales that season, only to be dropped for the first two matches. I didn't believe that anyone could drop me, such was my self-confidence. When they brought Barry in, it felt as though my world had ended.

'When players are dropped, they invariably say they want the team to win. Well, when I was dropped I didn't want Wales to win. I went to see that match, and while I wasn't delighted that Australia had won, I was glad Wales had lost. They then went to Scotland and lost again. I don't think Barry was fully fit. He played badly and I came back in for the next game as captain. Yet a few weeks before I hadn't been good enough to get into the side. Where was the logic in that?'

A few months later the writing began to appear on the wall, even though Wales had finished the season with a thumping home win over England, Keith Jarrett's phenomenal debut helping his country avert a whitewash. The selectors' decision to delay choosing their captain against New Zealand in November 1967 did nothing to ease the doubts gnawing away at the back of Watkins's mind. His antennae told him not to wait. When Wales finally got round to naming their captain, Watkins was adjusting to his new world in rugby league.

'They had never dithered over the captain before and that told me there had been some debate as to whether or not I was good enough. I had this offer to go professional. I was 25 years old and I'd done everything the game could offer. I'd played all over the world, I'd played for Wales, the Lions, the Baa-baas and all the other representative teams. I'd never seen a game of rugby league in my life but I thought, "Bugger it. I'm not going to wait again to be disappointed."'

Bill Clement, the Welsh Rugby Union's authoritative secretary whose tenure spanned three decades, took the trouble to send the departing fly-half his best wishes. 'Your energy, enthusiasm and dedication to Wales will be sorely missed on our rugby fields,' Clement wrote. 'But, as in the past, I am sure that in due time we will again be able to fill the serious gap in our playing ranks as a result of your departure. My sincere and lasting wishes for your future success, both in rugby league football and in life itself.'

Watkins would find out soon enough that such warmth did not extend to the Union itself. There was something of an apartheid in certain union circles where they demanded a league 'turncoat' be treated almost as a social outcast. Salford's twinkling little star experienced that for himself one night at Cardiff Arms Park.

'I was mingling with the fans outside the clubhouse after a Cardiff–Newport match, not knowing what to do or where to go. Hubert Johnson, the Cardiff chairman, saw me and took me into the members' bar. While he was ordering me a drink, another very well-known Cardiff official, Danny Davies, was on the opposite side of the bar. He said, "I see we are drinking with professionals tonight, Hubert, are we?" Hubert told him straight, "If you don't want to drink with us, Danny, I suggest you go and find somewhere else." That was very comforting, but it was typical of the attitude.

'On another occasion when I came home, it was to do some work with the BBC commentary team at a Cardiff–Llanelli game. I was sent my pass to the press-box but at eleven o'clock on the morning of the match BBC Wales phoned to say that I had been refused entry to the press-box. The BBC were sorry but they said they could not overturn the decision and had to accept it, however reluctantly.

'Then there was the time when I arranged to meet a photographer at the Arms Park for some pictures for my book. They wouldn't let me in! I was refused permission to go inside the gates by Bill Clement. It wasn't his decision. It was the WRU's decision. All the photographs had to be done outside the main entrance.'

A dressing-room incident the following year, 1971, left him in no doubt that the same sort of rugby apartheid could also be applied in reverse. It happened on the occasion of his first full appearance for Great Britain, as Alex Murphy's half-back partner against New Zealand, and revolved around a comment from Bill Fallowfield, secretary of the Rugby League. 'He was the most powerful man in the game. He came into the dressing-room, handed me my jersey and said, "Make the most of it, because it'll be your last." Bill Fallowfield was never slow to let it be known that he didn't like rugby union players.'

The old prejudices cut both ways. Watkins ignored it, hardly missing a chance to compile records of monumental proportion in keeping with his status as one of the very few Welshmen to have had a lasting influence on both codes. His figures still stand today, among them the most goals in one season, 221, and the longest run without failing to score at least once, 92 matches.

What he achieved made a mockery of his early anxiety and those who had questioned his ability to hack it. Over a period of 16 years before rejoining his beloved but struggling Newport as chairman, he kicked 1,342 goals and scored 3,117 points to rise to tenth position in the all-time list. Only four Welshmen scored more: Jim Sullivan (6,022), Gus Risman (4,050), Kel Coslett (3,545) and Lewis Jones (3,445).

Not bad for a midget from the valleys . . .

6

Chopping the Pine Tree

Delme Thomas made the long haul from the Carmarthenshire village of Bancyfelin to New Zealand in the spring of 1966 convinced he had only been sent there to make up the numbers. Some eight weeks later, the uncapped Welshman found himself standing in the middle of a line-out surrounded by some of the greatest All Blacks of all time. They were grouped all around him, Wilson Whineray, Brian Lochore, Kel Tremain, Waka Nathan and, standing there right alongside him, arguably the greatest of them all: Colin 'Pine Tree' Meads.

A second or two later, Thomas jumped for the ball and landed on his back, as if he had careered headlong into a real pine tree. By the time the soaring young Welshman came back down again, Meads had given him a thumping reminder that All Blacks do not like to be messed about in the line-out. The experience cost Thomas one of his front teeth.

'Meads was a hard player and I remember him giving me a clout, a real hard one. It was my fault. I asked for it. They didn't take any prisoners in that series and in the previous line-out I'd gone up on Meads's back for the ball. At the next line-out I should have known what to expect. I went up for the ball, he punched me in the mouth and knocked me to the ground. He didn't say a word. Neither did I. There was nothing to say. We both knew where we stood.'

Back-handed compliments in those days did not come any bigger. In the brutal language of the line-out, the old emperor had acknowledged an unknown young Welshman as something more than a nuisance, his opponent having wasted no time persuading him that he was a dangerous customer, one not to be trifled with. Meads had no way of knowing that Thomas would end up with the last laugh.

Far from making up the numbers, the Welsh-speaking convert from soccer had made a piece of history as the first uncapped post-war Lion to force his way into a Test match. What made his choice all the more unusual was that the Lions selectors had to drop one of the selectors to make way for him. Mike Campbell-Lamerton thus became the first captain of a Lions touring team since Doug Prentice in 1930 to be dropped from the Test team because he was not good enough to justify his place. An army officer, the London Scottish lock had been a controversial choice, his appointment provoking a public outcry – especially in South Wales, where they had spent weeks anticipating the appointment of their man Alun Pask.

When his father drove him to the Lions' assembly point in Bournemouth, Thomas at least knew where he stood. 'I was the fourth lock,' he said. 'I had no choice of making the Test team.' It was, if nothing else, a realistic appraisal of his rank. In the international pecking order, the other three locks were all some way ahead of him. Campbell-Lamerton had to be in because he was *numero uno*, and Brian Price would start off as the other Test lock if only for the very good reason that his presence went a long way towards explaining Thomas's uncapped status.

The third choice was none other than Willie John McBride, embarking upon the second of his five Lions tours. Little wonder, therefore, that Thomas felt more than a touch nervous at mixing in such company. He had never expected to be there in the first place. 'One or two papers had tipped me but, much as I wanted to believe them, I didn't think anything of it. I thought it would be a closed shop. Brian Price and Brian Thomas were the first-choice pair for Wales and I certainly thought they'd both be in.

'Llanelli were playing Richmond in London on the weekend when the party was being chosen, and we travelled back by train on the Sunday. I still hadn't heard a word when I got back home but everyone in the village must have known because they'd laid on a big celebration. You can only begin to imagine my surprise. I didn't know all the Welsh players, never mind the rest of the Lions from England, Ireland and Scotland. Being a village boy, I hadn't been about much.'

Whether by accident or not, it was McBride who eased the apprehensive new boy through the initial uncertainty of his initiation into the most élite rugby order in the British Isles. In pairing the 30 tourists off, the Lions management did Thomas the favour of putting him in the same room as a player whose sheer powers of endurance had elevated him to a class all of his own. 'I checked in, got my key number and went up to the room,' said Thomas. 'I had no way of knowing who I was rooming with until I opened the door and saw a suitcase with Willie John McBride's name on it.

'Going to the other side of the world was a big thing in those days, bigger than it is now in the sense that we were going away for what seemed like an eternity, four and a half months. Willie John knew how inexperienced I was. He said, "Don't worry. Everything will be okay." He really looked after me. I just felt my way and kept quiet for a couple of weeks and got on with trying to play to the best of my ability.'

It did not take the quiet man long to make a strident case for a Test place in tandem with his Irish room-mate. Thomas proved to be such a quick learner that he needed only four midweek matches to demand elevation to the Test team alongside his hitherto midweek partner McBride. A 'real hammering' in the first Test at Dunedin clinched their joint promotion, the consequent removal of Campbell-Lamerton a tacit admission from the Lions management that they had got it wrong. They had fallen into the trap of choosing a captain who, for all his unquestioned devotion to the troops at his disposal, was not good enough to justify his place as a first-choice lock.

Thomas had taken a shortcut to the summit of the British and Irish game, bypassing Wales to get there by the fastest route of all. Within a matter of months he had progressed from being not quite good enough for Wales to being a Test player for the Lions at 23, a comparatively early age for admission to the engine-room of the international game.

'It was a great honour, made all the greater by being picked for Great Britain before I had been picked for Wales. Mike Campbell-Lamerton realised he wasn't playing up to the mark and he wished me all the best. It must have been very embarrassing for him, being captain and not being able to hold his place. I have great respect for the man. Not many would have stepped down in those circumstances.'

During the course of his Test debut Thomas held his own, despite Meads using his extra-large fist to welcome the new boy to the real world of All Black rugby. In spite of the ensuing dental work, the introduction left him with a sense of admiration for the New Zealand game which the passing of time has not dimmed one iota. 'People talk about hard games but unless you have been to New Zealand you don't know what physical rugby is all about. It was a real eye-opener.'

Sadly, it was also a real eye-closer, literally so in the case of Sandy Carmichael, the Scotland prop who suffered more than anyone from the systematic violence used by the notorious Canterbury Butchers against the Lions during their next tour of New Zealand five years later. 'Hard' in Delme's book was not a euphemism for the brutality which guaranteed that match a place in the black museum of rugby mayhem. By hard, Thomas meant the ruthless, but acceptable, New Zealand attitude to rucking: that if you were caught on the wrong side, then you had it coming.

'If you tried to kill the ball, they rucked you back with the ball, and if you complained to the referee, he'd just say, "Serves you right, you shouldn't have been there in the first place." If any of their own players were caught on the wrong side, they'd be rucked back just the same.'

It's known in the trade as shoeing. Thomas survived the studded treatment and, what's more, he survived in the Test team despite Campbell-Lamerton's reinstatement to a touring side which found itself two down with two to play. Thomas had made such an impression in place of the non-playing captain that the selectors were determined to find room for him somewhere.

They found it in the front row, at tight-head prop, a choice which said little for the Lions' strategic planning and an awful lot about Thomas's emergence as a team man willing to play whenever and wherever it was required, even if it did nothing to enhance his reputation as a specialist middle-of-the-line jumper. He hurled himself into the strange new position with relish, but it turned out to be at the expense of his chosen career in the second row.

'They said they wanted to include me in the Test for my line-out work. I held my own in the scrums and jumped at four in the line-out, but then I got hurt playing at prop in a midweek match in the week before the last Test. The scrum went down, I twisted my back and that was that.'

If Meads thought he had seen the last of Thomas, he was badly mistaken. In Carmarthenshire they ignored the 4–0 Test whitewash and Thomas came home to a hero's reception as well as a place in the Wales team at the earliest available opportunity. It was against Australia at the Arms Park at the end of that year when he won his Welsh cap, on the same day that another Welsh-speaker from the same neck of the woods, Barry John, won his.

Ironically, while Thomas had embarked upon his first Lions tour as an uncapped player who would force his way into the second row, he left for the second two years later as a fully fledged Welsh international who found himself unable to make a single Test appearance in his specialist position. McBride and the beanpole Scot Peter Stagg emerged as the Test pair, but once more Thomas found an alternative route into the team.

Yet again he proved the old adage about not being able to keep a good man down. As the replacement lock for the first Test against the Springboks, Thomas played virtually the entire match in his role of emergency prop, the English tight-head Mike Coulman having been injured in the opening minutes. For Thomas it was to be as much a test of courage as it was of technique. The giant South African Johannes Marias was waiting to get to grips with him, all 19 stone of him. 'In that first scrum I thought he was going to kill me,' said Thomas. 'He took me right up into the air so that I was sticking out of the scrum, but he never did it again. I held my own after that.'

The other Welsh prop on the tour, John O'Shea of Cardiff, then ensured Thomas as much practice as possible between Tests – although such altruism was hardly uppermost in his mind when he landed an uppercut or two on an opponent in the Orange Free State match at Bloemfontein. The referee, H.J. du Plooy, from Orange Free State, decided to do something none of his more permissive colleagues had dared do on that tour. He sent O'Shea off.

Another lost cause did nothing for British rugby's recurring failure to win when it mattered most. No sooner had Thomas returned from a second abortive Lions tour than he was off on another punishing venture with Wales, on their pioneering journey to New Zealand in the summer of 1969. The All Blacks won both Tests by the proverbial street, but the experience was to provide the Lions with the foundation for their triumphant return to the Land of the Long White Cloud.

Only three had survived from the ill-fated expedition five years earlier: McBride, the Scottish back-row forward, Frank Laidlaw and the durable Thomas, off on his third Lions tour. By then he was on the wings of an eagle, his career soaring to so many peaks that over a period of 18 months he won a Grand Slam with Wales, followed by a Test series in New Zealand, followed by his most unforgettable victory of all, for Llanelli against the All Blacks.

For Thomas it was a classic case of cometh the hour, cometh the man, Carwyn James. He, perhaps more than anyone, had been responsible for exploding the global theory of All Black supremacy. In five matches against New Zealand as coach of both the Lions and Llanelli, James lost only once, the Scarlets' victory proving he could work the miracle with a club side as well as with the best players in the British Isles.

'Carwyn was a man far ahead of his time,' said Thomas. 'He saw things in players long before anyone else did. For example, he moved

Barry Llewelyn from No. 8 at Llanelli to loose-head prop, which was something nobody else would have dreamt of doing. The switch made Barry the first of the new breed of mobile prop forwards. Again Carwyn was miles ahead of the game.

'If he had lived, Welsh rugby would not be in the state it is today. People would have realised that his ideas made sense and done something about it. There is no doubt he should have been made coach of Wales after the Lions tour. The Union made a mistake in rejecting him.

'He made enemies in the Union because he wanted to do the job his way or not at all. He was a lovely man, Carwyn, but he could also be a loner when it came to pursuing his beliefs about the game. He wanted to pick the team and do away with the selectors, the Big Five. As he used to say to me, "How can you expect five people to agree on picking a side?" What a pity the Welsh Rugby Union were too set in their ways to listen to what he was saying.'

En route to New Zealand for the last time, Thomas had another good reason, besides having his club mentor at the helm, for thinking that this time it would be different. The All Blacks were over the hill and a fair way down the other side. 'They were a better team in 1966 than they were five years later. Most of the greats – Whineray, Gray, Meads, Tremain and Lochore – had all gone. I knew from the Welsh trip a couple of years before that they weren't as good as they used to be.

'There was one other big difference. The 1971 Lions was the finest team I ever had the privilege of playing for. It was a great side with a wonderful three-quarter line, the majority of them Welsh, but also with other world-class players like Mike Gibson. We don't seem capable of producing their like any more.'

Early results strengthened Thomas's conviction that this would be the tour to end all tours, that this time nothing would stop the Lions from achieving something which had been beyond every British and Irish team since the first party to carry the official title The British Isles Rugby Union Touring Team had blazed the trail almost half a century earlier.

As well as the right mix of management and players, the '71 Lions also had more than their fair share of irrepressible personalities, each guaranteed to keep the spirit bubbling. None more so than Chico Hopkins.

If Chico was ever tempted to wallow in self-pity at having to play second fiddle to Gareth Edwards, he had the consolation of knowing he would have walked into any other team in the world. There were other characters, like the Irish prop Sean Lynch. 'Hell of a boy, Sean,' said

Thomas. 'He'd be feeling so homesick at times that you'd think it would break his heart. We'd often go and have a drink together, and on this one night, when Sean had had one or two too many, Carwyn walked out of the bar with a smile and a wink and left him sitting there.

'He was never one for shouting his mouth off at a player. He'd quietly let it be but you knew he would get his own back on the training field. The next morning he'd put us through it as usual and we were trooping off when he called out, "Sean, you haven't finished yet." Then he'd have him doing sprints non-stop for about ten minutes. Sean used to swear that Carwyn would never catch him again having one beer over the odds but he did. Carwyn would catch him four times out of five. Sean was a great character who had the utmost respect for the man.'

As well as his smart use of psychology, James also had an instinctive knack of pre-empting the opposition. A late change to the Lions team chosen for the match against a provincial team whose name would become a byword for infamy is a classic example of how James could smell danger and react accordingly.

New Zealanders had never seen a fly-half like Barry John. Nor had they seen a Lions backline run so many rings around so many opponents in the approach to the first of the four-match Test series. Christchurch seven days before the opening international was supposed to be the time and place where the Kiwis would hit back, with boots, fists and anything they could lay their hands on. The Canterbury Butchers reacted with a savagery which confirmed the Lions' worst fears: that they had been sent in to give the tourists a good hiding. James's sixth sense told him to withdraw John from the firing line and save him for the more important business the following week, rather than take the unnecessary risk of exposing him to common assault.

'Carwyn pulled Barry out because he had a fair idea what was going to happen and he didn't want him hurt,' said Thomas. 'That's how shrewd he was. Whatever the New Zealanders tried, they weren't crafty enough to outwit Carwyn.

'I played against Canterbury and I have never played in such a terrible match in all my life. They were a disgrace, and "Grizz" Wyllie, the All Black in their back row, was the worst of all. He behaved like a wild animal. You can't respect a man who behaves like that. He was off his head, punching, kicking, the whole lot. He was arrogant off the field too. Not a nice guy.'

The systematic beating which the Lions took in the front row was such that neither prop, Sandy Carmichael nor Ray McLoughlin, took any further part in the tour. The photographs of Carmichael, his face smashed and ugly black and red lumps around what passed for his eyes, shocked the world. The X-ray examination revealed that he had suffered five fractures to the left cheekbone.

If Canterbury were a disgrace, as indeed they were, then the rugby Establishment was an even bigger disgrace for allowing such gratuitous violence to pass without a single player being brought to book. Not for the first time, the supposed custodians of the sport, the International Board, sat back and contemplated its navel.

As one who plied his trade in the engine-room of the game, Thomas had seen it all – or, rather, he thought he had seen it all. The events of Lancaster Park on Saturday, 17 June 1971 shocked him then and still do now, more than a quarter of a century later.

'I have never experienced filth like it in any game of rugby, to be honest with you. It was vicious. I remember taking the ball from a short line-out when I was kicked on the cheekbone. I was standing up at the time so that gives you some idea how high the boots were flying that day. Luckily, it was a glancing blow, otherwise it would have broken my cheekbone.

'I had never seen such a mess on a man's face as I saw on Sandy Carmichael's when I got back to the dressing-room. He was in a hell of a state, poor chap, with both his eyes closed. I've been a keen boxing fan, watched it all my life, but I've never seen anyone that bad in the ring. And to think that was done in the name of rugby football!'

The Lions did not, of course, take it lying down. In getting their retaliation in second, to paraphrase the subsequent '99' alarm call, they suffered one of their more severe injuries. Ironically, McLoughlin, then at the height of his considerable scrummaging power, broke his hand in trying to get a little of his own back. Once again, Thomas had been relied upon to answer a front-row crisis, as Carmichael's replacement prop. 'I thought, "That's it, I'm going to be buried in Christchurch!" We decided at the start of the tour that we were not going to take any nonsense. If you don't respond to any All Black intimidation they will just trample all over you.

'We were never going to let them do that. They had gone out to soften us up for the Test the following week and we knew we had lost two star players, a wonderful pair of props. John Dawes, the captain, said to us at the end of the game, "Now you know what we'll be up against, but you also know that no matter how dirty it gets, we've got the game to beat them."'

For the start of the momentous Test series the following week, the Lions replaced their fractured props with the reserve pair, another stubbornly effective Celtic concoction in Ian 'Mighty Mouse' McLauchlan and Sean Lynch, who found the prospect of making the All Blacks suffer for Canterbury a perfect antidote to his homesickness.

The Americans had been able to send men to the moon at that time but the blinding flash of inspiration required to order neutral referees for the biggest international event staged in the name of rugby football somehow had not occurred to the administrators. The Lions had to put up with New Zealand referees in all 24 matches, and Dr Humphrey Rainey, the official who singularly failed to deal with the thuggery at Lancaster Park, gave way to another local referee for the first Test.

The Lions had left nothing to chance. They won the opening contest, lost the second, their only defeat on the tour, won the third and clinched the series at Eden Park in Auckland, where the rarest of drop goals from J.P.R. Williams secured the ultimate in honourable draws. The Lions had won the series by two matches to one with one drawn, precisely as their prescient manager, the jovial Doug Smith, had said they would before leaving the UK.

For Thomas there was the huge personal satisfaction of appearing in that final match as a replacement and being there at the end to put one over on Meads, and while Delme would never dream of suggesting that he had uprooted the Pine Tree, the fact remains that the most revered of All Blacks had come to the end of the road.

'They didn't like it that they'd lost the series but they recognised that we had the better players,' said Thomas. 'We had Gareth Edwards and Barry John at their brilliant best, and in J.P.R. we had the best full-back I have ever seen. McBride was a wily old campaigner who knew the score, Mervyn Davies was outstanding, a class act. John Taylor was brilliant on that tour, likewise Fergus Slattery and so many more.'

The Lions having caught the imagination of the British and Irish public as never before, every one of them was given a homecoming fit for a king. Thomas appeared like a latter-day Caesar on the balcony of Carmarthen Town Hall to take the plaudits from thousands below during a civic reception hosted by the mayor, Councillor Ron Evans. Delme, an electricity board linesman all his working life since leaving St Clears secondary modern school, appreciated the gesture but, as a shy country boy, could have done without the fuss.

'I felt embarrassed that so many people had gone to such lengths to welcome me home,' he said. 'That's the aspect of rugby I didn't always appreciate. Some people thrive on that sort of thing but I've never sought the limelight. It's not me.'

When the other way of avoiding the limelight was to lose a big match,

Thomas had to run the risk of being catapulted back into the nation's spotlight again the following year as captain of a Llanelli team without peer in the club game. They had old Lions, young Lions and at least one Lion in the making, Ray Gravell, who, in addition to proving himself adept at eating soft centres, was building a reputation among colleagues as something of a hypochondriac.

Fifteen minutes before the kick-off in a big home cup-tie against Cardiff, Gravell sat in the dressing-room refusing to change, his head in his hands. Thomas, so the story goes, approached Phil Bennett, jabbing a thumb over his shoulder at his apparently stricken team-mate. 'Won't play. Says he's got a terrible headache and that he'll have a brain haemorrhage if he does. See what you can do, Phil.'

Bennett tried every approach, from the sympathetic to the hostile. With Gravell groaning and the minutes ticking by, Bennett spotted Bert Peel, the club's physiotherapist and general factotum, and gave him a wink: 'Bert, have you got any of those wonder tablets that the Olympic athletes take to clear their heads before a big race? I think Grav could do with a couple.'

Peel told him he could suck, chew or swallow the tablets. Gravell, still suffering audibly, closed his eyes and opened his mouth and Bert administered the 'medicine'. 'After about ten seconds, Grav shook his head, declared that he felt right as rain and rushed off to change,' said Bennett. 'Just before kick-off, I asked Bert on the quiet what he'd given him. "Two tic-tacs," he said, trying his best to keep a straight face. "Orange-flavoured ones."'

Thomas's long, loyal service to the Lions may have been over but there was still one more victory over the All Blacks to be chiselled out, and for the man himself this would be the greatest one of all: Stradey Park, 26 October 1972, Llanelli 9, Seland Newydd 3.

'That was *the* day of my rugby career. To captain Llanelli against the All Blacks at Stradey, I could not have asked for more than that. And most of all I was chuffed for Carwyn. A lot of people had been on his back ever since the business with the WRU when he wanted the coach's job on his terms and they wouldn't let him do it. Those same people had been trying to belittle what he had achieved, saying that it was easy to coach a winning Lions team because you had the best players from four countries at your disposal. At Stradey that day, Carwyn proved his point by beating the All Blacks again, only this time he did it with a club side.

'He had been planning for that match since we'd got back from New Zealand the year before. He knew exactly what he wanted every player to do, and when the big day came the atmosphere was even more electrifying that any of us thought. It was an overcast, gloomy sort of day but there was something special in the air.

'People still talk about it today, which is a bit embarrassing because it happened 26 years ago and a lot of rugby has been played since then. But if I had to choose one day from my rugby life, that would be the day.'

It is a safe bet that Stradey, then bursting at the seams with spectators craning for a view from every vantage point, will never witness anything remotely like it again, The official attendance was put at 26,000, although the myriad subsequent claims of 'I was there' would have you believe that the figure was nearer 126,000.

For Thomas, carried shoulder high to the dressing-room, victory brought Royal approval from Buckingham Palace, where he received the British Empire Medal from the Queen.

The citation might have read: 'For repeated gallantry on the rugby field in the face of overwhelming odds . . .'

7

Mervyn Davies:
The Full Case History

When he headed towards Cardiff on that fateful Sunday morning for the match that would leave him fighting for his life, Mervyn Davies had the rugby world at his feet. Nothing, it seemed, could stop him from leading Wales and the Lions to new peaks of excellence unreached by any captain before or since.

Three weeks earlier, in the euphoric aftermath of a Grand Slam win, he made no secret of his belief that his country would go on to achieve the first triple Grand Slam of the Five Nations as a lasting monument to the '70s and the finest decade in Welsh rugby. Davies, never one to indulge in hyperbole, had stated in public on the back pages of that morning's newspapers what the other home countries feared in private.

What he dared not reveal then is a secret which can be told now: that he had already been asked to captain the Lions in New Zealand the following year, 1977, and that he had accepted. The most glittering prize was his for the taking, justifiably so considering he had been a permanent fixture in the Test team against the All Blacks in 1971 and the Springboks three years later.

Davies's stature was such that the Lions coach John Dawes, then running the Welsh team, offered the position to him fully 14 months before the selectors sat down to finalise their squad. It was all done and dusted in strict privacy in the Welsh team's hotel in London after dinner on Friday, 16 January 1976, the night before the match against England at Twickenham at the start of the Five Nations championship.

'I'd been on two Lions tours and I knew how bloody hard they were, how you had to be at your peak for every minute of every match. There were no easy games, no opportunities to relax even for a single moment. At that stage I didn't honestly know whether I wanted to go off on a third Lions tour. I was undecided but unconcerned because it wasn't an immediate issue, or so I thought.

'John Dawes had been appointed coach and I was sitting alone in the team room at the hotel on the Friday night when he came in and said, "I want to have a quiet word. Will you come to New Zealand with me next year?"

'I said, "I don't think so, John."

'"Come on," he said. "You'd come as captain, wouldn't you?"

'"I'd seriously consider it. Let me give you an answer at the end of the season."

'"No. I want to know before then."

'"Yes, of course I'd be delighted to go as captain."

'He said, "I know this won't go any further."'

Four more wins over the next few weeks strengthened Davies's position as the outstanding candidate. As he prepared for Swansea's Welsh Cup semi-final against Pontypool at the Cardiff club ground, he had led Wales to eight victories in nine matches and become the world's most-capped No. 8 in the process. On top of that he had appeared in eight Tests for the Lions and been on the losing side just once.

At 29 years of age, it was reasonable to assume that he had enough time left for two more seasons with Wales and one more Lions tour. When he took up his familiar position for the kick-off that sunny Sunday afternoon, his beanpole figure made all the more recognisable by the trademark white headband, his hitherto irresistible career had precisely 28 minutes to run.

What happened at 3.28 p.m. on Sunday, 28 March 1976 resulted in a frantic struggle to save the player's life. Within seconds of the brain haemorrhage which brought his Himalayan career to a scything end, he had almost died before they could carry his breathless body off the pitch. Incredibly, it was the second such haemorrhage of his rugby life.

The first had taken place four years earlier, in April 1972, following a match between London Welsh, then unquestionably the finest club team in the British game, and London Irish. 'It was a very hot day and I had a terrible headache during the game. The game was an important one in terms of clinching the championship. No substitutes were allowed in those days and so I didn't go off.

'I got into the shower after the match and collapsed. There were several doctors in the London Welsh team at the time and they rushed me off to the nearest hospital, down the road at Roehampton. After various tests they identified the problem as meningitis, which is an inflammation of the membrane enclosing the brain. What I'd had was almost certainly a mini brain haemorrhage. That is what doctors have suggested to me since as the probable diagnosis.

'What the hell I was doing at Roehampton, an orthopaedic hospital, I don't know. They did a lumbar puncture and all sorts of things but there was no brain scan. Nobody said I should go for any brain tests. Therefore they did not detect that I had a flaw, a weakness in the nerve ends of the brain, which came to the fore in the match against Pontypool four years later. I left the hospital with a tremendous headache and for days afterwards I had problems coping with any bright light. I recovered in due course and forgot all about it.'

In hindsight, Davies's rugby career ought to have ended there and then. 'I have asked myself what would have happened had they done the brain tests. They would have found the cause of the problem. They'd have asked me what I did for a living and whether I had any hobbies. They would then very probably have told me to stop playing rugby and take up tiddlywinks instead.

'I suppose, in hindsight, it was a blessing in disguise because of what I would have missed for Wales and the Lions. Doctors have explained to me that, statistically speaking, a certain percentage of people survive one brain haemorrhage and far fewer survive two. I recovered from the first one without being any the wiser, forgot all about it and carried on playing rugby as if nothing had happened.'

Four years later, with nothing worse than the occasional sprained ankle or muscular twinge to interrupt their captain's winning way, the Swansea players *en route* to Cardiff and the semi-final against Pontypool filed into the dining-room of the Bear Hotel in Cowbridge for a light lunch. It is the last thing Mervyn Davies can remember with any clarity about the most traumatic day of his life.

'I have only a very vague recollection of being in the dressing-room prior to the game. People have told me since that they thought I was out of sorts, that I wasn't my normal self, but they put that down to the importance of the occasion. Before any match I'd always go into a little corner of the dressing-room so I could think alone and get myself organised.'

Baden Evans, then a back-row replacement, now Swansea's chief executive, had detected a slight change in the skipper's mood. 'Mervyn wouldn't normally show any sign of nerves before a game but he was a bit quieter than normal that day,' he said. 'We put it down to the tension of a cup semi-final. He was fine.'

Leading the Whites from the dressing-room beneath the north stand, he walked past the entrance to the Arms Park stadium and turned right into the club ground with no sense of foreboding. Roy Woodward had scored the second of his first-half tries when Davies, standing some yards from the nearest Pontypool player, collapsed. Evans was the first player to reach him.

'I couldn't get his gumshield out and I made a mess of his lips trying to rip it clear,' he said. 'At first we all thought one of the Ponty boys had clouted him because there'd been a few niggles. It was obvious there was something seriously wrong. For a few seconds there was no breathing, then some heavy panting, then nothing. I was worried in case he had swallowed his tongue. Then the paramedics arrived, opened his mouth and cleared the airways.'

Davies, the left side of his body paralysed, lay 'seriously ill' in the neurological unit of the University of Wales hospital for more than a week before being removed from the danger list. 'It was an absolute thunderbolt. I knew nothing about it until a fortnight later and nothing really about the week before. Three weeks of my life gone. The game was a total blank.

'I'm lucky to be alive and able to talk about it. If I'd been playing golf and I'd been on the sixth tee at any course in South Wales that Sunday afternoon, then one thing's for sure: I wouldn't be here today. If it had to happen, it was just as well it happened in front of 15,000 people and at least 12 of them were doctors. Luckier still, it happened at a ground where there were good medical facilities.

'I can only go on what the doctors have told me, that I stopped breathing immediately after I fell down. They gave me mouth-to-mouth resuscitation until they got me to the resuscitators in the changing-room. I then stopped breathing two or three times on the way to the nearest hospital, which was about half a mile away.

'They had to delay the operation because of my weakened state in the hope that I'd get stronger. Instead I was getting weaker, so they had to go ahead anyway. I seem to remember someone shaving my head and me cursing at a few people but I didn't know a thing about what was going on.'

There was no question of the damage having been caused by any blow during a full-blooded cup-tie. Robert Weeks, the neurosurgeon who carried out the operation, said, 'This could have happened just the same if he had been sitting at home in his armchair.'

The same conclusion would surely have been reached four years earlier, had the cause of his initial collapse been the subject of a deeper investigation. Davies, though, does not discount the theory that his exposure to an innately violent and physical contact sport increased the risk of a potentially fatal haemorrhage inside his skull. 'The brain haemorrhage could have happened anywhere, at any time,' he says. 'Other people would say that it was a result of taking numerous blows to the head over a long period of time, rather like a boxer. Medical opinion is divided.'

Six years later another famous Lion, former England captain Bill Beaumont, was forced to quit on a neurologist's advice because of the cumulative effect of the blows he had taken. 'The wear and tear to my neck was causing me to have blackouts. I was warned that I could end up suffering permanent damage which would affect the rest of my bodily functions. It could have affected the nerve ends of my brain and there was simply no point taking the risk.'

With an anxious nation praying for his recovery, Davies pulled through, but his life would never be the same again. There would be no more carnival days at the Arms Park, no more Grand Slams, no captaining the Lions against the All Blacks.

There would be no more rugby.

'A large part of my life was suddenly taken away from me. Rugby to me was a bit like a drug. It was something I did as a hobby. I went on to the field every Saturday and I didn't think about anything else. Family problems, work problems, any other problems, they were all blown away every Saturday.

'It was the perfect way to release all the tension of the week. It usually started at midday on the Saturday, when I left the house, and I didn't get back until gone eight at night after a few beers with the lads. It was a lovely, lovely way of getting rid of all the hassles of the working week. Suddenly, all that had gone. I could no longer play rugby.'

Nor could he play any other sport. More than 20 years later, the most elementary athletic pursuits are still beyond him and will remain so for the rest of his life. The inability to do all those things he took for granted caused such frustration that it is still hard to take, even after all these years, for someone whose nickname, Merve the Swerve, captured his knack of giving mobile obstacles a wide berth.

'It frustrates the hell out of me that I can't play squash and that I can't play golf. It's not because I'm not allowed to. I could play rugby and any other sport you care to mention but I haven't got the ability to do so. My co-ordination has gone. The brain still works. It's the limbs that don't. The message gets through, but the reactions aren't quick enough.

'The best example I can give is to imagine jumping over a three-foot wall. You trot up, one little hop and you're over. Easy as that. I can't do that. I have to climb over it because I can't react quickly enough to get into a position to make the hop. It's difficult to explain, but I'd have to stop at the wall and think, "Which foot do I use?"

'Beating your opponent has always been an essential part of my make-up. In any sport, all I want is to have a chance of winning. When you have no chance of beating anyone, you literally cannot compete. The only way I could console myself was through frequent reminders that I had done virtually everything the sport had to offer.

'Where else could I go? The pinnacle would have been captaining the Lions, but it could have happened when I was a lad of 18. At least I'd had ten wonderful years and done many things I would never otherwise have done. I'm not complaining. I'm still alive to talk about it.'

The physical effects of the haemorrhage are far from conspicuous. 'It has affected my eyesight dramatically. I also can't smell, which, having a baby at the time, was not entirely a disadvantage! They did tell me that my vision and my smell would get better, which it didn't, and that I could be impotent for six months, which I wasn't.' A case, therefore, of two rights and a wrong – not that the trauma has diluted Davies's sense of humour: 'I'll take the one they were wrong on!'

During that critical spell when nobody knew for sure whether he would live or die, the mail arrived by the sackful. 'I had in excess of 3,000 messages. There was another guy also called M. Davies in the next ward, and he didn't get any letters at all. Much later, I did find one or two in my pile which should have gone to him. Then, when I got back to Pontlliw, near Swansea, where I was living at the time, I saw there were two T.M. Davieses in the phone book for the village. Because the other chap's number was listed above mine, he got hundreds of calls meant for me. He was going bananas after a while!'

After six months Davies was back at work for W.R. Blyth and Company, the industrial clothing company then run by Len Blyth and now run by his son, Roger, both Welsh internationals. It had taken their famous sales representative six months 'to get back into the land of the living', although he is no longer able to work because of his deteriorating eyesight.

He still had to come to terms with the weekly problem of how to cope with Saturday. 'How do you release the tension? It's got to go somewhere, but where? Your life has changed forever. Inevitably, that alters you as a person. I suppose there's one moral to be taken from it all, though: don't play rugby on a Sunday!'

It is hard to believe that when Davies appeared from nowhere for the start of the 1969 Five Nations championship against Scotland at Murrayfield, there were plenty in Wales who had never heard of him. He arrived so completely out of the blue that even the selectors had caught him by surprise, to such an extent that the new No. 8 knew nothing until the day after the team had been announced.

That Friday morning, he and another teacher had been driving to their school in Guildford. 'We'd been talking about who they might have picked or not picked when my colleague said, "Do you want to find out if you're in this Welsh side or not?" I said, "No chance." With that he stopped to buy a paper. Of all the papers, he bought the *Daily Mirror*. And there, at the bottom of an inside page, in about an inch and a half right down in the corner, was the Welsh team to play Scotland. I thought, "Bloody hell . . . !" We turned round, made some excuse to the headmaster about flu in the house and spent the day celebrating. It was a total shock to everyone, including me.

'My rise from obscurity was traumatic for both me and the Welsh public. Only one question was being asked: "Who the hell is this bloke Mervyn Davies?" When I'd played against Swansea earlier that season, nobody in Wales had heard of me. It was a case of being in the right place at the right time. London Welsh were very much the vogue side, along with Llanelli, and Wales were looking for a tall, ball-winning No. 8 and I suppose I fitted the bill.'

He fitted it so perfectly that any Welsh defeat in the Five Nations took some believing. From his first match in Edinburgh on 1 February 1969 to his last against France at Cardiff on 6 March 1976, Davies appeared in 31 consecutive championship internationals, and 38 in all. Wales lost only five of them, delivering two Grand Slams, three Triple Crowns and four championship titles as outright winners, figures which exclude the 1972 tournament when the Welsh Rugby Union refused to send its unbeaten team to Dublin because of the troubles in Ireland.

If Davies thought it was all a bit too easy to be true after his initial season, a tour to New Zealand that summer exposed him to the harsher realities of life at the top. Wales finished a battered second in both Tests, but what they learnt from the experience would prove a decisive influence when the Lions, with their hefty Welsh contingent, played their historic series against the All Blacks two years later.

'That New Zealand tour with Wales was a real eye-opener. For the first time in my life I found out what it felt like to be given a right hammering. I learnt a lot: that we were not fit enough, we were not hard enough and we were not competitive enough. Every time I got the ball in any match I'd be knocked back by their big hits. The big hits I made on them didn't seem to matter. At the end of every match, I'd be absolutely knackered.

'I went home and worked on my upper-body strength, as we all did. I honed my game to a higher level because what was good enough to win a Triple Crown was nowhere near good enough to beat the All Blacks. If you wanted to compete against the best, you had to match them for fitness. Without that, you had no chance.'

Those two New Zealand trips represented a significant shift in attitude which brought a sea change in the entire British philosophy to rugby in general and touring in particular. The old 'it's only a game' approach was being replaced by a more disciplined policy, a game plan which left less to chance. Rugby union was still amateur but by the end of the '60s it had become a good deal less amateurish. The first steps were being taken towards generating a new brand of unpaid professionalism, and Wales were blazing the trail. The '71 Lions would be the first beneficiaries.

What Wales experienced in New Zealand two years earlier hit players like Davies with a force which could have been measured on the Richter scale. How appropriate that his first night's sleep on tour, in the town of New Plymouth, which nestles beneath the volcanic Mount Taranaki, should have been interrupted by something he had never experienced in Swansea.

'We'd spent 40 hours, yes 40, cooped up in an aeroplane so when we got to Taranaki late at night all we wanted to do was get to sleep. We stepped off the plane and couldn't believe our eyes. It seemed as if the whole town had turned out to welcome us, and they wanted us to sing. Sing? In the jet-lagged state I was in, that was the last thing I wanted to do.

'Then, in the middle of the night, all hell broke loose. Windows were rattling, doors were nearly coming off their hinges, the whole room was shaking. It was a bloody earthquake! And after all that we had to go out and play Taranaki two days after we'd got there. We were amateurs.'

Tremors of a different kind were about to revolutionise the British game, galvanising the Lions from almost perennial losers into stylish winners whose aggression, legitimate and otherwise, was too much for the All Blacks and the Springboks.

'The 1968 Lions lost the series in South Africa and yet I have heard stories that they thoroughly enjoyed themselves, which seemed a bit hard to understand, given the results. From what I was told, they put more of an emphasis on the social side of the tour than the playing side.

Whether that was down to weak management, the wrong choice of captain or what, I don't know. By the time we got to New Zealand three years later, those days had gone.

'This was a watershed in British rugby – yes, we would enjoy ourselves, but first and foremost we were there to win. There had been a big change in attitude. We became professional in outlook, and in Wales we were far more professionally minded in our approach to the game than the rest. We had an international coach and some sort of team organisation, which was more than England, Ireland and Scotland had.

'The backbone of the Lions side was provided by the Welsh team which had been out in New Zealand two years earlier. We had been hardened by that experience. We knew what to expect. It held no fears for us because we knew we had the ability to beat them. We would not accept defeat as, perhaps, our predecessors had done.'

He was as good as his word, the Lions winning the series 2–1 with the last Test drawn. For the first and only time, Welsh supremacy in the Five Nations had been transferred to New Zealand with spectacular results. In a Lions context this was, without doubt, Wales's finest hour. There were never fewer than eight Welsh players in any Test team, and eleven all told. Ray 'Chico' Hopkins's appearance for an injured Gareth Edwards took the Welsh representation in the winning first Test at Dunedin to ten, with Ireland's Mike Gibson the only non-Welshman behind the scrum. The Lions were more than happy to pitch an uncapped Welsh player into the series, Derek Quinnell's selection alongside Davies and John Taylor in an all-Welsh back row for the third Test contributing to a 13–3 win which guaranteed that the Lions would, at worst, share the series.

As if that wasn't enough, they also had a Welshman orchestrating the whole show, Carwyn James, who had flitted across the international stage against Australia in January 1958 during what was the briefest of interruptions to Cliff Morgan's occupation of the outside-half position. Davies acknowledges James as the man who made it all possible.

'He obviously knew about half-back play and, possibly, full-back play as well. But he'd never played No. 8 or second row. He'd never propped or hooked, and yet he was able to talk the best out of every player. He'd tap into the vast knowledge and experience of players like Willie John McBride and Syd Millar and he'd be constantly asking you questions.

'He'd never *tell* you to do something. He would *suggest* that maybe it could be done this way, and he channelled all your thoughts in such a positive direction that I found it quite fascinating. His most famous saying came after we'd been stuffed in the second Test. He told us, "Now I know we are going to win the series." I said, and I couldn't help laughing, "I'm glad you think so." But deep down I thought, "If the coach says that we're going to win the series, it must be because we are." Carwyn had an ability to talk to men. I have never experienced coaching like that before or since.'

Davies, like several of his compatriots, also played a leading role in the invincible Lions' tour of South Africa three years later. He is in no doubt that New Zealand was the greater achievement. 'The '71 All Blacks were better than the '74 Springboks. There were quite a few easy games in South Africa and the Tests turned out to be fairly easy as well. There were no easy games in New Zealand.

'If the truth be known, their pack knocked the stuffing out of us in the four Tests. They were the better side but they lost because of our superior three-quarters. We managed to gain just enough possession in three of the four matches for our backs, Barry John, Gareth Edwards and Mike Gibson in particular, to use their skills brilliantly. We were stuffed out of sight up front and yet we still won it thanks to our backs and an absolutely amazing defence.

'In South Africa we completely dominated the 'Boks up front. There's no doubt we caught them with their pants down. They had been in the international wilderness and they thought everything in their garden was rosy. Then we came along. They never expected what they got, the ferocity of the British forwards. We set out not to be roughed up. Get your retaliation in first, take no prisoners, all that stuff. They couldn't handle it.

'The South African players had lost their edge. They weren't as hard as they thought and in that respect it was a total role reversal. The '74 Lions pack was pretty awesome. They were big and aggressive and they threw their weight around a lot. I'd never played in a series of rugby matches where we were so completely on top.

'The South African public were totally shocked. They could not believe what was happening because it had never happened before. The selectors chopped and changed their team and after one match the Springbok manager said, "I hope they don't pick any more because we're running out of green blazers!"'

The aura of supremacy which had lingered all over New Zealand since '71 disappeared rapidly after the arrival of the '77 Lions. Fate having decreed that he could not return as captain, Davies saw all the petty bickering at first hand while combining a lecture tour of the country with a journalistic role for the *Daily Mirror*. By the end of the tour, he too had become a victim of John Dawes's running feud with the press.

The plan had been for Davies and Dawes to run the tour as captain and coach. It ended with Dawes ordering Davies to leave an official New Zealand Rugby Union reception after the last Test in Auckland, a sorry end to a sorry expedition. As one who had flourished under Dawes's leadership since the early days at London Welsh, Davies found it hard to understand why the whole tour had gone belly-up in such a big way.

'The management of the '77 Lions got it wrong in their attitude to the press. I spent my entire playing career with John. He was my captain at London Welsh, my captain with Wales and the Lions and then my coach with Wales. I thought he would be a great Lions coach. He had done it all and knew what it was all about. I don't know why it went wrong.'

Davies discovered that whatever the special nature of his rugby relationship with Dawes, it did not provide him with immunity from the coach's almost paranoid hostility towards those commenting on the tour. He first noticed the hostility after one of the players, fellow Welshman Allan Martin, had invited him into the team room for a beer. 'Who should walk past but George Burrell, the Lions manager. He said to Dawes, "What's he doing in here? Get him out."'

'The climax to the whole thing came after the last Test. There was a party in the Lions' hotel in Auckland, paid for and organised by the New Zealand Rugby Union. I had been invited as one of their guests. I was standing at the bar with Clem Thomas, who was reporting on the tour for *The Observer*, when John Dawes came up and said, "Merve, no press are allowed in here."

'I said, "John, I'm leaving, but the only reason I'm leaving is that I don't want to cause any hassle. You haven't invited me here. The New Zealand Union have invited me. Not you. It's got f*** all to do with you." With that I walked out. It's wrong to say that I had tears in my eyes but it shouldn't have been like that.

'I've never blamed John for that and it hasn't affected our friendship. I honestly believe that Burrell had a tremendous influence on him. I don't know why. I felt quite guilty, in a sense, that I wasn't there as a player, even though that was a physical impossibility. New Zealand were ready for them in '77. They'd waited a long time to get their own back.'

The good times rolled on a little longer for Wales but it could never be quite the same. Within two years the team which their stricken captain had talked of leading to a Grand Slam treble had begun to break up, although only France in Paris prevented them from achieving the unprecedented three Slams in a row. Whether a team lead by Jacques Fouroux would have stopped them with Davies still at the helm, nobody will ever know.

At the Arms Park, the question in the home dressing-room was not whether Wales were going to win but by how many. 'There was an arrogant self-belief that we were going to win. We knew we were better than the opposition. The question of losing never arose. The main focus when I was captain was on how much we were going to win by. I'd say, "Let's win well. Let's show them how rugby should be played." The opposition could rant and rave beforehand but it would count for nothing. By the time they stood for the national anthems their legs were liable to turn to jelly. The volume of noise from the crowd at Cardiff Arms Park was soul-destroying for the opposition.

'What we had was a Welsh team which had hardly changed. There'd be the odd new face now and again but nothing startling apart from when we brought in six new caps in Paris in 1975, and they were all a bit tasty. There was this professional attitude about the players. They got on well together. The only problem would be between the Pontypool front row and anyone who wanted to take them on.

'There'd be the occasional fracas, which was healthy. Usually it would be between Geoff Wheel and Bobby Windsor arguing the toss in training sessions. They were at it hammer and tongs one day. Windsor would say, "Are you trying to make me look a **** or what?" And Wheel would shout back, "Throw the ball in when I tell you to throw it in." And so on.'

Davies never allowed any international occasion, no matter how important to the well-being of the country at large, to obscure the fact that it was still only a game of rugby. He could never subscribe to the tub-thumping rhetoric of those captains who demanded that it be treated as more than merely a game.

'I've heard some liken rugby to war, telling the players they are going into battle. In the trenches of the First World War, some idiot would blow a whistle, you'd get out of the trench, you'd start running towards the enemy and your chances of survival were virtually nil. Well, rugby isn't like that. When the whistle goes, you come out pumped up for action and nothing is going to get in your way. You are fighting for your country and your survival. That's what rugby is like.'

Terry Cobner, the former Pontypool captain who almost salvaged the 1977 Lions tour by taking belated charge of their pack, could never have been accused of underestimating the importance of any major contest. '"Cob" would say, "This is war." I know because I overheard him giving his team talk at Pontypool when I was there with Swansea. John Dawes, on the other hand, would never dream of speaking in those terms. Always cold and cool, he talked quietly. No blood and thunder. No banging the table. No effing and blinding.'

Davies's elevation to the captaincy coincided with Dawes's appointment as coach in succession to Clive Rowlands. 'Top Cat's' stirring of the emotions in support of his own brand of patriotism had served Wales well, although having a hefty dose of match-winners all around him often made the result appear a foregone conclusion.

Rowlands had his own fire-and-brimstone style. 'He'd get us in the hotel room before leaving for the match and he'd say, "What are we going to do today, boys?" We'd say, matter-of-factly, "We're going to win."

'"What did you say?"

'"We're going to win," we'd say, turning up the volume slightly.

'"Can't hear you."

'"Win, Clive," we'd shout at the tops of our voices. "We're going to win."

'One day he said to our prop John Lloyd, who tended to have a big appetite, "What are you going to do today, Mr Greedy?" John would say, "I'm going to eat them, Clive."

'Then he'd really get going and say, "Are we all on the same beam-length?" I think he meant to say wavelength. Clive would be standing there, hands on his knees, fag in the mouth, puffing away. When he talked of beam-length, Barry John could hardly keep a straight face.

'"Barry, what are you laughing at?"

'"I'm not laughing, Clive."

'"Barry, you are laughing." And the room would fall apart . . .'

Davies still follows the game despite it being no longer to his liking. 'After 20-odd years, I've got used to it. The game is faster, the players are bigger, but the skill levels don't exist. The only skill that exists nowadays is staying on your feet after the tackle. That's about as far as it goes.

'Careers at the top level are going to be shorter and a lot of players are going to end up crippled unless they're careful. The power in the game now raises the danger of serious head injuries. There is a cumulative danger as there is for a boxer.

'The game is tailored for television. When I played the game, there were far more 50-50 balls in the set-pieces, rucks and mauls. Today it's been changed so that one side dominates possession for such long periods that the biggest cheer now is for a turnover. It's a different game now and I find a lot of matches boring. I don't think I'd enjoy playing rugby today.'

At times of late he would gladly have settled for Wales being boring. He found them so bad, especially against France at Wembley in April 1998, that for the first time in his life he found himself walking out at half-time. 'I didn't want to be there in the first place, watching Wales play rugby in a concrete jungle. Having said that, there was a lovely atmosphere walking from the tube station to the stadium. But once the game started, I kept thinking, "These guys are representing Wales. Where is their pride? Where is their passion?" I walked out at half-time because I couldn't take any more. I got a taxi to Paddington to catch the train home and the taxi driver said, "You're Welsh, aren't you, mate?" And then, with great glee, he told me that Wales were losing by 40-something. Only when I got home did I find out that it was 51.

'We talk about a learning curve but we've been on that for 20 years. The worst thing that ever happened to Wales was finishing third at the World Cup in 1987. Things were desperately wrong then but people allowed themselves to be deluded into thinking that we were still the third-best team in the world.

'Professional rugby sounded the death knell for the game in Wales. There isn't the financial clout to enable us to compete. I don't want to sound too despondent but I fear Welsh rugby will go the way of Welsh soccer, where all the best players play for English clubs. I sometimes despair of seeing another Grand Slam. It's 20 years since the last one and it may be another 20 before the next one.'

It takes a lot to win a Grand Slam, and Davies need only look at his right shin for surely the most satisfying scar of his rugby life, as inflicted by the French in his last big match. That they set out to boot him into oblivion made the victory all the sweeter.

'I remember being run over by the entire French pack in the first five minutes and thinking that I might have to go off. Someone's stud had gone through a muscle in the front of my shin and left a hole in my leg which I've still got. That was fairly standard French practice. Pick on one player and give him the treatment. The ball was 20 yards away at the time. Typically French.

'Gerry Lewis, the trainer, came on and said I'd have to come off. I said, "I'm not bloody well going off, mate." When the adrenalin is pumping, there is no pain unless you start thinking about it. By the end of the game I was struggling, but by then we had it pretty well sewn up. The Lions was a fantastic experience but successes for Wales are far closer to my heart. If I had to single out one game it would be that last one, against France.'

They carried him shoulder high from the pitch, ecstatically unaware that they would never see his like again. Davies, at 51 much in demand on the after-dinner speaking circuit, never received a cent by way of compensation but, thanks to the surgeons and his natural tendency to beat the odds, he is at least able to tell the tale.

8

From the Slagheap to Everest

Ever since they chose the first one during the '20s, the Lions have finalised their touring teams in central London at the East India Club, the gentlemen's establishment where the Prince Regent was being entertained the day in 1815 when news broke of Wellington's victory at Waterloo.

When the selectors went into conclave there on Sunday, 28 March 1971, almost half a century had elapsed since the pioneering tour, and throughout all that time the representatives of the Four Home Unions had maintained an odd consistency in their policy regarding the picking of the captain. They had consistently failed to pick a Welsh one.

They kicked off with two Englishmen, Ronald Cove-Smith in South Africa in 1924 and Doug Prentice in New Zealand six years later. The next four tours were all under Irish leadership from both sides of the border, Sammy Walker and Robin Thompson from the north, Karl Mullen and Ronnie Dawson from the south.

The Scots took over for most of the '60s, first through Arthur Smith and then through the controversial Mike Campbell-Lamerton. Both had been appointed at the expense of such outstanding Welsh candidates that the decision fuelled speculation that the persistent refusal to give the most prestigious position of all to a Welshman was perhaps more than coincidence.

Bryn Meredith, for instance, captained Wales in 1962 during the weeks before the selection of the tour party for South Africa that summer. As the outstanding hooker of his generation who had stood the test of time at the highest level over a period of eight years, the Newport player was a Test certainty, just as he had been on the previous tour of South Africa seven years earlier and just as he would have been in Australasia in 1959 had the Lions not given the captaincy to his Irish counterpart Ronnie Dawson, a celebrated player in his own right but not, according to some shrewd judges, as good as his Welsh rival.

Meredith, as fine a team man and tourist as he was a player, took it all in his stride, refusing to let whatever disappointment he felt affect his sense of sportsmanship. The same went for another Gwent forward, the tragic Alun Pask, similarly overlooked four years later in favour of a player who was unable to satisfy the principal criterion of any Lions captain: that he must be good enough to justify his place in the Test team strictly on playing merit.

Pask, who lost his life at the age of 58 when fire engulfed his home at Blackwood in November 1995, had been considered the outstanding candidate, not least because he had been there and done it for the Lions in the previous tour. There had been three instances of how the management had been only too happy to turn to Welsh players in times of trouble. Bleddyn Williams, Cliff Morgan and David Watkins had all captained the Lions in Test matches, but only in emergencies caused by a lack of form or fitness affecting Messrs Mullen, Thompson and Campbell-Lamerton respectively. Morgan's decision to put himself out of contention for the captaincy of the 1959 tour still left Wales with a formidable candidate in the mighty presence of a man described as the best lock in the British game during the '50s.

Rhys (R.H.) Williams contented himself instead with the distinction of being the only Lion to match Tony O'Reilly Test for Test by playing in all ten between 1955 and 1959. Colin Meads, his New Zealand opponent during a series when the All Blacks won the first three and lost the last one in Auckland, where Williams performed heroics, paid the Llanelli lock the supreme compliment of picking him in his Best-in-the-World XV alongside a former Springbok captain. 'Rhys Williams, the Welsh Lion, and Johan Claassen of South Africa, won ball, scrummaged strongly and hit rucks like rams,' Meads wrote in his autobiography. 'Too many have won ball, leaned in scrums and hit rucks like lambs. Many locks have been good line-out forwards and little else, but Rhys was more than that. Rhys always kept going for the ball and always did the right thing when he got it.'

There was no escaping the fact that, for all the admiration they attracted in the hardest school of all, at that time no Welshman had ever got nearer than being an occasional deputy. All that, and a great deal more, was going through the mind of another Gwent player as he sat that night and waited for any news of white smoke billowing from the East India Club. Carwyn James, the first Welsh coach of the Lions, had assured Dawes in Paris only the night before that he would do his best to give him a call.

For John Dawes, it was to turn into one of the longest days of his rugby life. A Grand Slam won in the grand manner in Paris the previous day would surely make him the first Welsh player to captain the Lions. The telephone in his flat in west London had been ringing all day long, but the call he so badly wanted to hear never came and it was now midnight.

His mind went back to a day earlier that month at Northampton, where he had captained the Barbarians against East Midlands in the annual Mobbs Memorial match to commemorate Lt.-Col. Edgar Mobbs, the former England three-quarter who had been killed in the First World War.

'All the Baa-baas committee were in the dressing-room to hear my team talk. Seeing them all there made me feel that this was a bit of a trial run for the Lions. It was pouring with rain and I told the players to try and enjoy themselves and give the ball a bit of air. In dreadful conditions we scraped through 3–0 with a penalty from Bob Hitler, and Carwyn told me afterwards that my team talk had nearly cost me the captaincy of the Lions. I had felt at times that they were looking for excuses not to have a Welshman in charge and obviously what I said that day at Northampton wasn't what they wanted to hear.

'I must have had what seemed like ten thousand phone calls that day from people asking me whether I'd heard anything. As time went by, I prepared myself for the worst. Carwyn had never gone beyond hinting that I was in with a good chance. I was 30 years of age, which was quite old, and I had almost convinced myself that they had picked someone else when the phone rang five or ten minutes after midnight. It was Doug Smith, the tour manager, with the good news.'

Never in the history of sport can one man have received as spectacular a reward for running up and down the biggest slagheap in his native Gwent valley. Dawes began flogging himself through the dusty exercise in masochism at the age of 17, his imagination fired by one of the sporting icons of the late '50s, Herb Elliott. Dawes had read how the Australian 1,500-metre runner trained by running up and down sand dunes under his celebrated coach Percy Cerutty. There being a distinct shortage of sand dunes in Gwent, the future Lions captain settled for the next best thing: a dirty big coaltip. Not any old coaltip, but the dirtiest, biggest one he could find in his native valley. There could hardly have been a more revealing example of how he began laying the foundations of his climb towards the rugby stratosphere.

'There was a tip between Newbridge and Abercarn which was so steep that every time I got to the top my legs felt so weak I had no control over them. I would have to walk around on top of the slagheap for a few minutes until I recovered the strength to go back down. I'd go up and down ten times at a stretch and go home looking as if I'd spent the day at the coalface. It still hurts every time I think about it.

'I suppose I was lucky in one respect because there were no distractions. In the valleys in those days there wasn't much else a young fellow could do. There were no tennis courts, no golf ranges, no swimming pools. I ran every day because Herb Elliott inspired me. Reading about him, I learnt the importance of what it meant to be really fit.'

Dawes always was ahead of his time. He entered senior rugby at 18, for Newbridge in an Easter Monday local derby against Cross Keys, an occasion enhanced by the guest appearance for the opposition of two Irish forwards who between them would make a towering contribution to Lions history: Syd Millar and Willie John McBride. Both had played for their club, Ballymena, at Abertillery the previous Saturday, and they stayed in the neighbourhood for another game.

Having graduated from Aberystwyth University with a degree in chemistry, Dawes set about creating his own brand of the stuff which would transform London Welsh into *the* team in Britain. Ironically, he had gone there to further not his own career but that of his wife as a singer of some repute, anxious to make the most of her talent.

Meanwhile, at Old Deer Park, the non-singing Herb Elliott aficionado set about knocking a haphazard club into some sort of shape. 'There was no formal training when I went there in 1963. We met at ten to three on a Saturday afternoon and kicked off at three. That was it.'

The organisation which he promptly initiated may seem primitive by modern standards but back then it again illustrated his knack for seeing the next development in the game and bringing the future to the present. It may not sound terribly visionary, but Dawes, in tandem with John Ryan, another London Welsh player who would be one of his successors as national coach, introduced midweek training. 'It was fairly basic but it was a start. We just ran round the park. The new sodium street lighting had been installed in the road outside and that gave us sufficient light to be able to practise our passing and handling skills.' In next to no time, before the end of that season, Sydney John Dawes – 'Syd' to his friends – was playing for Wales.

He flew to Dublin from London on the Friday morning as the reserve, not knowing that he was already in the starting line-up. Ken Jones, the stylish Llanelli Lion not to be confused with his namesake, the record-breaking wing and Olympic medal-winning sprinter with the Great Britain team at the 1948 Olympiad, failed a fitness test and Dawes was to partner Keith Bradshaw in midfield.

'In the Ireland game I touched the ball twice and read in the paper the next day that I had revelled in a dream debut. Well, it didn't seem like a dream debut to me. With my first touch I passed the ball out to Peter Rees on the wing. He hit about five people out of the way, got the ball back to me and I fell over for the try. That was my contribution. We won and they kept the same team, which meant that DK [Jones] didn't get back, and he was a far better player.'

Dawes's total exclusion from the 1966 Five Nations meant that the returning Jones made the Lions that summer while his rival did not. Nor did 'Syd' make it on to the next Lions tour, to South Africa in 1968, by which time he had succeeded Gareth Edwards as Wales's captain. He took his country to Argentina instead, and although he may not have felt so at the time it turned out to be a blessing in disguise, if only because it enabled him to recruit a teenaged colossus for London Welsh before anyone in England had even heard of him.

J.P.R., then about to begin medical studies in London, joined the Welsh under Dawes's captaincy. 'He played his first game for us by accident against Richmond after someone dropped out. The rest of the team wondered who he was and viewed him with some suspicion, because Gareth James had been our full-back and you had to be very special in our eyes to replace him because he ran everything. J.P.R. was the most fiercely competitive player I have ever seen, though, and once they'd seen him in that first match there was never another question asked about him.'

The Grand Slam team was taking powerful shape. When they had finished assembling it in January 1971, six of its members were from London Welsh: Dawes, J.P.R., Gerald Davies, Mike Roberts, Mervyn Davies and John Taylor. All six went with the Lions. All bar Roberts were fixtures in the Test team throughout the series victory, an achievement which Dawes acknowledges as surpassing anything that he achieved with Wales.

From the start, James and Dawes were on a wavelength beyond the comprehension of the All Blacks. 'Carwyn was specific about the type of game he wanted to play, one which he felt only two clubs in the British Isles were playing to his satisfaction: London Welsh and Llanelli. His view fitted in perfectly with my philosophy of the game and that was adventure. I didn't mind if the opposition scored ten tries so long as we scored twelve.

'My whole game was based on attack. At times in the '60s London Welsh won games without any set-piece ball because we could make the most of what scraps came our way. With the Lions, Carwyn knew what he wanted and had enough great players to put it into operation.

'The players in that Lions team of 1971 would have fitted into any international team in any era and that is what made them truly great. And I'm talking about J.P.R., Gerald, Gibson, John Bevan, Duckham, John Spencer, Barry, Gareth, Mervyn, John Taylor, Slattery, Willie John, Delme, Gordon Brown, John Pullin, Sandy Carmichael, Sean Lynch, Ray McLoughlin and the "Mighty Mouse".'

As a player, Dawes never had real pace. A plodder, perhaps, compared with some, but the exquisite timing of his pass created space for his wings or J.P.R. thundering into the line from full-back. In addition to an organisational flair which invariably enabled him to be in the right place at the right time, Dawes never allowed himself to be flustered, even when defeat stared him in the face.

Murrayfield, halfway through the '71 Grand Slam, was a classic case in point. When the Scots led 18–14 with time rapidly ebbing away, Dawes managed the crisis by refusing to give anyone the slightest excuse to panic. Gerald Davies remembers it well: 'He had the ability to keep his wits about him when the pressure was at its most severe, as it was that day. He was like that in New Zealand. Always calm, never ruffled. There must have been a lot of tension beneath the surface but he never showed any. At Murrayfield he was the one who said, "We have enough time to win this game." He had the presence of mind to point out that there were three or four minutes left when all seemed lost.' Davies responded with the try, but not even Dawes could have envisaged that it would be won in a manner which is still talked of today, his London Welsh colleague John Taylor firing over a left-footed conversion from the touchline.

Dawes was never a rant-and-rave merchant. 'I never banged the table and neither did Carwyn. He'd just smoke 500 cigarettes instead! I never heard him lose his temper or bawl anyone out. And if someone made a mistake, I'd just say, "Bad luck." At that level, they knew when they'd made a mistake. They didn't need me to point it out to them.'

In all his years captaining London Welsh, Wales and the Lions, Dawes never faced a more daunting challenge than the one the All Blacks presented him with in the second Test at Christchurch. With ten minutes left and New Zealand virtually out of sight at 22–6, a lesser man would have been only too relieved to settle for the comparatively soft option of kicking a penalty or two to improve the losing margin. Not Dawes. This was the acid test of his adventurous spirit, the moment of truth. He believes that what the Lions did under his command in those final ten minutes at Lancaster Park was of such significance that they won the series as a direct consequence. Barry John dropped a goal, Gerald scored a try and the Lions would probably have had another had their opponents retreated ten yards after conceding a penalty in front of their posts.

'That was the turning point of the series. We started running what ball we got, including two penalties, and when Gerald scored his marvellous try I thought to myself, "They can't cope with this." In the first Test we didn't know there was a ball on the field, but as soon as I got back to the dressing-room after the second match I knew we would win the series.

'We were releasing so many potential matchwinners that I was sure that if the match had gone another ten minutes we'd have wiped out the deficit. I said to Carwyn, "We've found the way to beat them. We've just got to make sure we use the full range of Barry's skills and start in the next Test where we left off in this one." That's exactly what we did and we were 13 points up in next to no time. There was never any question of letting it slip.'

His contemporaries are quick to pay tribute to Dawes as 'a brilliant thinker'. For example, in one Test he deployed his troops with sufficient precision to ensure that the Lions would have both the kick-off and the choice of ends. In those days, whoever had won the toss could delay his decision until he could see which way the wind was blowing immediately prior to kick-off. 'On this occasion, Syd took us out on to the field with instructions to go away to the far left and chuck the ball around in front of the posts. He'd won the toss and wanted to play into the wind, so when he told the referee he would take the kick-off, Colin Meads had the choice of ends for the All Blacks. He could see how the rest of us were all at the far end and decided to stick where he was. A smart bit of thinking, that, by Syd. It was like winning the toss twice, for kick-off and choice of ends.'

En route from their hotel to the stadium in Wellington by bus ('it wasn't posh enough to call it a coach'), Mike Roberts led the Lions in a rendition of their battle hymn 'We Shall Overcome', adding a verse of his own to tease his captain with the words 'Syd will make a break, one day-ay-ay-ay'. Dawes remembers it as an example of how the Lions prepared for a big match in a relaxed mood, something which he attributed mainly to Barry John and his catchphrase: 'Nothing to worry about here, boys.'

It held true until the glorious finale, John spurning a late try by kicking when he should have passed – which, in the grand scheme of things, mattered not a jot. A draw, 14–14, was as good as a win in that it clinched the rubber. Dawes had climbed his Everest, and if that was the perfect time to bow out as a player, he still had one last shot at the All Blacks left in his locker. That winter he led a Lions team under the guise of the Barbarians to a famous win over the All Blacks at Cardiff Arms Park. He also had a hand in *that* try, the unforgettable epic launched from in front of his own posts by a dancing Phil Bennett, something which took almost as much nerve as succeeding Barry John. It had taken the next great Welsh stand-off all of three minutes to obey the dressing-room instructions as laid down by Carwyn James.

Dawes looks back on the match as 'a tribute to Carwyn's philosophy. He showed the world that day what he stood for. It enabled us to show everyone in the UK the kind of rugby we had played in New Zealand, which was important because there wasn't the mass coverage of the Lions that there is now.

'I can remember what he said to Benny before the match. Carwyn had more faith in him than the rest of us because Phil at that stage was still relatively unknown. He said to him, "Look, Benny, the All Blacks don't like anyone who takes them on. They can't cope with it, so at the earliest possible opportunity I'd like to see you take them on."'

The rest, as they say, is history. Regrettably, the same can be said of Dawes and the Lions, because when he returned in charge of the next British Isles touring team in 1977, the trip turned out to be the antithesis of 1971. For Dawes, bogged down in a morass of issues, many stemming from the incessant rain and the unnecessary war with the press, this was his nemesis.

Six years before, Dawes had been lauded by tour manager Doug Smith. In his report to the Four Home Unions, the genial Scot described the Welshman's appointment as 'probably one of the main reasons for the success of the tour. A charming and knowledgeable man who held the respect of everyone in the team, not only for his own outstanding ability but for his friendliness.'

'Friendliness' is not a word which springs to mind when talking about '77. Hindsight being a wonderful thing, Dawes will now admit that in picking 17 Welsh players the Lions picked at least two too many. Far from approving the list, he makes it clear that on several occasions he was outvoted by the selectors, one from each country, over the precise composition of a party which suffered its first blow almost 18 months before departure.

Mervyn Davies, whom he had privately briefed about the captaincy the previous January, had been cruelly removed, leaving Dawes to wrestle with the tricky problem of finding an alternative. 'The two candidates were Roger Uttley and Phil Bennett. I thought of Benny because Wales had had a good season and because we had a large nucleus of Welsh players. Uttley was certainly a strong candidate. Maybe he should have been made captain with Benny as his right-hand man. Fran Cotton and Peter Wheeler were then emerging as players and, of course, both went on to become captains in their own right. But I thought Uttley was the only other candidate at that time. I'd have been quite happy with him as captain, and losing him with a back injury just before the tour began was a big blow. It was also a relief that he did not come, because I had a feeling that maybe the captaincy should have gone his way. It was difficult because I was not sure in my own mind.

'Benny got it because he would have a bigger rapport with the Welsh players. But without Uttley, he didn't have the support of an outstanding pack leader. I thought Terry Cobner would have been the man to pull it all together in that role but he was injured early on. I must have used five or six different pack leaders in the first five or six matches. I thought that if I appointed Cobner that wouldn't have helped, given the big number of Welsh players in the party.'

Their exaggerated presence hung round their national coach like an albatross. The '77 Lions had got off on the wrong foot by picking the wrong party. Whereas selection had been impeccable in '71, the party put at Dawes's disposal left ample room for criticism. He concedes that the selectors got it wrong.

'I think there were too many Welshmen, probably two or three too many. I'm not going to name names but there were some I would not have taken had the choice been mine and mine alone. It meant that there were better players in some positions who were left at home. I had to live with that. If I'd had my way, I would have taken "Mighty Mouse"[Ian McLauchlan]. The argument against him was that he was 33 or 34, but he was a good, hard prop who could hold his own anywhere and he knew what was required in New Zealand. He was a positive bloke who would have taken the bull by the horns, and we missed that sort of attitude.

'When we were selecting the Welsh side and I was undecided about a player, I had total confidence in the other selectors, R.H. [Williams],

Rod [Morgan] and Clive [Rowlands]. With the Lions selectors, I didn't feel I had that total confidence. I had one vote on selection with five others. Whenever I was undecided, the vote went against me.'

Ironically, Dawes had been hit hardest not by those Welshmen who did go but by three who did not. Gareth Edwards, Gerald Davies and J.P.R. Williams had all made themselves unavailable and nobody's absence was more critical than Edwards's. 'If Gareth had been there, we would have won the series, no doubt about it,' says Dawes. 'I tried to persuade him to change his mind during that season but the trouble was that he'd achieved everything. He had won a series in New Zealand, then topped that by what he'd done in South Africa, totally fulfilling his personal ambitions. He was playing at a slightly lower level that season but was still the best around. But he felt that he'd done it twice and that it wasn't going to happen again, which was perfectly understandable. Without him, we didn't have a top-class scrum-half. It was a real shame, because we had developed two of the finest Test packs I have seen, a luxury we never had in '71.'

Until then there had been no stopping Dawes. One of the rare breed to have both captained and coached the Lions, he made the transition with Wales in such a seamless fashion that the Grand Slams and Triple Crowns kept rolling off the conveyor belt as if they would never come to an end. The '77 Lions are the one blot on an otherwise spotless copybook. They lost the first Test and won what proved to be a Pyrrhic victory in the second at Christchurch, where flanker Kevin Eveleigh gave Bennett a clobbering by fair means and foul. 'He must have late-tackled Benny at least half a dozen times. Even the New Zealand press called for Eveleigh to be dropped, which they did for the next Test. But the damage had been done.

'You could do that to Benny. You could really knock him off his game. You could not do that to Barry John or Cliff Morgan, which is what made them great. Benny still played well but what he had lost from the rest of the series was his ability to control the game. With our scrum-half weakness, we needed that kind of dominance at fly-half all the more.'

Trapped in one of the wettest New Zealand winters on record, their leisure-time options reduced to snooker or mooching around the hotels of a country not noted for its glittering range of entertainment, the Lions developed a siege mentality. It wasn't helped by the management's paranoid attitude towards the press, resulting in a blanket policy of non-cooperation which foolishly extended to those anxious to give their boys a sympathetic hearing.

The Lions are always fair game as far as the Kiwis are concerned, hence the scurrilous article in the weekly paper *Truth* claiming that the Lions were 'lousy lovers'. All par for the course and not to be taken seriously, but subsequent decisions turned the tour into a public-relations calamity. Tour manager George Burrell, a former Scotland full-back-cum-international referee, took draconian action.

'That was the start of non-rugby journalists covering the tour and the management decision was that because these guys were ridiculing our players at home, when we went to any social function we didn't necessarily want them around. The line was drawn and nobody writing for a newspaper was welcome to any social event. It was a case of, "They can't be trusted, so we won't give them anything." That was a mistake, especially as I was in the firing line.'

Ironically, the blanket ban extended to the man who had originally been earmarked as the captain, Mervyn Davies. 'I was the one who had to ask guys like Mervyn to leave the party after the last Test. I did it because I was told to do so. I was responsible to the manager, not the players. If the manager said something I disagreed with, we would debate it. If I lost the argument, I would have to carry out his instructions. Unfortunately, everyone was tarred by the same brush. It was George's interpretation. Sometimes I wish we could have diluted that particular decision in some way.

'Mervyn was one of a number of people at that particular function in a press capacity. I said, "Listen, Merve, this is something I have been asked to do. It would help me if you could leave without making a fuss." It was difficult for me because there was no way out. I just felt the relationship with the media was something we could have done without. Maybe, in hindsight, we should have tried to sort it out earlier in the tour.'

Away from the training field, Dawes changed his tour tipple from gin and tonic. 'I was drinking Scotch, which I never drink. I drank it to win the manager's confidence, because he was a big Scotch drinker and that was my way of showing him my loyalty.'

Long before the end he discovered that the Lions did not have the calibre of tourist to lift them out of the mire. There was no 'Chico' Hopkins or Bob Hiller or John Spencer to raise spirits, and yet their domination in the set scrums was such that they reduced the All Blacks to packing down with nothing more than the front row on their ball. The point is clearly still a sore one with Dawes.

'They did that because they knew they were stuffed, but we didn't know how to combat it. On our ball we could have held it and marched them over from anywhere. Why didn't we do it?'

The Lions lost 3–1 and Dawes went back to winning Grand Slams and Triple Crowns with Wales. Appointed coaching organiser of the Welsh Rugby Union in 1980, he knew the conveyor belt was beginning to creak. 'My budget as coaching organiser in 1981 was £6,000. By the new millennium we'll have spent something like £200 million on stadia and if we'd only had 10 per cent of that for encouraging more youngsters to play the game, we would not be in the mess we are in now.

'It seems to me that a lot of players are just playing for the money. There's no pride there. What has happened, and it's a horrible thing to say, is that there is no shame in them when they lose so badly. Fifty per cent of the team which lost to France at Wembley probably didn't care. When they woke up on the Sunday morning, it didn't matter.

'It hurts me greatly as a Welshman to say that. I took a sadistic delight in England losing 76–0 to Australia, never thinking that South Africa would give us an even bigger hiding a few weeks later. Yet the passion for the game is still there. It's just been dormant.'

9

The King and his Abdication

When the invitation to join the British Isles Rugby Union Touring Team on their tour of New Zealand dropped through his letter-box one March morning in 1971, Barry John ignored it. He had made up his mind. He would not be going with the Lions because he was in no fit state to go, and that, sadly, was that.

Unluckily for the All Blacks, Carwyn James was not in the habit of taking no for an answer. In the end it took a special deal to ensure that the fly-half from Cefneithin in charge of planning the campaign would have another fly-half from the same village to put it into dazzling operation on the field. The deal took some striking, even for a coach of James's calibre.

'A few weeks went by and then Carwyn asked me why I hadn't replied to the invitation. Normally it would have been done by return of post with grateful thanks, but I told him straight. "I'm in a bad way. I need three months off. I'm not going because if I did, I wouldn't be much use to you."'

John was still suffering the effects of what he had done at Stade Colombes in Paris a few weeks earlier, tackling the marauding French back-row forward Benoit Dauga, all 6ft 5in of him, head-on five yards from the line. It had saved a try and left the tackler with a broken nose – a small, if painful, price to pay for securing a Welsh Grand Slam.

In attempting to go about his business, John suffered recurring nausea over the next fortnight or so. 'I would feel so groggy at times that I'd have to pull into lay-bys and try to snooze for half an hour. I used to sleep a hell of a lot. I can remember one occasion when I must have looked so white-faced and unsteady that one chap and his wife were so concerned about me they asked me in for a cup of coffee.

'I'd taken two big bangs playing for Wales and they were obviously affecting me. I had tests done fairly frequently and the message from the doctor was always the same: "Come back and see me in ten days' time." And so it went on, spasmodic attacks followed by spasmodic visits to the doctor.'

The invitation went on gathering dust. James, under pressure from the organisers, the Four Home Unions Tours Committee, was running out of time. He needed a decision, preferably in the affirmative, and with that in mind he was prepared to make a special case for a special player. Recognising the physical battering John had taken during that season's Five Nations, James was smart enough to acknowledge that his prize asset was worth protecting.

At the eleventh hour, he got the answer he wanted. 'I didn't decide until ten days before departure in early May. In the end my wife Jan was the one who sorted it out. She said, "You might as well go because you will only be sorry for what you're missing in a few weeks' time when you're clear of this trouble." I rang Carwyn and said, "Okay, count me in." He said, "If you don't want to train, you don't train. You will play whenever you want to play. That's a promise."

'I was concerned. You can easily wreck the party by making allowances for one person, and the last thing I wanted was for the others to think I was some sort of prima donna. Carwyn, of course, had thought of that. He said, "I've told the manager, Doug Smith, what the score is, and if the other players want to complain, we'll deal with it. There's no need for you to worry about a thing."'

And with that, rugby's prototype superstar was on his way, a player who by the sheer poetry of his movement would transcend the old game and take it to new heights of popularity. What some of England's higher-profile players achieved in the '90s, Barry John had been there and done two decades earlier. They had never seen anyone like him in New Zealand before, and it will be a long time before they see his like again.

The impact he had on his fellow Lions still leaves them in a state of bewilderment even today. The Welshman, whose outrageous skills, fearless vision and ability to glide through gaps that only he saw, never gave the opposition the ghost of a chance. They were bamboozled by a man one of his compatriots at the heart of the battle in New Zealand describes as 'a laid-back, obnoxious, arrogant little toad'.

In speaking of him in such glowing terms of endearment, Mervyn Davies shakes his head in disbelief at the mention of his name. Barry

John was the nearest thing he had seen to a genius on the rugby field. 'I have never seen anything by anybody in the game of rugby to equal his performances over a sustained period of time,' said Davies. 'He played rugby on a different plane from anyone else I ever saw. He was on a different, superior wavelength.

'We'd all be in the dressing-room thumping the wall and he'd be there in such a relaxed state that you'd think he was going out for a stroll. He was so laid-back he'd say, "Don't worry, boys, it's only a game. Just give me the ball and I'll win it for you. It's only the All Blacks. How many points do you want me to score today?" He had a tremendous influence on all of us because he had such confidence.'

It did not take long before the wonder boy's frequent absence from training became a topic of discussion, as well as potential rancour. It was a tribute to Barry's importance that nobody complained, although that didn't stop them from inquiring about his absence from much of the daily grind of the practice ground. Davies was one of the first to raise the question. 'I was told, "Barry's got a bad back. He's having a jog." Then you'd look round and see him in goal in a knockabout game of soccer, diving here and diving there. There was bugger all wrong with him. Carwyn wasn't daft. He'd say, "Barry doesn't like all this training." He knew his men and no one complained.'

In the dressing-room at Carisbrook Park, Dunedin, immediately prior to the start of the series, his innate belief in himself and those around him provided striking reassurance that these Lions were not going to be denied. It was not so much an impromptu little speech, more a case of thinking out loud. 'I've just had a thought, boys,' he told them, pulling the red jersey over his head, gumshield in hand, just before they had been called out by the referee. 'I wouldn't swap anyone in this dressing-room for anyone else. I'm happy with my shirt. Let's go.'

He then went out and kicked the Lions to victory, two penalties on top of a charged-down try claimed by the Mighty Mouse Ian McLauchlan. Nothing could now spoil John's *annus mirabilis*, which he had launched that January with two drop goals in the ritual beating of England at Cardiff. Never one to hog the limelight, he had the uncanny knack of inspiring others to new heights, chief among them a three-quarter whose greatness was never questioned after that tour.

If anyone freed Mike Gibson from the shackles and opened his mind to a daring new game where anything was possible, it was Barry John. The performance of the Lions in the match against Wellington, then New Zealand's champion province, on Saturday, 5 June 1971, is considered by experienced observers who witnessed it as arguably the nearest thing to perfection ever achieved by a British Isles team. The Lions won 9–0 on tries, with four from Cardiff wing John Bevan, and by a points total of 47–9, or 65–9 under today's scoring system.

Barry's capacity for catching the opposition by surprise was never better illustrated than during the first half of the Wellington match. 'We were almost underneath our own crossbar just before half-time with our ball at a scrum. Their backs had come up and Syd [John Dawes] said to me, "Fancy it?"

'Mike was standing next to me. "What do you mean?" he said. "What are you going to do?" I said, "I'm going to chip them," and Mike said, "No, no. Don't."

'"Look," I said. "That's all I'm telling you. If you want to come with us, it's up to you."

'And that was it. The ball came out, I did a little dink over the top with the left foot. Mike was off like a greyhound. The ball stood up and he angled away to the left, gave it to John Bevan and he was in under the sticks. After that there was no holding Mike Gibson. He had found his stage and come of age.

'When he was playing for Ireland, more often than not they were geared to losing. Everything was a dogfight and Mike rarely had the opportunity to show what he could really do. That Wellington match was the making of a lot of us. But most of all it was the making of Mike Gibson.'

It helped having a fly-half whom no New Zealand team could ever catch, let alone nail. It also helped having a fly-half who could make the ball sit up and almost talk. As a kicker, he had such an extensive armoury that he tormented the All Blacks throughout the series with the variety and deadly accuracy of his footwork. Every time he went on to the field it was as if he had armed himself with a private arsenal. Goalkicks, grub-kicks, punts, chips – you name it, he could do it, and he could drop every one on the proverbial sixpence. A speciality was to take aim at a colleague 40 yards away on the training ground and fire the ball 'down his throat' so he didn't have to move more than the odd muscle to catch it. Most of all, he perfected the garryowen, the up-and-under, in a way that it caused mayhem. Barry had programmed it to deceive the catcher in the last seconds of its flight by drifting mysteriously away, making it fiendishly difficult for the opposition to repair the damage.

'If you cut the ball in the right way for the up-and-under it goes spinning up and when it comes down and the full-back or the wing thinks he is right underneath it, the spin makes it drift away and leave the catcher floundering. In order to cause the maximum chaos, the kick must drop in front of the wing or the full-back so they are having to run towards it, which increases the chance that they will take their eye off it. I'd say to our centres and wings, "Whatever you do, don't spoil it by tackling the man without the ball, because he won't have the ball!"

'When I was chipping over the top of the opposition backs, I'd hit the ball a touch more on the bottom so that it would spin in reverse, giving it a better chance of sitting up for our runners. The grubber is particularly effective because it gets defences turning, and nobody, least of all the French, fancies having to fall on the ball. I found kicking very simple. It was all a question of applying the perfect weight, as if you were using a nine-iron or a wedge.'

The tour made him *the* player of his day, a rugby George Best, with whom he once spent a weekend. It might not have been mere coincidence that both chose to leave the global stage at an early age. Barry, astounded to learn that he had become a folk hero across Britain in his absence, would ultimately find the adulation more than he could handle, but for the rest of the tour he remained on top of the world.

It was as if his whole life had been geared for that summer and that tour. As a boy he had been gliding around obstacles ever since he could remember, swerving through the kitchen, out of the back door of no. 14 Heol Tabernacle, Cefneithin, and over the hedge into the field for a game of make-believe, whether it was Spurs versus Aston Villa or Wales against England. 'It was only four and a half yards from the kitchen to the field but I was into a stride pattern from the word go. Right from the start I was always quick in thought and movement. I could see things early, whether it was rugby or soccer, and that enabled me to claim my opponent's space before he knew it. To me, it was always a game of chess. A case of checkmate.

'I could drop a goal with my left foot and rifle a 60-yarder with my right foot. I could pass either way, but to break, that was the secret. Making a break means you must have the same balance on either side. The right angle, the right bending of the body and the right show of the ball are all crucial. The fly-half is the orchestrator, but first of all he must create doubt in the minds of the opposition waiting to confront him. Any fly-half taken for granted by the opposition is useless. It's all about angles and creating space, what I call the geometry of the game.'

For someone who will confess to being technologically challenged, John made a remarkably good fist of working his own in-built computer throughout his five years on the international stage. 'I still can't understand any of these hi-tech machines, but on the rugby field I was lucky to have the means of picking up signals very quickly. If a winger standing 70 yards away was a yard or two out of position, I'd spot it. But spotting it is one thing. Being able to take advantage of it is another matter.'

If it all seemed to come to him with ridiculous ease, the young Barry John seldom missed an opportunity to perfect his art, and as his reputation grew, so the Carmarthenshire Police were only too happy to put the sixth-former into a man's game, under an assumed name. It meant skipping most of a triple lesson in zoology and botany every Wednesday afternoon at Gwendraeth Grammar School.

'I used to leave my satchel at my desk and wander out to the toilet never to be seen again until the next day. The police used to say that if anyone asked any question about what I did in the force, I was to say, "Special Branch." Imagine that, an honorary Special Branch officer for the day!

'I'd walked out two Wednesdays in a row and when I went to leave again a fortnight later, the teacher, a lovely lady called Miss Nancy Gravelle, barred the way. She'd run to the door and stand in front of me. "Barry," she said. "You are not going anywhere."

'"I'm sorry, Miss Gravelle. I have got to go."

'"If you don't come back to this classroom right away, I am going to have to report you to the police."

'"You can't do that, Miss Gravelle."

'"And why ever not?"

'"Because I'm going to play rugby for them!"'

He would then rush out to be whisked away in a waiting panda car.

Weeks later Llanelli signed him, but not everyone in Wales at that time considered him the best around. The Welsh Secondary Schools, for example, chose not to pick him despite the fact that he had made his debut for the Scarlets at Moseley while still a schoolboy. With delicious timing, Barry played for Llanelli against Harlequins at Twickenham on the day that the Welsh Secondary Schools were beaten by their English counterparts. Both teams ended up on the same train back to Wales. 'I'd done the business for Llanelli in the citadel of English rugby against international players and yet I wasn't good enough for the schools side. The selectors had some very red faces when they got on the train and saw me. They couldn't look me in the face.'

Two years later he was playing for Wales, the selectors having delayed his entry until a month before his 22nd birthday rather than take a chance by picking him sooner. Despite a losing start brought about largely by his taking a few selfish options, the new boy took it pretty much in his stride as if it was part of his destiny.

'Once I finished that match, I knew this was my stage. I had been comfortable out there, not frightened. It was just a question of fine-tuning my game, and I could tell that the other players were happy for me to be in the team. I knew how to orchestrate the game because I knew what was required.'

With Barry, there was never any questioning his ability, never any risk of his instincts being afflicted by any fleeting anxiety or self-doubt. 'Temperament in international sport is worth 99 points out of 100. Very little ever bothered me in any rugby match. I made mistakes, lots of them, but they never bothered me. I was too busy thinking of the next move.'

It hadn't all been plain sailing. His first Lions Test, against South Africa at Loftus Versfeld in Pretoria, ended after 15 minutes in a freak accident which left the most creative back in the British Isles with a broken collarbone. Typically, Barry had disobeyed skipper Tom Kiernan's instruction to 'bang it into touch', running the penalty instead. While it might not have been clear to anyone else, he could see a yawning gap down the middle of the field as plain as a pikestaff, and he was off in a flash.

Keith Savage, the England wing, had the pace and wit to offer him support on the wide outside when Barry, some 60 yards on from his starting point, decided, fatefully, to go for the line himself. 'I could see a shadow coming from behind me but I still thought I'd check inside because the full-back seemed to be standing there as if frozen. I thought I'd be in under the posts. Lovely. And that was when Jan Ellis caught me with one finger under my collar.

'The crazy thing was that before the Test we'd had new jerseys, so the collar was starched whereas the old one wasn't. Anyway, there was enough starch for him to get enough of a grip. One little mistake and it threw me clean over, and I landed on my shoulder. To make it worse, I came down right at the end of the cricket square and I knew it had gone straight away.'

Deprived of their most creative player for the rest of the trip, the Lions' hopes of rescuing the series had gone too. Reduced to the harmless role of duty boy, Barry returned home that summer to discover how fickle life can be, even for an embryonic national hero. Having given up his job to make the tour, he was stuck at home fretting over the inescapable fact that nobody seemed to want him.

The BBC, via the powerful voice of David Coleman, highlighted his plight in what amounted to a buckshee advertisement. 'It was a real tear-jerker and I was very grateful because my pride wouldn't let me pocket any dole money. I thought after the BBC plug that they'd have to hire a JCB to bring me all the job offers. I didn't get one. I was feeling cheesed off before that, so you can imagine how much worse I felt afterwards. I was a qualified schoolteacher and yet nobody seemed to want to know. It made me wonder whether this was what people really thought because I was injured and not of any use to them.'

Such despondency made him susceptible to rugby league, and while he waited for a job offer, who should come up with one but Wigan. For a short time, Wales and the Lions were in grave danger of losing their prize asset simply because nobody could bother offering him a job. Today, judging by what is paid to players hardly fit to lace his boots, clubs would be falling over themselves to pay him £300,000 a year, but back then nobody bothered.

'I arranged to meet the Wigan directors at a hotel in Hereford and when I got there they rolled out the contract and gave me a beautiful pen. All I had to do was sign. At the last minute I gave them the pen back. No offence to Wigan, but it dawned on me that I was taking the coward's way out. I was going to league for the wrong reasons, because I felt nobody was helping me out at home.'

No sooner had he turned Wigan down than Gwyn Walters, the distinguished former international referee, saved John's rugby union career, solving his unemployment problem at a stroke by securing him a job as a representative in the financial company Forward Trust. His immediate future secured, John proceeded to take his game to a level which astounded his peers, among them those who were the undisputed masters of their own particular art. Mervyn Davies put it succinctly: 'Barry beat people by sleight of hand or sublime movement of the body which gave an almost lackadaisical impression but which was done at great pace. He was like Stanley Matthews. He did things which made me think, "How the heck did he do that?"'

The most outrageous, even by Barry John's standards, took place at Napier on Saturday, 17 July 1971. As a personal protest against the Stone Age behaviour of the local cavemen, it took some nerve even for one who was never lacking in that department. 'Cocky? You had to be . . .'

And yet all Barry got for his trouble was a condemnation for the arrogance of his behaviour. Rather than lowering himself by indulging in any skulduggery, he chose an original way of showing his contempt for the opposition. He sat on the ball, and when the Hawke's Bay mob, already incensed at being given the runaround, bore down on him, he was still sitting there. If some in the Lions party feared for his well-being,

Barry knew exactly how he would apply the *coup de grâce* to the ultimate in ridicule, what you could call 'taking the Barry'.

'Hawke's Bay that day just wanted to take people out, mainly Gareth Edwards. I've seen some awful things on a rugby field in my time but nothing to compare with what I saw in that match. I saw one of their props try and kick Gareth's head off. Gareth was trapped in a ruck, the ball was a foot and a half away from him and this bloke tried to kick him. If he had connected, I shudder to think what the consequences would have been. Fortunately, all Gareth could feel was the draught of the boot as it missed him by a whisker.

'When Gerald scored his four brilliant tries, the crowd did nothing to acknowledge any of them. They were pathetic. So when they kicked downfield with about ten minutes to go, I ran back to get the ball. I trapped it with my backside and then I sat on it. They were charging at me and it sounded as if the whole crowd of 25,000 were shouting, "Kill! Kill!"

'I had taken the precaution of making sure I was inside the twenty-five before sitting on the ball. I left it as late as possible, picked the ball up and slammed it right back behind them so they all had to turn around. I was showing them, in a more subtle way, what I thought of them. I was totally disgusted by what had gone on. If this was rugby, what was the point in playing it?'

His point made, John hurled his boots across the dressing-room. His anger had only just subsided when he learnt that some of the British journalists covering the tour were less than bowled over by what he had done. 'They thought I was petulant and one paper made a reference to the effect that the halo was slipping. I never asked anyone to put a halo there in the first place.'

It was another disturbing reminder of something which he would be made increasingly aware of: that the public had come to expect almost impossible standards from him. The penalties of fame would drive him into early retirement all too soon, and the first warning that his rugby life had begun to undergo an irrevocable change had come a fortnight before the Hawke's Bay game in the town of New Plymouth.

In deference to his performances on tour, the players had given him a regal soubriquet, 'The King'. The 'coronation' took place, much to HRH's embarrassment, in a restaurant beneath the brooding shadow of Mount Egmont. Entry to the restaurant was via an elevated ramp which led to the dining-room below, and John, arriving late, paused on the ramp to scan the sea of faces below for an empty seat.

'I stood there for about ten seconds or so. I was late because I'd been writing a few letters home and it was just a question of trying to see if there was room for one more at any of the tables. Anyway, the next thing I knew they burst into a chorus of 'God Save the King'. I felt so embarrassed I didn't know what to do with myself.'

Terry McLean, the distinguished New Zealand journalist who had seen them all come and go from the year dot, wrote about the coronation the next morning, the analogy between John looking down on the diners and a king appearing before his subjects too powerful to resist.

Shortly afterwards, on the eve of the third Test in Wellington, John had begun to realise what sort of an impact he and the Lions were making back home. He had a rough idea because Clem Thomas, recently arrived to beef up the press party, kept telling him how every Saturday morning the lights were going on all over Britain as the country tuned into the Lions.

'Clem was going on about how people were naming babies after me and how I'd be crowned when I got home and all that nonsense. I never realised it was that big, that it had captured the imagination of the public in such a way. For the first time in my life, the pressure got to me. Normally before a big match I'd stay in my room until 11 in the morning, have some coffee and toast and then wander around. On the morning of that Test match I was downstairs in the foyer of the hotel by half past eight. Terry O'Connor of the *Daily Mail* was there and he thought to himself, "What's wrong with BJ? Why's he up so early?" I went for a walk and he came with me. We got talking and he got a good piece for the paper about the pressure of playing for the Lions with the whole country willing you to succeed.'

His response was to drop a goal, convert a Gerald Davies try and follow with one of his own, all within the first 20 minutes. The Lions won 13–3, drew the last Test and took the series. On their return they were fêted like conquering heroes, and none more so than 'The King'. The scale of the welcome and the reverence with which he was treated wherever he went flabbergasted him.

'The whole security system at Heathrow had to be reviewed because so many thousands turned up to see us home. They reckoned we were as popular as The Beatles. It was so hectic that in order to do one radio interview, the only quiet place I could find was the ladies' toilet! The *Evening Standard* had pictures of us on the front page. I thought, "What the hell's happening here?" And then there were the letters, delivered by the sackful.'

When he next played for Wales, against England at Twickenham in

January 1972, he walked off to be ambushed by Eamonn Andrews and whisked away to be the subject of *This Is Your Life*. At that stage he was thinking seriously of getting out, of finding an escape from the public adulation which had been bothering him ever since a public engagement a little earlier in North Wales.

'I opened the extension of a bank and after I'd been introduced, this little girl came forward and curtsied. Everyone thought it was wonderful. They were clapping like mad. That was when it came home to me that this was all getting out of hand. If I needed something to show me that it had all gone way over the top, that was it. That is in no way meant as a criticism of the little girl but it embarrassed me. It meant that some people had put me on such a pedestal that it was as if I was from another world.

'Nobody could touch me on the rugby field, and I don't mean to sound as though I'm bragging. I had to finish because of my rugby, because of what people had made of me through rugby. It got to the stage where I couldn't book a table in a restaurant in my name. Jan always had to do it for me. It was all getting too much. I decided I would retire at the end of that season. I'd had a gutsfull.'

He confided in three people: Gareth, Gerald and Gerry Lewis, the Welsh team's loyal physiotherapist-cum-magic-sponge man. He sold his story to the *Sunday Mirror* after bowing out a few days earlier in a special match, Barry John's XV against Carwyn James's XV in aid of Urdd Gobaith Cymru, the Welsh League of Youth. Almost 40,000 turned up. There would have been 140,000 had they known beforehand that they wouldn't be able to see him again.

Barry John had quit at the age of 27 to write for the *Daily Express* and exploit his fame. The abdication shocked those around him. 'Barry was just about reaching his zenith then,' said Mervyn Davies. 'He should have stayed in rugby a damned sight longer than he did. The world never saw the best of Barry John. I had no idea he was going to retire, and even if I had known I don't know whether I was close enough to him to have been able to persuade him otherwise.

'He was the first rugby superstar and he wanted to cash in on his fame. But there's no doubt he could have kept going for another three years. I think his early retirement was a mistake. When I had to retire I was thinking, "I'm just getting the hang of this game. I can take it on to a higher plane." Barry would have done the same.'

Gerald Davies, born one month after John in February 1945, understood the demands which went with his compatriot's escalating fame. His lavish skills, allied to a pleasant, easy-going nature, made him a perfect advertisement for an often brutal sport. He was the first to change the public's perception of rugby players, blazing a trail for future generations.

'Suddenly, after that Lions tour, rugby players were beginning to be thought of in a showbiz sense. They were being sought after to make television appearances and write newspaper columns, things which had been unheard of before. Barry had become a cult hero, the most romantic figure in the sport, and in order to make the most of that commercially, he had to retire.

'There was a sense of fulfilment in Barry after that tour. Whatever he touched turned to gold and there was simply no stopping his success. He had a kind of swagger about him, almost in a self-mocking way, because he laughed at himself. Nothing was too great for him. There is no doubt in my mind that he should have gone on. Without doubt, he retired too soon.'

John, now separated from his wife and no longer working for the *Express*, is embarking upon a new business venture. Whatever happens, he is assured his place among the most revered figures in the game, a Pied Piper who enriched the sport worldwide and never received a bean for playing it. Had he been born a quarter of a century later, he would have made millions.

'Yes, of course I had regrets. I'd love to have gone on for three more years at least but, as an amateur, I had a job to do as well, and whenever I went back to the office it was chaos. People came in just to stand and look at me. I never sought adulation. That's probably why I ran away from it.'

Since then he has witnessed the decline of the fly-half factory and the creation of a new cottage industry in the valleys: making caps to keep pace with the increasingly quick turnover in personnel. Nobody who saw Barry John will ever forget him.

They didn't call him 'The King' for nothing.

10

Gareth the Great

The reports from various scouts hired by Swansea Town Football Club to scour the locality for new talent were beginning to pile up on the manager's desk when Trevor Morris decided he could afford to wait no longer. One of the great soccer salesmen of his time reached for the appropriate registration forms and headed out of town towards a little place called Gwaun-cae-Gurwen.

Swansea had a long tradition of producing exceptional footballers, from John Charles and Trevor Ford in the '40s to Cliff Jones, the Allchurch brothers, Terry and Medwin, and many more in the '50s. In the spring of 1963, the homely Second Division club which Morris would take to within one freak goal of the FA Cup final the following year was about to sign another embryonic star.

The 16-year-old left winger had just scored twice for Swansea in the final of the Welsh Youth Cup, and Morris had assumed personal responsibility for going out that morning to sign him before someone else beat him to it. He considered the player in question to be a 'special case', although nobody then could have realised just how special he would become.

Morris had a rare eye for signing players nobody had ever heard of and turning them into internationals. A few years earlier he had bought a part-timer from Kidderminster, Gerry Hitchens, who in next to no time was playing centre-forward for England. But for all his charm and natural eloquence, Morris was getting nowhere fast in Gwaun-cae-Gurwen that morning until he suddenly shifted the conversation into his native tongue.

'We met in his grandmother's house and the atmosphere was not all that convivial until I asked for a cup of tea in Welsh,' said Morris. 'We were sitting there talking about the virtues of soccer and rugby and not getting very far when that one request suddenly changed the whole atmosphere. The grandmother's eyes lit up and I even got an extra lump of sugar! I could sense that, like my own grandmother, she only trusted Welshmen. The rest were all foreigners.'

Half an hour later, Morris left the house with a spring in his step and a contract in his pocket. He had signed Gareth Edwards, albeit on one condition. Even so, the Swans manager drove back to his office at the Vetch Field, tucked away behind the local prison, genuinely excited at having done everything he could to secure the services of quite a prospect.

'Gareth was a special case. I realised he had got something and all the reports bore that out. He had all the requisite skills. He was strong, he was fast, he had two good feet and he wasn't afraid. He would have made a really good professional soccer player but at that time he was undecided about furthering his education. So before he signed we agreed to a condition that if he chose to stay at school, I would release him from the contract. When he changed his mind, we were very disappointed to lose him.'

Edwards had played in the same Swans youth team as an Italian boy from Cardiff, Giorgio Chinaglia, who also signed professional forms for the club in the same year. He went on to become an international goalscorer, a millionaire businessman, the president of the New York Cosmos, for whom he played alongside Pele and Beckenbauer, the owner of the Lazio club in Rome and much more – and all that after Swansea had given him a free transfer!

Had Edwards not been offered a scholarship at the last minute to arguably Britain's most sports-conscious public school, Millfield, he would have joined Chinaglia, and the course of Welsh football history in both codes would probably have been very different.

'I was just about to start a soccer career with the Swans when I got an eleventh-hour reprieve to go to Millfield,' said Edwards. 'If that opportunity hadn't arisen, I'd have gone to the Vetch. I had the chance of trials at quite a number of bigger clubs but I'd have been happy to start at the Vetch because they had such a good reputation for developing local players.'

Bill Samuel, Edwards's mentor and coach from the age of 14 when their paths first crossed at Pontardawe Secondary Technical School, tells in his book *Rugby: Body and Soul* how he discussed at some length with

Gareth's parents the prospects of his protégé pursuing a career in professional football. 'I had no objection to Gareth becoming a soccer apprentice,' Samuel told Mr Glan Edwards and his wife, Annie. 'It would suit Gareth perfectly. No more schooling. An idyllic existence. Ever since I have been in the Tech, I have seen excited boys going on trials to some of the top clubs in the country. Not one of them made the grade.

'I am a qualified soccer coach and referee. What would Manchester United do if I recommended a promising boy to them? Not only would they thank me, they'd send me a cheque as well, providing the boy was any good. Name your club, Gareth. I'll fix a trial period for you.'

When asked by Mrs Edwards what he would do if it were his son, Samuel said, 'I am sorry, Mrs Edwards, he must make that decision for himself. I can write on his behalf to Manchester United, Arsenal, Spurs. Or he can work for his O-levels to become a PE teacher and play rugby for Wales.' According to Samuel, both parents scoffed at the idea. 'Play rugby for Wales, indeed! He'll be lucky to play for Cwmgors.'

There was more, far more, to Edwards than an above-average ability in one football code if not in the other, judging by his failure to convince some fairly shrewd judges that he was anything more than an average scrum-half. It was an observation which clearly had a lot to do with rugby falling behind soccer and athletics in the pecking order. As a gymnast and an athlete, the teenaged Edwards made such an impression among the *cognoscenti* that they believed he could have represented Great Britain at both.

Luckily for Wales, he reserved his gymnastics for Saturday afternoons, almost exclusively but not quite. Once, when the Big Five were in a bit of a tizz over a suggestion that their scrum-half might not recover from a dodgy hamstring in time for the international, Cliff Jones, the chairman of selectors and pre-war idol, bumped into the man himself, reminded him of the Friday morning fitness test and asked how he felt. Without batting an eyelid or even taking off his jacket, Edwards did ten back somersaults on the spot.

'I'm very well, thank you, Mr Jones,' he said. 'Very well.'

His athletics prowess had earned him, among others, the Welsh national long-jump title before Bill Samuel smoothed his path for the longest jump of all, one which took the miner's boy from a council house in Swansea valley to an English public school in Somerset with a reputation for taking the privileged sporting élite and making them more élite.

Millfield was not exactly bowled over, pardon the pun, by the

Edwards curriculum vitae as outlined by Mr Samuel which included his winning distance in the long jump, 21ft 6in. The reply, leaving no doubt that Millfield was not in the business of awarding sports scholarships, also put his long-jump effort into perspective: 'We have a 12-year-old boy from Brazil who jumps 25 feet.'

Before completing his two years at the school, Edwards had developed from a Welsh schools field events title-holder into a British track champion, and a record-breaking one at that. In winning the sprint hurdles, he beat an English boy who would make a name for himself as a Olympian of some renown before making a similar name for himself in the field of sports marketing: Alan Pascoe.

Within a year of leaving Millfield and beginning a teacher-training course in Cardiff, Edwards was playing for Wales, at the age of 19, against France in Stade Colombes. It was hardly the gentlest of initiations, yet the experience did not bother him one iota. He slept so well the night before that his father, so the story goes, had to wake him up at half past nine the next morning.

'There have been so many great moments over the years but one I'll never forget was my first international at the Arms Park. All the singing, and you know they're on your side. When you come out of the dressing-room, you feel like Popeye after the spinach. You don't feel frightened.'

Ten months later, after a run of four matches, he was no longer merely playing in the team but in charge of it, the youngest Welsh captain of all time. He may not have held the job for long but, over a period of 11 years, only one other player was allowed to take his place at scrum-half in a championship match, and then for not much more than 20 minutes. As it turned out, it was long enough for the irrepressible Ray 'Chico' Hopkins to transform a lost cause against England at Twickenham into an improbable win.

Hopkins, a Lion in his own right who deserved a stack of caps, had gone north when Edwards left his post for the last 90 seconds of the 24–0 win over Australia in 1973, long enough for Clive Shell of Aberavon, another who lived long in the master's shadow, to gain the international status worthy of his all-round skills. Edwards was never injured again.

When he vacated the position after the 1978 Grand Slam at the end of 53 consecutive internationals, he had, by common consent, established himself as the greatest rugby player certainly of his time, probably of the century. The facts are astounding, all the more so given his country's fall from grace during the '80s and '90s. Of 22 Five Nations matches at Cardiff Arms Park with Edwards at the nerve-centre of operations, Wales won 20 and lost 1, to France in 1968, ironically under their scrum-half's captaincy. In 63 Tests for Wales and the Lions, he won 40, drew 8 and lost only 15. His 20 international tries stood as a record for a scrum-half for more than 20 years until the South African Joost van der Westhuizen eclipsed it in 1998.

Yet statistics alone cannot do him justice. A global poll of many world authorities on the game conducted by *Rugby World* magazine to rank the hundred greatest players of all time put him at number one in a top ten which included, in descending order, Serge Blanco, Colin Meads, J.P.R. Williams, Gerald Davies, Mike Gibson, Barry John, Philippe Sella, Frik du Preez and Willie John McBride.

Cliff Morgan, ranked a mere 69th in that particular list, did not need anyone to tell him what he knew about Edwards all along. 'I've always said that of all the players I've known during 50-odd years' involvement with the game, Edwards stood out head and shoulders above the rest. Not only was he a great gymnast, he also had all the physical attributes, not least a strong pair of shoulders and a strong neck. And he was fast.

'What Edwards also had, and it's one thing which I believe is essential to great sportsmen, was 250-degree vision. Even if he was looking straight ahead, he could sense when there were players on either side, and what they were doing. He was unbelievable.'

The unbelievable stuff created a worldwide mystique. You don't get to be Sean Fitzpatrick's sporting hero for nothing. As a nine-year-old boy he sat at home in Auckland, transfixed before the television set, watching the Welshman score that sensational try for the Barbarians against the All Blacks in January 1973. If he hadn't seen it, the young Fitzpatrick would never have believed it.

'My dad got me up in the middle of the night so I could watch the match with him and what I saw was just sensational,' he said years later. 'It made such an impression on me that from then on, whenever my brother and I played footie out in the backyard, I was always Gareth Edwards.'

Terry McLean, the celebrated New Zealand journalist who had seen them all come and go for most of the century, recorded the final stage of the try as follows: 'At about 45 yards from the All Blacks' goal-line, [Tommy] David passed to Edwards. Kent Lambert, a Clydesdale type, gave chase to Edwards, who was Thousand Guineas stuff. Whether the try was the greatest ever, as is still contended, is unimportant. Simply, it was perfection.'

A masterpiece like that, which many hands stitched together once Phil Bennett had started the counter-attack in front of his own posts, had not been uppermost in anyone's mind when the Barbarians trained at their spiritual home in Penarth. The omens, as Edwards remembered them, were not good.

'We'd had the worst sort of preparation we had for any game. We practised for two days on a sloping pitch and a muddy field. If I threw a decent pass to Phil, he dropped it. If he actually caught it and passed it to Mike Gibson, he fumbled it. J.P.R., of all people, actually dropped passes, and no matter what we did it was clumsy. Bloody awful!

'In the actual game, all I can remember was my energy being sapped. I was thinking, "The ball's got to go to touch so we can get our second wind." So when the ball went deep into the corner and Phil went scampering after it, I thought, "Thank God. He'll put it into touch."

'Then, all of a sudden, Phil had to run with it because he was surprised at how quickly their flanker had come up. So I had to let the players go past me. I thought I'd better follow up because, as a scrum-half, if the ball goes to ground and I'm not following up, they'd all say it was because I hadn't been training hard enough.

'By the time I turned around and started to go after them, I was generating some pace. So when Derek Quinnell went to pass to John Bevan, who was outside, I was picking up pace and their full-back was expecting the ball to go to Bevan. When I came into the line, I shouted to Derek, "Give it to me." I took the ball and that injection of pace took me round the full-back.

'I can remember seeing someone out of the corner of my eye closing on me, and I can remember praying, "Don't let my hamstring go now!" My PE master always told me to dive from five yards out because it is harder for them to tackle you. So I just dived into the corner.'

He had dived into a different corner of the same stadium the previous season for another try which was an epic of the solo variety. No try, not even the one against the Baa-baas, better encapsulated all of Edwards's qualities, not least his stamina, than the one he scored from a range of fully 85 yards against Scotland in February 1972. In the end he made it against almost impossible odds, sheer will-power taking him past two Scottish players before his gymnastics enabled him to touch the ball down a split-second before it could squirt into touch. 'All I was thinking at the time was, "Please, God, don't let it bounce over the dead-ball line." It could have done and nobody would have remembered the moment. There's such a fine line between success and failure.'

He had almost drowned in a morass of mud when Gerry Lewis reached the scene of the glory and got his magic sponge to work on the prone body. 'You know what, Ger,' Edwards said when he had finally found the breath to say anything, by which time the faithful Lewis was easing him out of a muddy hole.

'What, Gareth? What's the matter?'

'You know, Ger, there'll be millions of people watching this on television.'

'So what?'

'So give us a kiss, Ger!'

Throughout his eleven years with Wales and the Lions, Edwards had only five outside-halves: David Watkins, Barry John, Phil Bennett, John Bevan and Mike Gibson, the last a brief partnership which took place during the first of Gareth's three Lions tours, to South Africa in 1968. John, against whom he had first played during a regional schools trial as a 16-year-old, had broken his collarbone during the first Test of that tour.

The partnership with Gibson lasted for one full match, the 6–6 draw at Port Elizabeth, because something then happened to Edwards which had not happened before and would never happen again. Astonishingly for a player who relished such physical combat, he picked up the only bad injury of his career. A torn hamstring against Boland at Wellington on the Monday before the third Test meant that not even he could avoid missing the last two Tests.

Denied the chance to prove their partnership on the world stage, the Welsh half-backs were reunited in New Zealand three years later, and this time there was to be no denying them. Edwards had gone to punishing lengths to extend the range of his pass, and its distance gave John that extra bit of thinking time in which to work the magic.

Bill Samuel tells in his book how his pupil did it. 'Gareth never had any difficulty in finding his man. He would practise with a leather rugby ball filled with sand to develop distance. He used a car tyre attached by a rope to a hook in the ceiling to create a pendulum through whose centre he would pass the ball as it moved to and fro. He was pressure-trained for reflex action.'

The then uncapped Edwards and the newly capped John, then 19- and 20-year-old college boys respectively, first played together for the Probables in a Welsh trial in January 1967. Their partnership began in less than promising circumstances a few days before the match when they arranged to meet on a rugby pitch at Johnstown on the outskirts of Carmarthen for a fairly primitive introductory session.

Barry John remembers it well. 'I'd been out with the boys the night before with the result that Gareth had to knock for me at about half past eleven on the Sunday morning. I thought, "Do we really have to?" It was pouring with rain but we went out and threw a few balls around. I was out there in a pair of gym shoes and slipping all over the place in the mud.

'At one point we had a discussion and I said, "Look, Gareth, you throw it, I'll catch it," and he said, "Listen, I'll get passes out to you that nobody else would think of. So be prepared." And with that we called it a day. We'd been out there for only 15 minutes but by then we were like two drowned rats!'

Edwards kept his word and John was never more grateful than against the All Blacks in 1971. 'Some of the passes were so long and accurate that I felt a bit like the man at the counter of the post office, rubber-stamping each one as I moved it on. I could have played at times in a duffel coat and still done my job without any problem because he made it so easy.

'I had the greatest scrum-half on the inside and arguably the greatest centre on the outside in Mike Gibson. People talk about Gareth's long pass but in many cases the shorter pass had an even greater impact. He had such terrific upper-body strength that even when he was badly off balance and his whole weight was in the wrong direction he could still get the ball out to me. Some of those passes only travelled five yards but they would take about ten players out of the game because nobody believed he could possibly get the ball out to me from such hopeless positions. He could flick it with his fingertips. Nobody else could have done it. He was a fabulous player. Absolutely out on his own, even if at times he had a short fuse off the field.'

The reflex action which Samuel had spoken of proved a crucial factor in putting British and Irish rugby on top of the world for the first half of the '70s. Not for nothing does Edwards describe Bill Samuel as 'the instigator of everything'. Largely true, but not entirely. He had his own sense of humour and he could always be relied upon to lighten the occasional grind of a training session, as happened when Wales were halfway through their Five Nations schedule in 1976. This particular example revolved around Edwards calling the back-row moves for the flankers, Tommy David and Trevor Evans.

'We wanted to keep the signals simple. Tommy was from Pontypridd and Trevor was from Swansea, so we based them around P and S. Anything with a P was for Tommy, anything with an S for Trevor. We had a few easy shouts like Sugar and Salt, Play and Pepper. Couldn't be simpler. Everything was going like clockwork. So at the next set scrum they waited for me to call the word.

'I shouted, "Psychology!" Well, talk about mayhem. Tommy ran smack into Trevor and ended up on the floor. Trevor was a bit sharper and avoided the worst of the contact. They weren't allowed to forget that one in a hurry . . .' It did nobody any harm. Wales went to Dublin the next day and flogged Ireland by a record margin, 34–9.

Edwards could have made even more history while he was at it, gone on a fourth Lions tour in 1977 and given the All Blacks another beating. Heaven knows, they could have done with him, but he had been there and done it and by then he knew he was on borrowed time. Besides, he felt he had taken enough time off from his job as a management executive with the Neath-based company Dynevor Engineering.

'I didn't think there was too much more left to prove. I thought it was time to make a decision. Jack Hamer, my boss at Dynevor, had always been very supportive. He always urged me to go on the Lions tours, as did Maureen and the family. I gave it a great deal of consideration and decided not to go. It's a decision I've never regretted.'

By then he was juggling with the trickier question of retirement and trying to get the timing right. 'There had always been such a thrill every time I played for Wales, but by '77 it was no longer quite what it used to be. You always wonder whether you are going to play too long and outstay your welcome. On the other hand, you've got to make sure you don't pack up too soon because you're a long time retired.'

One match, more than any other, convinced him that the time had come, that he had only one more international left if he wanted to get out at the top. The match, Ireland 16, Wales 20 in Dublin on 4 March 1978, clinched the Triple Crown hat-trick.

'Physically, they didn't come any tougher than that. I wasn't enjoying it as much as I used to, to the point where at one stage in that match in Dublin I thought to myself, "What am I doing here?" I decided that the game against France a fortnight later would be my last. I came to the conclusion that after that there was nothing left to go for. There were other things to do in my life and the time had come to start doing them.'

Fishing had always been a passion and now he had time to pursue a sport which he had begun with nothing more sophisticated than a jam jar. 'I started with little mountain streams, fishing for trout, and moved up to salmon. People used to think it was a bit odd I had such a gentle hobby compared with the hurly-burly of rugby but I haven't had a minute to miss the game. I never dreamed fishing would play such a big part in my life.'

In his retirement, the nation showed its appreciation of a unique player in a unique way. They made a statue of him and strategically placed it slap-bang in the middle of the capital city in the St David's Centre, not far from the statue of another crusading Welshman, Aneurin Bevan, the father of the Welfare State who came from a valley to the east of Gwaun-cae-Gurwen.

'I am very honoured and overwhelmed, really. It's too difficult to put into words how I feel, but whenever I'm in the centre I'll try and find a way of avoiding the statue. I don't want people to think I'm going past it just to have a look at myself! What makes me really happy is when people come up and thank me for the enjoyment I gave them as a player. That makes it all very worth while.'

Even Edwards, though, has to play second fiddle in one aspect of Lions history to a front-row forward. The indefatigable Graham Price played in more Lions Tests, 12, than any other Welshman and made more consecutive Test appearances than any Lion, dead or alive, with the sole exception of Willie John McBride. Price started against New Zealand in Wellington on 18 June 1977 and finished against the same opposition in Auckland on 16 July 1983.

A tight-head prop of world renown who played on until well into his 40s, Price was the only contender for the tight-head prop position when no less an expert in the art, Fran Cotton, picked his World XV to mark the 25th edition of *Rothman's Rugby Union Yearbook*. 'There's only one name which really jumps out and that's Graham Price,' Cotton wrote in nominating a team which included five other Welsh Lions: J.P.R., Gerald, Benny, Gareth and Merve. 'I've played with him and against him and he's a great, great player.'

Price, from the same school, West Monmouth Grammar, which produced two other famous Gwent Lions, Ken Jones and Bryn Meredith, was the archetypal strong, silent type. No matter how hard the going, he never complained, not even when he spent more than 24 hours flying halfway round the world the day after an Australian broke his jaw at the Sydney Cricket Ground in June 1978. The Front Row Union had a vow of silence about the more brutal aspects of business and Graham Price never broke it.

Five other Welsh players stood the test of time long enough to make three Lions tours: Bryn Meredith, Delme Thomas, Jeff Squire, Ieuan Evans and Derek Quinnell, a Test player at Wellington during the 13–3 victory over the All Blacks in 1971 before he had been capped by his country. Outstanding players one and all, and yet none made as great an impact on the game in its widest sense as Gareth Edwards.

It makes you wonder what would have become of him had he not asked that nice Mr Morris to tear up his contract with Swansea Town. Even if he had gone on to play for Manchester United or Liverpool, it is safe to say that they would not have to put his statue up in the centre of Cardiff. What Gareth Edwards did, he did for Wales.

11

Gentleman Gerald and a Twickenham Strike

The late Tudor Davies never went quite as far as banning his small son from kicking a football around the fields of his native Llansaint, but he seldom missed an opportunity to remind him of the goal which mattered most if he was to make his way in the world beyond Carmarthenshire.

Education was far more important than sport. Education offered an alternative to the coalmine and Mr Davies's determination to ensure young Gerald's escape from a working life in the pit was such that he tried to dissuade him from football activities, whatever the shape of the ball. His father, a noted local practitioner of both codes, spoke from experience.

'He used to tell me he had broken every bone in his body playing soccer and rugby and that the same was going to happen to me. He'd say that to put me off because he wanted me to concentrate on school and getting the best possible education. He had broken arms and legs playing on the wing for the village football team and in the centre for the Kidwelly rugby team.

'My father tried very hard in the early days to get me to give up sport so that my education wouldn't suffer, telling me that if it did I'd end up in the mine like him. He'd tell me off but you don't always follow your father's advice, do you? When I insisted on playing and started to make progress, nobody was more interested than my father. He followed me everywhere.'

Striking a balance between sport and studies has been the undoing of countless boys over the generations, many making the discovery, often too late, that ability in the former had been achieved at the expense of the latter. Gerald Davies struck such a perfect balance between the two that he excelled in both rugby and academia beyond his wildest dreams, never mind his father's.

Balance, of course, was one of the attributes which made him the most mercurial wing of his generation, yet as a boy he found every 100-yard school sprint such an ordeal that he would be physically sick before almost every race. 'I enjoyed watching athletics but I hated taking part. I suppose, deep down, it was the fear of failure which every sportsman has inside him. I didn't like any individual sports because they made me more self-conscious. I much preferred team sports and the shared concept.'

The young Davies was ten years old when he saw something on the Pathé News at the local picture-house one Saturday morning which hooked him on rugby in general and the Lions in particular. What he saw in a brief newsreel clip of the 1955 tour of South Africa and an Irish boy, Tony O'Reilly, who would become one of America's ten richest businessmen, left an indelible impression.

'For me, that was the romantic tour of all romantic tours. Each week I'd go to the cinema, fingers crossed that the Lions would be on the newsreel, because there was no television in those days, at least not in my part of the world. I remember seeing Cliff Morgan score his great try under the posts in Johannesburg and pictures of R.H. Williams and Alun Thomas from Llanelli among the palm trees in Cape Town. It was as if they were on some sort of fantasy island. There was something very magical about that particular tour and the Lions drawing the series in an exotic, faraway land. The realisation that rugby could make all this available was a huge source of personal motivation. Tony O'Reilly became a hero of mine there and then.'

There was no immediate clue that Davies would succeed the tomato-ketchup tycoon on the right wing against the All Blacks and outscore him on Test tries into the bargain. Too small, even by Welsh outside-half standards, he made the national Under-15 schoolboy team at centre, where his opposite number turned out to be a junior Goliath, Terry Price, who won his full cap the following year, 1965. Price was still there in December 1966 when Davies eventually joined him at the start of an international season during which caps were presented to a few other useful performers, among them Barry John, Gareth Edwards, John Taylor and Keith Jarrett. Why Gerald, newly qualified after three years' teacher training at Loughborough, was kept waiting quite so long was one of the mysteries of the time.

On the night they chose the team for the Australia match at the Arms Park, Davies was in a pub in Cardiff with a few friends from back home in Llansaint when the news broke on television. 'Nobody informed the players in those days so you had to find out by whatever way you could. It was almost stop-tap time when my name came up, and that was the excuse my friends had been waiting for to shower me with beer.

'I felt I'd had a good run the previous season and might have played then, and while there was a certain sense of anti-climax, it was the realisation at last of something which I had dreamt of ever since I could remember. Sport was everything in our village, even if soccer was the main game. At every spare moment, down went the jerseys to mark the goals and out came the ball.'

At the age of 21 he had won his cap and completed a form of higher education good enough to qualify him for what Cliff Morgan calls 'that most noble of professions, schoolteaching'. Making his entry into international rugby at a time when Wales sank into their last trough before the advent of their second Golden Era, the new centre three-quarter began by experiencing a rare consistency, four consecutive defeats, before opening what was to become a record-breaking account with two tries in the home beating of England.

Even then, education was still gnawing away at the back of his mind, and this time he needed no prompting from his father to understand the need to strive for better qualifications. While lesser individuals would have allowed their rugby fame to distract them from pursuing studious ambitions off the field, Davies was never going to allow the glory of playing for Wales, however intoxicating, to deflect him from higher academic honours.

'During two years' teaching in Cardiff, I found that unless you had a degree there was no chance of climbing the ladder to become a head of department or a deputy headmaster. A diploma in physical education from Loughborough was not sufficient. A degree was what mattered. I made inquiries about getting one and Billy Raybold, my fellow inter-national centre then at Cambridge, encouraged me in that direction.'

Confirmation that he had been accepted on to a three-year course in English literature at Cambridge University reached him during the Lions tour of South Africa in the summer of 1968. Another famous Cambridge graduate, fellow Lion Mike Gibson, was on hand to offer him an immediate inside track on life at such a renowned seat of learning.

'I was with Mike on the coach going to training the day my accept-ance for Cambridge came through. He told me, "There are three things you can do at Cambridge. You can play sport, you can concentrate on your academic work and you can socialise. All three are available but you can only do two. Attempt all three and you will fall by the wayside." That was a very astute way of putting it. I knew there and then that, at some stage during my time at Cambridge, the international aspect of my rugby would have to go.'

As a Lion fulfilling the dream inspired by those black-and-white pictures on Pathé News 13 years earlier, Davies suffered recurring frustration caused by factors beyond his control. Other black-and-white issues of a disturbing nature which he witnessed at first hand would trouble his conscience and result in him declaring himself unavailable for the next trip to South Africa six years later.

The effects of an early injury put him out of contention for the first two Tests and the unfailing inability of physiotherapists in a whole succession of towns and cities from the seaboard to the high veldt drove him to distraction. 'As the tour wore on, there were times when the failure to cure the injury brought tears of frustration to my eyes.'

When acupuncture provided a sudden and complete cure to his ankle condition, Davies replaced Barry Bresnihan in midfield for the third Test at Newlands, where the Springboks clinched the series in one of those matches which deserved a ranking near the very top of the what-might-have-been table of Lions matches.

Davies's tour ended in further anti-climax at Bloemfontein the fol-lowing Saturday against Orange Free State, a trip to stop him gathering his grub-kick resulting in a dislocated elbow. His tour was over after a paltry nine appearances out of a maximum of twenty and the Lions had been deprived yet again of their most creative back. Not for nothing does he write it off as 'an unhappy tour'.

The physical blows were a further reminder – not that he needed one – of the importance of his degree course. He entered Cambridge later that year and spent most of that season negotiating the long, pre-motorway trek across almost the full breadth of the country, from eastern England to South Wales, for squad training at Port Talbot. Port Talbot had been chosen as a halfway house for players drawn from opposite ends of the Welsh rugby belt, an area stretching no more than 60 miles from Llanelli in the west to Pontypool in the east.

For Davies the weekly journey from the serene cloisters of Cambridge to the grime of what was then one of the biggest steel towns in Britain must have come as a bit of a culture shock. His rugby flourished, albeit from the centre alongside Keith Jarrett, in a Welsh Triple Crown team featuring a Lions Test player on each wing, Stuart Watkins and Maurice Richards, whose four tries against England at Cardiff made him the first Welshman to score as many against the English this century. Judging by more recent events, the record is probably safe for another century.

When Richards decided to cash in his chips later that year with Salford, where in 14 seasons he scored 297 tries in 498 matches, Davies had declared himself unavailable. The only threat to his international future had been self-inflicted, as he worried that the almost weekly cross-country marathon would leave him in a state approaching exhaustion. He did not need to be Albert Einstein to work that one out.

'During that season, from the start of the Michaelmas term through to the Lent term, I was not in Cambridge for one weekend. I spent them all travelling to play for London Welsh or going to squad training in South Wales, a journey of five hours, sometimes six. At the end of it, I'd ask myself, "What am I doing this for? What is the point of being at Cambridge if I am never there? I am fortunate to have been accepted by Cambridge in the first place. Why, therefore, am I not making the most of it? The whole object of my being here is to get a degree, so why put that in jeopardy?" I decided that something had to give. International rugby had to go.'

And go it did. Rather than allowing his degree in English literature to be run over somewhere between Cambridge and Port Talbot, Davies wrote himself off for the entire season. At a stroke, he had removed himself from all five international matches in 1970, starting against South Africa in January and finishing with France three months later Ray Williams, in overall charge of national affairs as the Welsh Rugby Union's coaching organiser, received his letter and, naturally, attempted to talk him back into the team. Davies refused to waver, sticking to his decision with a single-minded strength of character. It cannot have been easy, but once he made his mind up there would be no changing it.

'I like to make clean decisions and stick to them. Ray wrote me a long letter, trying to persuade me to change my mind. He was very good about it, pointing out that it was a very important period in Welsh rugby history, that the team was coming together nicely, and generally appealing to my competitive instincts. It was very persuasive but there was no going back on my decision.'

His Cambridge studies completed successfully and a degree in the bag, he returned in 1971, reclaiming his place in a way which left no doubt about his elevation among the great wings of the game. Eight tries in eight Tests that year for Wales's Grand Slam XV and the Lions in New Zealand guaranteed his admission to rugby's pantheon.

No defence in the world could cope with his mesmeric ability to turn an opponent inside out on the proverbial sixpence, least of all the All Blacks. In two matches halfway through the tour he scored six tries, two in the one losing Test to New Zealand and twice as many against Hawke's Bay seven days later at Napier, suitable punishment for the provincial team's brutish behaviour.

The fourth try, after Davies had reverted to centre in a reshuffle caused by Gibson's injury, stood comparison to any scored by a Lions three-quarter anywhere, the Welshman shredding the opposition before accelerating clear and side-stepping the full-back. That such a masterpiece should have been greeted in stony silence by almost 30,000 mean-spirited spectators amounted to a deafening indictment of their crass behaviour. The executioner laughs at the memory. 'They do tend to take umbrage, if that's the word, when they lose. The non-playing Lions sat in the stand and waited for a clap of appreciation. Instead there was nothing but a deathly silence.'

The smallest wing in the international game at 5ft 9in, as well as the lightest at less than 12 stone, he had used his innate footballing ability and burning pace from a standing start to leave the rest of the world in his wake. If Barry John was 'The King', the darting Davies was unquestionably the Crown Prince of a Test series which the Lions could never have won without the individual brilliance of the Welsh backs.

'The tension of a British Lions Test match was far greater than the tension of playing for your country. At least, it was in my experience. There was a lot of tension playing for Wales but it was something you became comfortable with through time. It was nothing like the overwhelming tension of playing for the British Isles in Johannesburg, Cape Town, Wellington and Auckland. At every one of those grounds you know that 99 per cent of the crowd are supporting the opposition. It's an extraordinary feeling. Gareth Edwards and I used to look at each other in the dressing-room on big-match day and say to each other, "Why aren't we back home in Porthcawl enjoying the summer? What are we doing here?"

'We were there, of course, because as international sportsmen we wouldn't have been anywhere else. If you wanted to succeed at the highest level, you had to cope with the tension. It was a shared experience and that's what I liked about it. We were all in it together.'

Now unchallenged as a master craftsman, Davies never lost sight of the fact that it was only a game after all, that there were other more important matters, chief among them his newly acquired status as a family man whose wife, Scilla, had just given birth to their first child, Emily. Gerald was also that rarity among international footballers of whatever persuasion during that particular time: a sportsman with a social conscience.

In South Africa with the Lions he had experienced apartheid at first hand and been appalled at what he saw. His abhorrence of the regime was another major reason why he refused to revisit the country with the Lions in 1974, a loathing of the regime which he shared with John Taylor but which, unlike his London Welsh colleague, he chose to keep to himself until now. No matter how strong the temptation to have adopted a strictly selfish stance and gone on what was always likely to be a successful tour, there was never any question of Davies compromising his principles on any family or social issue.

He had more critical decisions to make in the months leading to the departure of the Lions in May and he made them in much the same way as he scored his tries, sharply and swiftly. After three years' teaching at a public school in Sussex, he had applied for a job as a technical officer with the Sports Council of Wales in Cardiff and had been offered the job. For once, his timing had been less than perfect.

'Could I ask my headmaster for two months off to go on the Lions tour and at the same time say, "Sorry, I won't be coming back. My time is up. I'm going somewhere else"? I could not do that, but there were other reasons for making myself unavailable to the Lions. There were domestic responsibilities in that I had to find a house for our move back to Cardiff. And then there was the question of South Africa and apartheid. I'd had one or two bad experiences out there in 1968 and my conscience was asking me whether it would be right to go back.

'One of my fellow students at Loughborough was a South African who was, in the horrible language of the system, a Cape Coloured. When I got to South Africa, I invited him to the hotel where the Lions were staying and he said, "Sorry, I cannot meet you there. I'm not allowed in." I said, "I'll meet you in your house instead." He said, "You can't come here because the apartheid laws won't allow it."

'In the end we met in the garden of the hotel. That to me was a very significant moment. I had known him socially in this country and yet it was impossible for us to meet in the same way in his country. That was something I could not stomach. I then saw other things which left a very nasty taste in my mouth. I saw the way the black waiters were treated in the streets outside the hotels. I will never forget seeing a black man who was selling newspapers being kicked on a street corner in Cape Town and everyone turning a blind eye. Those incidents stuck in my mind because they were so horrendously different from anything I had seen at home. And yet there it was accepted as normal behaviour. I found that quite frightening.

'It affected John Taylor in a major way and he took a strong anti-apartheid position by refusing to go to South Africa. I did not do that because I did not think I was in a position to try and persuade people not to pursue their sport. For that reason I didn't make a public stand. Sportsmen can make up their own minds, and they tend to be selfish. They want to compete against the best as often as they can and, yes, it's a short life.

'In the end it was a combination of reasons which made me say, "No, I am not going to South Africa." This was the country which as a boy in Llansaint in 1955 had appealed to me as a magical place, and yet when I got there I found a beautiful country applying such horrendous laws to the human race.'

As the tour gathered momentum and the Lions began sweeping all before them, Davies could have been forgiven for torturing himself over the decision to opt out when one of the principal roles in a glittering cast would have been his for the taking. But he had the moral fortitude to avoid the quicksands of self-doubt.

'Of course it would have been great to have been part of the other most successful Lions tour of all time but I didn't dwell on that. My policy in life has always been the same: "Never look over your shoulder at what might have been." Those are the four worst words in the English language, "what might have been". You always have to look towards tomorrow. There is no point reconsidering something in hindsight. At the time it was the right decision. It was the only decision.'

Even when the Lions pleaded with him to join them as a reinforcement halfway through the Test series, Davies stuck to his guns. When injury to Scotland's Billy Steele left them one wing short of a squadron, the crafty management pulled a cunning trick in delegating Gareth Edwards to make the impassioned phone call to his fellow Welshman.

'They got Gareth to ring me because we were the best of mates and they no doubt figured that such an approach would be as good a way as any of getting me out there. He rang me at my school in Horsham. "We need you," he said. "Can you come out as quickly as possible?"

'I thought, "There's this great tour happening and yes, okay, I might go out." I hesitated. Then I said, "Give me time to think about it." At that precise time, I was swaying. Then I sat down and thought, "No, I can't go back on my decision. This is a very successful tour and I'd be going out on the coat-tails of others. How can I go back on a decision which I was so firm about? I have to stay firm."

'Gareth rang back two or three hours later, as arranged. I told him straight, "No. No way." I only debated it with myself. I had very strong reasons not to go and to have gone out there at that stage would have been like climbing on to the bandwagon. There would no doubt have been plenty to assure me otherwise but that was the way I felt.'

With that the Lions became a closed book. In the next four seasons before his retirement, Davies was a permanent fixture on the right wing, ensuring that Wales cleaned up as never before, stacking two Grand Slams on top of four Triple Crowns. Nothing, though, could match, let alone surpass, the Lions' feat in New Zealand. 'Grand Slams have been won before and since. What the Lions did had never been done before.'

By the look of things, it will be a long time before it is done again. Davies, his record of 23 Test tries for Wales and the Lions then second to none, had played 46 times for his country when he decided to call it a day in September 1978. He could have gone on but the thought of outstaying his welcome and finishing up some way down the hill was anathema to him.

'A lot of people have asked me why I didn't stay on for four more games to get to 50. It never occurred to me. What matters is the competition, the next opponent, the next match. If I'd played on just to get to 50 caps, I'd have been playing for the wrong reasons. In the end my competitive instinct may not have been strong enough and I could never justify lowering my standards just to hang on. I was 33. Time was up.'

It may sound trite but with Davies it was all about playing the game as it was meant to be played. Above all, he had style, a commodity in seriously short supply during these troubled times. There were no tantrums, no professional fouls, no bending the rules, no controversies, and yet, for all his goody-two-shoes image, there is one untold story which, had it been revealed at the time, would no doubt have been a source of permanent embarrassment.

Gerald Davies would never have qualified for the Militant Tendency but on Friday, 19 January 1968 he joined in the unanimous threat of serious industrial action by the Wales team heading for London and the match against England at Twickenham the following afternoon. They had informed the selectors that they were going on strike over their miserly ticket allocation. The issue revolved around the travelling reserve, an uncapped 19-year-old from Llanelli by the name of Phil

Bennett. 'We travelled up by train the day before and had taken the decision not to play by the time we got to Paddington. The row was over tickets. Each player had one complimentary ticket plus one he paid for. But the reserve, for some strange reason, only had one ticket, which he needed himself.

'Phil should have been treated the same as everyone else. We explained his predicament to the selectors on the train. They were adamant. They said it was "impossible" to get him another ticket. We felt very strongly about it and that was when we decided we would refuse to play. It sounds a bit far-fetched but we were absolutely serious about it.

'We told the selectors what would happen and the penny dropped after we'd checked into our hotel just off Oxford Street. One of the Welsh Rugby Union officials, and I'm not naming names, produced a bundle of tickets from his breast pocket and said to us, "Right, then. How many do you want?" End of strike!'

Davies maintains a keen interest in the sport, both as chairman of HTV Wales and as a perceptive rugby journalist for *The Times*. Not surprisingly, he is less than enamoured of much of what he sees, both the deteriorating standards of on-field behaviour and the decline of Wales as a rugby nation. For one who always had too much respect for the opposition to indulge in any overexuberance at scoring, he has no truck with those who do as, for example, the England hooker Richard Cockerill did after the Calcutta Cup match against Scotland last season. 'I don't see any point in an English forward going to the stand and lifting his fist in a gesture of jubilation and intimidation. Quite often in approaching the crowd there is a kind of threatening "up yours" attitude. I don't think any sportsman should behave like that.'

His fears for the game in Wales are infinitely greater. 'We are on the road to oblivion. There has been an inescapable downward trend in recent years and professionalism has accelerated that decline. When the International Board declared the game professional in August 1995 they had no idea what effect their decision would have on the game worldwide. They didn't look that far. It was as if they were just saying, "Okay, now you can take your brown envelope above the counter instead of beneath it." They never visualised the repercussions of their decision when they should have done.

'The condition of the Welsh game is so serious that unless it is addressed very quickly we will never recover. Neath against Llanelli in the quarter-finals of the cup last year attracted 1,600 people. Five years ago you could not have printed enough tickets for such a match.

'The idea of rugby being a professional sport is not something easily accepted by many people in Wales. They don't like the idea of the players being paid vast sums of money to play a game which had been amateur. Suddenly they were asked to pay £12 to £15 to see an inferior product, whereas before they paid £2.50. There is no longer a feel-good factor about Welsh rugby.

'I feel sorry for the players. I sympathise because they are having to play in an atmosphere which is neither optimistic nor encouraging. They are playing a game which is deteriorating. Yes, they have money, but are they treated like heroes when they walk down the streets of their home towns? I cannot imagine that is the case.

'The Welsh Rugby Union's duty is to govern the game. In order to do so you must take the views of all the people, but I don't think they have taken sufficient cognisance of the clubs and their needs. I don't think a governing body's role is simply to deliver tablets of stone and demand that everybody adhere to them. They have lost touch.

'The collapse of the steelworks, the mines and the grammar-school system were put forward almost 20 years ago as the reasons for the decline. Instead of addressing them when they were valid reasons, the WRU allowed the decline to take root. They have now become excuses for our continued failure. Too many people seem quite happy to reiterate the same old excuses, and I don't think that is good enough.

'When I was a boy growing up, I wanted to be a Welsh rugby player. There were thousands upon thousands like me. I just wonder how many of the youngsters think like that nowadays. I was lucky to have been part of something very special. But today there is no vitality about the game, no buzz.'

And nobody to match the master in the moustache who, jersey buttoned to the neck, once had the effrontery to score four outrageous tries from inside his own twenty-five in winning a cup-tie for Cardiff at Pontypool Park when the locals were the most fearsome team in the game. It was as close as he ever came to the faintest whiff of a scandal.

12

The Grand Slam Lunch Bill

Nobody had any way of knowing back then that it would never happen again, that the old Arms Park would never see another Grand Slam occasion. The crowd were far too busy raising the roof, blissfully unaware that Saturday, 18 March 1978 marked the end of something far more sobering than another Five Nations championship of Welsh invincibility.

Only two people knew it could never be the same again. One was Phil Bennett, the other Gareth Edwards. The famous half-backs had played their last match for Wales and yet neither had a clue about the other's decision until, quite by chance, they happened to be the first players to reach the dressing-room after the unforgettable match against France.

And there, far below the North Stand, while the old tunes of glory cascaded around the stadium, Bennett shook his partner by the hand. 'Gar, I just want to say that it's been a privilege and a pleasure these last few years,' the captain of Wales told his partner, 'Brilliant. But that's it, and I wanted you to be the first to know. That's my last game for Wales.'

Edwards, nonplussed at the coincidence, had time to confide that he, too, had played his last match for Wales before the rest of an ecstatic team piled in to start the celebrations. They kept their secrets to themselves for long enough, rather than hijack the third Welsh Grand Slam of the decade. It was the end of an era and, for a whole generation at least, the end of the Grand Slam.

In the finest showbiz tradition, Bennett had left them laughing, even if it meant taking his leave at the age of 29. He had always promised himself he would go out at the top, a promise which countless players make in their youth, few of whom are good enough, lucky enough or strong enough to resist the temptation to stay for one game too many.

He may have failed as captain of the Lions in New Zealand the previous year, but for Bennett this was the perfect time to go, the holy grail of the European game safely delivered under his leadership and the Welsh nation in its heaven. Had the crowd known that the two supreme match-winners would never be seen in harness again, their mood would have been different. Perhaps it was just as well. Ignorance is bliss.

Bennett had been all over the world and, to this day, he considers that French match to be the classic example of how a crowd could lift its team. 'We were hanging on and the fans could sense we were tired. There was still 15 minutes to go and I was pleading for the players to hang in there, but we needed something extra. All of a sudden the singing broke out, and I'd never heard anything like it. I can remember saying to the players, "God, listen to this." It flowed around the stadium. It was absolutely electric. I'd never heard emotional singing like it. The crowd won the game for us that day. Yes, the boys played with huge spirit, but, for me, that emotional singing made it. Once they started, there was no way France were ever going to score.

'I'd decided before the game that I would retire. I'd had a couple of good seasons, the crowd were very nice to me and I thought, why spoil it by hanging on? Perhaps one or two players stayed on a year too long, lost a few games, and it's easy for people to forget the great years. I knew this was the right time to get out. Wales were going to Australia at the end of that season and there was no way I could have faced that.

'We in Wales can be very emotional. We can become very close but also we can go the other way and shoot each other in the foot. It was a decision I felt at the time was right. I felt something was coming to an end, something marvellous. It was nice to go out on a high and nice to be able to remember that game. It would have been awful had we lost that last game, but it wouldn't have affected my decision.

'But I'd thought long and hard about whether to have one more season because we were doing well. I'd made up my mind that, whatever happened, the French game would be the last, and after that there was never any turning back. I didn't want to take the chance of staying on too long, risking a bad injury and being remembered as the bloke who was carried off in his last match.'

The Grand Slam came free of charge. Bennett, whose two tries made all the difference in a 16–7 win, belonged to another time when Wales could be relied upon to win with such a regularity that, had professionalism come a generation earlier, the Welsh Rugby Union might have been put out of business paying the win bonuses. Nowadays, more often than not, it costs them a small fortune paying their team to lose.

What perks there were back in the '70s did not extend to expenses, not if the WRU accountants had anything to do with it. When it came to scrutinising every claim, nothing much got past the formidable WRU secretary Bill Clement, a Lion in his own right as a member of the team led to South Africa by the Irish prop Sammy Walker.

It was not exactly to Bennett's advantage that Clement had also been brought up in the village of Felinfoel, near Llanelli. 'I handed my expense sheet in on this one occasion and Bill said, "Eh, I used to live in Felinfoel. You've charged 60 miles. I know it's 55." Bill was a lovely man even though he ruled with an iron fist. I had a lot of respect for him, but I wished at times that he could have seen the bigger picture.'

Expenses, or rather the lack of them, were a sore point, as Bennett went on discovering to his cost at the start of the 1978 Grand Slam campaign. Three penalty goals from the skipper on a wet day at Twickenham eased Wales over their first obstacle, only for the players to find out that beating England was easier than getting the Welsh Rugby Union to buy their wives lunch on the way home the next day.

Rugby being one of the last bastions of male chauvinism, the players' wives and girlfriends were left to fend for themselves. They were excluded from every international occasion and it didn't make a blind bit of difference where the match was being played. Not before time, Bennett used his position as captain to do something about it.

'Before the England match I asked Cliff Jones, the chairman of selectors, if it would be possible for our wives to travel back to Cardiff with us on the team bus, which was empty, instead of travelling on their own by train. They gave it the okay at their meeting.

'We stopped somewhere in Swindon on the way home for lunch. We had a pint or two, which we felt entitled to, and all the girls had was a fairly modest plate of gammon and chips. It all went on the Welsh Rugby Union bill, we got back on the coach and we thought nothing more of it.

'Then, a few days later, I had a letter from the Welsh Rugby Union. I could hardly believe it. They'd sent me a bill for £4.50 for Pat's lunch. I thought that was a bit mean, but I paid it.'

The sequel to the episode turned out to be to Bennett's advantage. The following week, after beating Scotland at the Arms Park, the Welsh team woke up on Sunday morning to find themselves marooned by blizzards which had paralysed the country overnight.

'We were so badly snowed in that we couldn't get out until the Sunday night but I had to leave my car stuck in Cardiff. By the time I got it out a few days later, I was lumbered with a parking bill for about seven or eight quid. Now, beforehand I would never have dreamt of charging the Union for it, but if they could send me a bill for Pat's lunch, then I could certainly send them the bill for the car. Fair play, they paid it.'

Bennett did have the last laugh on expenses, not in a calculated way but in a spontaneous response to a crisis which reared its head without warning during the dinner at the Angel Hotel in Cardiff after the Grand Slam victory over France. The opposition had run out of red wine and Jean-Pierre Rives was making it fairly clear that his lot had not had their fill.

When he informed Bennett that his table had run dry, the Welsh captain realised he had one last function to perform, one which would require a few delicate skills if the French were not to be offended by a sudden drop in the warmth of Welsh hospitality.

Rather than risk being told that the French had had their quota of wine for the evening, Bennett assumed responsibility. 'The head-waitress was a lovely lady, a real character, but she was terrified of Bill Clement. When I asked her for a few more bottles of wine, I told her that I'd had a word and there wasn't a problem.

'The French boys got their wine. Crikey, if we couldn't have a party after winning the Grand Slam, when could we have one? I heard on the grapevine the next morning that the Union weren't very happy when the bill came. I explained that the French had had this and we had had a drop of this, that and the other. So what? Every time we went to Paris we were so well looked after by the French that we could drink as much as we wanted, all night long if we wanted to.'

An earlier claim had caused such ructions that three Llanelli players, Norman Gale, Delme Thomas and Bennett, were called before the Union. The three had travelled from their homes to join the Wales squad at Cardiff Airport *en route* to Dublin.

'We went together in one car but we felt entitled to make separate claims,' Bennett said. 'We were all losing vast sums of money from taking time off work and all we wanted was to get a little of it back. The mileage allowance they gave us was peanuts anyway, so we were only talking about a few quid.

'Anyway, we were called before the WRU, and when they asked us about the claims Norman went berserk, letting them know in no uncertain terms that they were making a fortune while we were losing money, and here they were quibbling over a trivial amount of money.'

When he first appeared in the Wales squad towards the end of the

'60s, Bennett lost sums which were anything but trivial. The price to play for Wales was never too great, but every international weekend in the early days meant missing the biggest pay days of his week as a steelworks clerk.

'Saturday and Sunday were the days when you could earn a lot of money,' he said. 'Eight to twelve on Saturday morning was time and a half. With double time on Sunday, your pay would rocket. In those days I'd lose around £40, an awful lot of money back then, but you never complained because that's how the game was.'

Had he been in it for the money, the young Bennett would have gone north before he had even been old enough to make his debut for Llanelli. Halifax recognised his blossoming talent before anyone else and dispatched a high-powered team on the improbable journey from Thrum Hall to a council estate in Felinfoel.

At 17, Bennett was still playing youth rugby for his village team, which put the Halifax delegation seriously ahead of the game. 'This big car pulled up outside the house, and you can imagine what sort of interest that stirred on the estate where I lived. They sold the club to me in a very persuasive way, and then they offered me £8,000.

'I had to stop and think, because you could have bought a lot of houses in Felinfoel for that kind of money. The north of England was six and a half hours away by car in those days and, to be perfectly honest, I wouldn't have had a clue where Halifax was on the map.

'They were very courteous and very keen for me to sign that night. I said I would have to think about it, and the following week I decided I wanted to stay and see how far I could go in rugby union. I had to be very careful about the Halifax business, though, because in those days if you even talked to a rugby league club you could have been banned for life, which was very sad.

'The joke was that very often the scouts acting for league clubs were well-respected figures in union, so whenever they put something to you, they'd always say, "Now, for God's sake, whatever you do, don't breathe a word about this." It was one of those well-respected union figures who approached me in 1974 after the Lions tour with the biggest offer I ever had.

'St Helen's were prepared to pay me £40,000 over a three-year period. The league clubs were keen to cash in on the success of the Lions by signing a few of us, and I'd decided long before that that if I ever went to rugby league, St Helen's would have to be the club. They were my team. I loved them, mainly because they had great Welsh players like Roy Mathias, John Warlow and Kel Coslett.

'After they'd made their offer, I went up and stayed with Roy and had a look round the ground at Knowsley Road. I wanted to see the area before making the big decision. The money was so good that if I'd invested it properly, I'd have been well off for the rest of my life.

'I thought long and hard before making up my mind to stay where I was. I'd lived in West Wales all my life and the thought of uprooting made me realise how lucky I was with my quality of life. I had the Gower, the Pembrokeshire coast, the countryside, my family and Pat's family all around me.

'I thought very seriously about going but, deep down in my mind, I knew I could never leave this part of the world. I could never have been as happy living anywhere else. I didn't want to end up in the north of England feeling homesick.

'I count myself very lucky. We were all lucky in that Welsh team. True, we didn't get paid for playing, but we had such great quality of life. There was no recession then, certainly not in rugby. Wales were on top of the world, right up there with New Zealand in terms of ability, even if we weren't able to beat them. It was such a wonderful, wonderful era that not even a small fortune from rugby league could tempt any of us to leave it all behind.'

And so he stayed to become a legend instead. Barry John's sudden abdication at the ripe old age of 27 gave the rest of the rugby world a fleeting hope that Wales had lost some of their magic. Instead they pulled another one out of the hat, and if everyone else considered outside-half for Wales an impossible act to follow, Bennett not only proved them wrong but hardly missed a trick to enhance the mystique of the most demanding position in the game.

He had been proving all sorts of people wrong for most of his life, never more so than during a sickly infancy when doctors advised his father that the poor boy would never be strong enough to play rugby. Within two years of succeeding John, he had achieved Test victories over all the major rugby-playing powers with the sole exception of New Zealand, a fact for which the All Blacks ought to have been mighty grateful, considering the mesmeric effect the little sorcerer from Felinfoel had on them in launching the try of the century for the Barbarians at the Arms Park in 1972.

In South Africa two years later with the invincible Lions, he left nobody in any doubt that he had courage as well as class, refusing to take the easy way out after a despairing Springbok attempt to prevent the darting Welshman's dazzling try in the second Test in Pretoria left him with a wrenched knee and a gashed ankle which refused to heal.

When it came to the decisive third Test at Port Elizabeth a fortnight later, Bennett played with not one pain-killing injection but two. 'My left foot was so numb it felt like a block of ice. I had no feeling for the ball because I couldn't feel my foot, so I had no way of knowing what weight to apply to any of my kicks.'

It didn't stop him from dropping two goals as the Lions played their way towards one of the most cherished landmarks in British and Irish rugby history, the rout of the Springboks which won the series a fortnight before Willie John McBride's storm troopers preserved their unbeatable status by drawing the final Test. Ironically, Bennett had been advised to withdraw from the tour as a protest against the reviled South African apartheid regime, a request which had come from one of Prime Minister Harold Wilson's bright young men, Neil Kinnock.

The Lions came home to a heroes' ovation at Heathrow, and when Bennett arrived home they drove the conquering hero and his wife, Pat, through crowded streets in a pony and trap. Several thousand people turned out at Felinfoel RFC. Nobody could ever remember as many gathering there, before or since. No American president could have had a bigger welcome.

For the Bennetts, there was no warning that their lives were about to be shattered by impending tragedy. Within weeks of the ecstatic home-coming, the family had been stricken by such grief that Bennett, in his deepest despair, refused to play rugby again. 'Pat and I lost our first child, Stewart. He died three days after he was born and we were both absolutely devastated. I'll always remember the joy of having the baby because we were so desperate to have a child. Pat had carried the baby all summer while I was in South Africa. It was hard enough for me but it was so much worse for her.

'We had bought a house and made it into a beautiful new home for our beautiful new boy. I was so thrilled when he was born and then I got the phone call from Morriston Hospital with the dreadful news. Rugby had always been the biggest thing in my life after my family, but after that it didn't matter. It just seemed so trivial.

'I went through several phases of guilt. I'd been away for four months playing rugby and a lot of things went through my mind. In the end I was grateful to rugby because, eventually, you realise that life has to go on. The first two or three games I played, I was just going through the motions.

'We'd seen the doctor at Morriston and he'd assured us that the baby had died from a heart defect which was really a one-in-a-million chance. He advised us to try for another child and Pat became pregnant again fairly quickly.

'Then in the December we were away to Northampton, which was always one of the biggest games of the season. We went up on the Friday and at twelve o'clock the next day I'd more or less made up my mind that I couldn't face it. I wasn't going to play until the rest of the team made me realise how important it was for them to get a big English scalp. We had a great win and they pulled me through the night.'

Steven arrived the following year. 'Pat always seemed to be rushed in at night, and seeing her in the same ward in the same hospital brought the memories flooding back. While she was in labour, I waited in the corridor outside. They gave me a glass of brandy because I was pretty exhausted and told me to rest because it would be some while before the baby arrived.

'I went into the chapel in the hospital and prayed to God that this time everything would be all right. They gave Steven a complete check and when they told me he was fine I was so overjoyed I just wanted to let everyone know.'

A second son, James, was born three years later. Both are now in their 20s but their parents will never forget Stewart. They visit his grave twice a week, as they have done for the best part of the last 25 years.

When Bennett and Pat were driving home from hospital one Saturday morning with their precious cargo, the Llanelli team coach was heading east for a cup-tie at the mining village of Senghenydd. Bennett's value to their cause was such that they broke their journey to ambush his car as he drove in the opposite direction! 'They recognised the car and flashed me to stop. Carwyn James got out of the coach saying that Bernard Thomas, my replacement at outside-half, was injured and pleading with me to play. Pat looked at me and said, "You'll only be bored out of your mind at the house this afternoon so why don't you play?"'

Llanelli made light work of the mud to win by a street and headed for home not unduly bothered by a stamp on Bennett's ankle in the last minute which required ten stitches. It was to be the root of arguably the single most controversial decision taken by the Welsh selectors during the Golden Era. They kicked Bennett out of the squad.

The clumsy boot at Senghenydd put him out of the opening international of the 1975–76 season, against Australia. The late John Bevan won his first cap and played for the Probables in the Welsh trial on the first Saturday of the New Year, which Bennett missed rather than risk aggravating his ankle. His mistake was to play for Llanelli against Bath the following Monday. He insists he never meant it as a slight to the selectors but acknowledges that they clearly saw it as such. 'Bath then were nowhere near as strong as now and although I wasn't able to do any kicking, I thought it would be a good runout. I should not have played out of respect for the Welsh selectors. As it turned out, I had a good match and I don't think they liked it very much.'

In fact they took such a dim view of Bennett's New Year arrangements that they not only dropped him for the opening Five Nations match, against England at Twickenham, they also removed him from the entire squad. Bevan was the new number one and an uncapped 20-year-old from Swansea, David Richards, was promoted as the second choice. Bennett, a central figure with the unbeatable Lions some 18 months earlier, suddenly found himself the third-best fly-half in Wales.

Hell hath no fury like a selector scorned, or, in this case, five selectors scorned. Their treatment of a player who had become a folk hero provoked a controversy which raged throughout the country all week. It was still raging when Bennett discovered the following weekend that seven days in rugby are liable to be infinitely longer than they are in politics. Wales had dumped him at a selection committee in Cardiff on the Saturday night without extending Bennett the basic courtesy of letting him know. I broke the news to him instead, assuming that he had already been informed and given some hint as to why he had appeared to have become *persona non grata*.

He was about to leave home the following Sunday for a family day out when the phone rang. The president of the Welsh Rugby Union, Handel Rogers, a Llanelli man from top to toe, was on the line with some startling news. 'He said, "Where are you off to?" I told him it was such a glorious day that I was heading out with Pat and the baby. Then he said, "We'd like you to be at Aberavon this afternoon for training. You're in the team to play England on Saturday."'

Bevan and Richards had both been injured playing for their clubs, leaving the not-so-Big Five' no option but to reinstate a bemused Bennett. When he arrived at the leisure centre on Aberavon beach which Wales used as their base, more than one senior player greeted his return with the same reaction: 'You jammy so-and-so . . .'

They never dropped him again, which was rough on Bevan, an outstanding player in his own right as well as a courageous one who went on to coach Wales despite the ravages of the cancer from which he died at the tragically young age of 41. Who knows how different it might have been had 'Bev' been fit to take his place as scheduled at Twickenham that January afternoon.

Over the last two years of his international career Bennett played in a way which made a mockery of the decision to drop him. From England in 1976 to his swansong against France in 1978, he appeared alongside Edwards in all 12 matches. Wales won 11 of them, losing only to France under the wily direction of the Napoleon-like Jacques Fouroux in Paris.

When he clinched the Triple Crown against Scotland two months later with a classical Welsh try under the posts at Murrayfield, Bennett was as good as past the post for the ultimate honour, or so it seemed at the time: captaincy of the Lions on their tour of New Zealand at the end of the season. Instead it turned out to be 'mental agony', the worst three and a half months of his rugby life. Even Welsh friends who toured with him admit they did not consider him up to it and that the redoubtable Fran Cotton would have been a better choice. Nobody ever gets it wrong in hindsight, and Bennett had the recurring misfortune of being caught in the crossfire of the feud generated by coach John Dawes and his attitude towards the press, some of whom, like Barry John and Mervyn Davies, had been in the trenches with him on previous tours.

It was bad enough trying to cope with the wettest, coldest New Zealand winter for decades, without opening a war on a second front. Bennett had never spoken of the fact that, right up until the final selection meeting, he had not really wanted to go. How he wished he had not been persuaded to change his mind. He was honest enough to concede that he had been 'a bad choice'. 'I admit that I should never have accepted the captaincy, even though I came back a better man for the experience.'

The captaincy would have been Davies's but for the brain haemorrhage which had almost cost him his life the previous year. 'I was in the process of trying to fill the great man's boots with Wales. I've never said this before but I was in two minds about whether I wanted to go on the Lions tour. I'd been on one, I'd been away from home virtually every summer and I kept saying to myself, "Am I right mentally for three and a half months in New Zealand?" I talked to a few close friends and they said that to be captain of the British Lions was everything. Pat and I sat down and she said, "You must be mad. You've got to go and captain the British Lions."'

The selectors had blundered at the start by picking too many Welshmen. They had a Welsh coach, a Welsh captain and 17 Welsh players which, by common consent, was at least 3 too many. Ironically, the tour would probably have still succeeded had three different Welshmen been there: Edwards, J.P.R. Williams and Gerald Davies. All three had declared themselves unavailable.

The tour went wrong from the start. Memorial Park in Masterton, where the Lions opened up with a 41–13 win over Wairarapa Bush, proved to be memorable all right, if only because nobody died from exposure. The very mention of Masterton still brings a chill to the bones.

'Despite the icy wind and the rain and the mud, we hammered them with a great exhibition of running rugby. At the end we rushed into the showers only to find that they were stone cold. The boys had to be wrapped up in blankets, taken back to the hotel and filled with brandy to save them from hypothermia.'

There was little warmth elsewhere on the tour. Bennett had been to New Zealand with Wales eight years earlier and noticed a sharp change in attitude towards the tourists. 'In '69, everyone had been friendly towards us. In '77 there was an open hostility, and a hostility towards the Welsh in particular, which made it even worse. They weren't so much anti-British as anti-Welsh.

'The Lions had been there in '71 and done the unthinkable of beating the All Blacks in their own backyard. They hadn't been forgiven for that, and the controversy over Keith Murdoch being sent home from the '72 tour of the UK hit us as well. Because it had happened in Cardiff, we got some of the backlash as if it had been something to do with us, which was ludicrous. There was a lot of bitterness and animosity.

'We were spat at as we came off the pitch after some matches and sometimes we'd have beer cans thrown at us. J.J. [Williams] got back to the dressing-room from one game drenched in beer. We were fairly physical, as you had to be out there. People like Frannie Cotton, Gordon Brown and Windsor showed incredible guts. They never stepped back an inch.

'The saddest thing of all was the way the relationship with the press, so good in South Africa three years earlier, had been stretched to breaking point. There were stories about the Lions wrecking hotels and nonsense like that, which left us with a siege mentality. John [Dawes] thought that certain journalists had gone against us and he cut them off completely. Then there was a run-in with Mervyn Davies, who was doing a bit for the *Daily Mirror*. Allan Martin, who wouldn't buy a pint if he was a millionaire, suggested to Merve that he go into the team room and help himself to a beer. George Burrell, the tour manager, saw Merve and there was a big row with all sorts of flak flying.

'Pat was sending me photos almost every day of my little boy sitting in the sunshine back home. I really began to think, "Do I really need to be here?" I didn't know if I was mentally strong enough.'

He also had to contend with accusations of a Welsh bias. 'One or two did think that you had to be Welsh to get into the Test team but that wasn't true. We dropped Bobby Windsor after the first Test because Peter Wheeler was playing out of his skin. We also dropped Allan Martin for Bill Beaumont in the second row.'

As the tour deteriorated still further, Bennett even found himself having to cope with the rumblings of an internal rebellion. 'One player packed his bags one afternoon and said, "I'm off." He'd had a bit of a barney with the management and I had to talk him out of it. I said, "If you go, you'll be letting yourself down as well as everyone else. You'll be accused of jacking it in. You've got to tough it out the same as the rest of us."'

Yet, despite everything, the '77 Lions are still kicking themselves for losing the series, which ended 3–1. They lost the first Test at Wellington in galling circumstances, throwing an overlap away for Grant Batty to score an interception try. They won the second, lost the third by a distance and were three points clear going into injury-time in the fourth at Eden Park, Auckland, only to suffer the cruellest twist of all. Another mighty performance from their pack demanded a kinder fate. Instead New Zealand prop Lawrie Knight applied the punishing finish, so condemning a miserable tour to the margins of history. For Bennett, there could not have been a more vivid contrast between successive Lions tours.

'South Africa in '74 had been all glamour. After New Zealand in '77 I felt so bad I didn't really want to play rugby again. I'd gone through three months of mental agony. I gave the tour my best shot even though, deep down, I was hating it, what with all the things that were happening out there. Whether I'd have taken the captaincy in hindsight is another matter. It was a very rough three and a half months. When I got back home, all I wanted was to be with Pat again, grab my son and spend some time in the sun with them. It was very sad it didn't go our way. Whenever I look back on that tour, I say to myself, "God, that was the one low point of my career."'

It did nothing to dilute the pride bursting out all around Felinfoel. They turned out in their thousands to give their favourite son a homecoming which, if anything, outstripped the one they had given him three years earlier. Bennett, overwhelmed by the reception, could hardly believe it.

Relationships between Wales and New Zealand had degenerated from friendly to frosty. How typical of the man that Bennett's spontaneous reaction to one incident when the All Blacks returned to Stradey Park the following year should save those relationships from slumping into a deep freeze. His intervention to dissuade Scottish referee Allan Hosie from sending off the All Black lock Graham Higginson in the final minutes of the Llanelli match earned Bennett the gratitude of many New Zealanders. It even moved one of their more provocative players, the abrasive Grant Batty, to send him a letter. 'Thank you for what you did,' Batty wrote. 'You have tried to keep relationships between our countries alive.'

He was more than merely a great player.

13

Drunk in Charge

Bobby Windsor's official CV contains eleven major titles: four international championships, two Grand Slams, four Triple Crowns and one invincible Lions tour. It is eleven major titles more than most players ever achieve, and yet the list does him scant justice.

The sanitised statistics stand as a monument to his period as the best hooker in the British Isles, and yet they do him a disservice because they tell you nothing about one of the most unforgettable characters of a sport which used to be full of them. His unofficial CV, the one the rugby authorities would have moved heaven and earth to suppress, paints a more colourful picture of his thunderous journey across the global stage.

The real Bobby Windsor, for instance, confesses that on one bizarre occasion in New Zealand he was drunk in charge of the Lions front row, a sobering episode which will be revealed in due course along with the reason why on a tour which set the rugby world ablaze the one Welsh component of the pack became known to the rest of the troops as 'the Fireman'.

He admits to having been embroiled in an expenses row with the English Establishment, to having walked out of a Barbarians tour in angry protest at being ordered to bed by the Baa-baas' president at ten o'clock on a Sunday night, and to having pulled the odd scam simply to ensure that the mortgage would be paid while he was overseas fighting for Queen and country.

A steelworker who was never averse to a bit of what he called 'ducking and diving', the lovable, roguish Windsor was the Arthur Daly of the

Lions. True to form, he had pulled his first stroke before the Lions left their London hotel for a tour which the organisers, the Four Home Unions, had refused to abandon in protest at the apartheid regime in South Africa. The Pontypool hooker and arch symbol of the working-class game could not have cared less. 'I didn't even know what apartheid meant,' he said. 'And that's the truth.'

Windsor arrived from South Wales in a state of some anxiety, fearful lest he would suffer from an inferiority complex and, more to the point, worried about whether he would be able to make ends meet. 'All of a sudden I was mixing with great players and I was still in awe of them. That wasn't the only difference. I was a steelworker and they were all collar-and-tie chaps. I was skint. They all had a few bob.

'I'd travelled down to London with 40 quid in my pocket. I was worried how I was going to manage but, as luck would have it, I picked up something straight away. The first thing we did was to go into this room to get kitted out for the tour. They said, "Go along the table, pick up your Lions sweater, your Lions shirt, your Lions this, your Lions that." I noticed that when you came to the end of the table, nobody checked what you had. There was loads and loads of stuff, so I went round the table two or three times.

'The chap who had driven a few of us up in a minibus was staying overnight before going home in the morning. I flogged the stuff to him and he flogged it when he got back. He made more than I did but I was happy enough. Nobody said anything. Nobody missed anything. Everyone had their gear. Somebody was going to do something with it. I just happened to be the first. Until then, all I had was £40 to last 15 weeks. I felt a bit happier because I never wanted to be so hard-up that I would have to borrow off someone. My pride would never let me do that.

'The funny thing was that at my kids' school all the other kids reckoned the big stars were millionaires because they had seen them so often on the telly. One of my kids even said that they reckoned I was a millionaire as well. Imagine that, me a millionaire going off to the steelworks at six o'clock every morning in my overalls and wellies.'

Now there is nothing unusual about players being carried out of tours on stretchers. Windsor reversed the trend in unique fashion. When the Lions landed at Jan Smuts Airport in Johannesburg, he had to be carried off the plane into South Africa on a stretcher. This time it was no laughing matter. A dodgy bit of seafood and a large amount of gin had conspired to render the Lions hooker legless before he had the opportunity to strike a ball, or an opponent, in anger. Windsor had a phobia about flying but he had never experienced anything quite like this.

'I made sure I sat next to J.P.R. because he's a doctor. After we got through the second bottle of gin, he passed out. Not long after that, I felt as though I was collapsing. I was in such a state I couldn't get out of my seat and the stewardess was trying to move me to the back of the plane where there was more room. I was in a bad way by the time they laid me out. I remember them asking if there was a nurse on board and calling for a doctor who, in J.P.R.'s unavoidable absence, turned out to be Ken Kennedy, the Irish hooker and my rival for the Test team. The nurse got to me first. She said, "He's burning up. Get his temperature down." So they stuck a couple of lumps of ice in my mouth. When Ken Kennedy came along, he put his thermometer in my chops. Then Syd Millar, the coach, came up and said, "How is he?" Kennedy didn't know I had the ice jammed in my mouth. He pulled the thermometer out, looked at it and said to Syd, "Well, according to this, he should be dead!"'

Windsor's hopes of making a grand entrance had long gone. 'Everyone else got out of the front of the plane to be met by 25,000 people all giving them a cheer. While all that was going on, I was being taken out of the rear of the plane and put straight into an ambulance to be taken to hospital.

'Whatever way they had me on the stretcher, I was sliding up and down. Every time they stopped at traffic lights, I'd shoot up one way and hit my head against something. And every time they drove off, I'd shoot down the other way and hit my head against something else. The two coloured blokes driving the thing were talking in a language of their own so I didn't have a clue what was going on.'

It took him six days to recover from what he insists was food poisoning, with a bit of the alcoholic sort thrown in. Six other players went down with a rather less severe attack, confirming Windsor's suspicion that they had all been victims of a prawn cocktail prior to departure. That he had never clapped eyes on the Egon Ronay Good Food Guide soon became blindingly apparent.

To his credit, Windsor tells the story himself. 'I was brought up on good, plain food like bacon and egg. Nothing fancy. I didn't go for all this spaghetti and tuna nonsense. So when the boys picked me up from hospital and we stopped at this restaurant on the way to the hotel, they said, "Have an omelette." When the waiter came to take the order, he asked me what sort of omelette I wanted. I said I wanted an egg one! I didn't know you could get other kinds. They've never let me live it down.'

As soon as he had regained sufficient strength, Windsor was punching his weight, in every sense. The Lions, weary over the years of being good tourists and nice losers, had decided they would waste no time in letting the Afrikaner know where he stood in the general scheme of things – which meant that he would start off flat on his back.

The tour to beat all tours began out on the wheat fields of Potchefstroom against Western Transvaal. There would be no pussy-footing around. 'Syd Millar said, "First line-out, turn round and belt the bloke next to you,"' said Windsor. 'I thought, "Fair dos." I like Syd, he's a good man, so I got stuck into them right away.

'And it worked. It worked because our next opponents would ask the last lot about us, and when the word got back that we were a bunch of nutters it put the opposition on the back foot. There's always been a lot of intimidation in rugby, especially up front, and that worked to our advantage. We went out to do a job.'

They did it in ruthless style. As the Lions followed one landslide win with another, Windsor's harder physical edge gave him the vote over Kennedy as the hooker for all four Tests. When it came to the third, at Port Elizabeth, the Springboks turned to their hard men in a final, desperate attempt to save the series. Moaner van Heerden replaced John Williams in the second row, with Johann de Bruyn in the back row. Not inappropriately for a blindside flanker, he had a glass eye.

'We got out on to the pitch a good while before the 'Boks,' said Windsor. 'It was always the same, the coloured people at one end of the ground giving us a cheer. When the South African team appeared, they came like bats out of hell, like they were all trying to beat Linford Christie. Somebody said, "Where are they going?" I reckoned they were running to get away from Cyclops! He was an ugly b******.

'We were chuffed to bits when they dropped Williams. Van Heerden punched us every time we won the ball but we were up for that. Mind you, he could punch his weight. He walloped me from behind once and I went down like a sack of spuds. I thought I'd been hit by the side of a house. Then Gordon Brown came charging in and Moaner dropped him with another beauty. I got up and said, "Eh, Broonie, what are you doing down there?" I was still sore but I could hardly keep a straight face.'

Windsor and the Lions – or, more specifically, the 1974 vintage – were made for each other, and not just because the rugged Welshman, hewn from the coalface in Gwent, provided one of the cornerstones of an élite squad responsible for setting records which can never be beaten. When the occasional celebration threatened to get out of hand, it would usually be a case of no smoke without fire.

One of the more spectacular pieces of horseplay resulted in a bed, thought to have belonged to Tommy David, the Welsh flanker from Llanelli via Pontypridd, being shoved out on to the canopy of the team hotel in East London. A grinning Windsor just happened to be walking out beneath it when the local paper's photographer took a shot of the bed dangling precariously above him, the (incorrect) implication being that he had had something to do with putting it there.

There were other times when he lent more than a hand to shaping some of the more uproarious events, claiming, hand on heart, that but for his intervention the Lions would have caused as much damage off the field as they did on it. 'I was known as "the Fireman" because I was the one who put the fires out,' he said. 'In East London some of the boys had piled up a few cardboard cases from empty beer packs. We never drank during the week but we used to have a skinful on Saturday nights, and this particular Saturday night someone had set the cardboard alight. I got the fire extinguisher off the wall but it didn't work. I got a hose pump and used that instead.

'When I turned round, thinking I'd done well, the hotel manager was standing there. He was a right prat and he started shouting at me, so I turned round and gave him a good drenching. He stormed off and said he was going to call the police. When he told Willie John McBride what he was doing, Willie John said to him, "Tell me this: how many of them will there be?"'

For someone used to the daily grind of working life in a depressed part of the country, life with the Lions proved to be a real eye-opener. 'Over the last few weeks, some players would say, "Won't you be glad to be going home?" I couldn't understand that. I didn't want the tour to end. I'd come from a place where you had egg and chips and gone to a place where you could have fillet steak twice a day if you wanted to and then apple tart and custard. As much as you could eat.

'When they asked me about going home, I'd say, "This is brilliant. I'm staying at a first-class hotel, everyone says I'm a nice bloke, I'm having free grub and free booze." I loved it so much that I wanted it to go on and on. I knew there'd never be anything better than this. Playing for Wales was fabulous but I always reckoned playing for the Lions was better, because we were on tour. It doesn't half annoy me today when I hear of some Welsh players opting out of going to South Africa because they say they are too tired to go. That's the difference, I suppose, between them and us. We loved rugby. They love what they get out of rugby.'

Windsor didn't exactly return from South Africa empty-handed. The perks included what could loosely be described as the first win bonus paid to a British team, after the Lions had beaten Northern Transvaal at the Loftus Versfeld stadium in Pretoria. Almost a quarter of a century on, the story can be told for the first time of how Bobby used his entrepreneurial skills by dropping the right word in the right ear at the right time.

'Jannie le Roux, then the president of Northern Transvaal, was a rich man. We called him Danny la Rue. He'd said before the game that they wanted to give the Lions a present. I said to our liaison officer, "Tell him to give us some money and then we'll buy our own present."

'"Good idea," said the liaison man. Then le Roux said he would come into our dressing-room after the game. In he walked with a briefcase, and it was full of money. As soon as I saw him, I started to sing, "Jingle bells, jingle bells, jingle all the way!" He went round us all one by one and we got between £50 and £60 each, which was a lot of money then. I came back with more than I'd had when I went! I had about two hundred quid, plus two suitcases full of pressies. I was flipping delighted. Really chuffed.'

He would have been even more 'chuffed' had his final coup not been foiled in hilarious circumstances as the players were heading towards the departure gate at Jan Smuts Airport at the end of the tour, prior to their acclamation at Heathrow as conquering heroes. What happened next perhaps went some way to suggesting that Windsor was not entirely joking when he listed the two most essential tools for a rugby tour as a screwdriver and a pair of pliers!

He was carrying a large object wrapped in brown paper, a painting which he had seen in the foyer of the team's Johannesburg hotel and which he had taken rather a liking to. Imagine his chagrin, therefore, at bumping into the manager of the aforesaid hotel just as he was about to go through passport control.

'The manager said to me, "What have you got there?"

'"Just a present," I said.

'"Why don't you let me send it over to Wales for you? Save you all the bother of carrying it."

'"Thank you very much, but it's no trouble. No trouble at all."'

At that point, according to Windsor, a senior member of the Lions party said, 'Bobby don't be so silly. Give it here and the manager will send it on for you.'

Windsor reluctantly handed the large brown paper object to the hotel manager, who appeared to be genuinely oblivious as to what was inside it. 'I never saw it again until a few years later, when we were at a bit of a reunion do at the house of the bloke who'd persuaded me to hand the painting over so that it could be sent to me. And, blow me, there it was, hanging above his fireplace!'

For all his fears about going bust on tour while making sure that his young family were not going short at home in Newport, he managed to balance his books despite a miserable daily allowance. 'We got 75p a day, which was enough for a postcard and a stamp. One phone call home and I'd be cleaned out. Some of the players had wealthy friends but I was never going to ask someone to lend me a tenner so I survived on my wits.

'One way of getting round the phone bill was to ask the duty boy to go to reception and ask for the Lions' bills just before we checked out. He'd put them on the counter. I knew which one was mine so I'd put it in my pocket with the duplicate and then dole out the others. I was caught out once when we were leaving the hotel in Cape Town. The coach was pulling out when the hotel manager came running up. Syd stopped the bus and talked to the manager. Then Syd asked, "Who hasn't paid his phone bill?" Nobody answered. Then he said, "Look, the number is 0633 . . ." etc. I was stuffed, because that's a Newport number and I was the only Gwent player on the tour. So I stood up in the middle of the bus and said, "Which one of you b******* has been phoning my wife?" Syd began to laugh his head off, along with everyone else. The manager got off, we drove on and, as far as I know, someone somewhere is still waiting for the bill to be paid.'

There were times, more than he cared to remember, when the boot had been on the other foot, when the Welsh Rugby Union, like the other home Unions, demanded their players turn up for weekend squad training while still ensuring a strict enforcement of the regulations. In other words, 'Behave like professionals and we will treat you as amateurs.'

'In the hot mills at the steelworks you got a bonus for tonnage and weekends were double time, a chance to put some jam on the bread. I went to Bill Clement [the WRU secretary] one day, explained the position and said, "Any chance of doing anything for me and Charlie [Welsh prop Charle Faulkner]?" He was in the same position.

'Bill said, "You don't have to go to training with the Welsh team if you don't want to. But if you don't go, you won't be picked." We used to give up 16 hours' work every Sunday to run around those b****** sands in Aberavon. In the end it didn't really matter that much because I was playing rugby and playing for Wales. I loved the game.

'I swear on my children's lives, we never got a cent from Pontypool to play rugby. We didn't want it. The only money I ever got was 25 quid to wear Adidas boots when I played for Wales. Boots would cost you £30 a time, so if someone gave you a free pair you were happy to wear them. For a while, nobody told me that you could get a few bob as well. Then Derek Tapscott, the old Arsenal footballer, was working for Gola and he gave me a pair of their boots. When I went training with Wales, Gareth Edwards said, "Why are you wearing that make of boots? We all wear Adidas." That's when I found out that you got £25 a match for wearing them, although the figure later went up to £50. I'd been in the team for two years and had had nothing.

'I had an argument with Edwards over that. I said to him, "I'll tell you something. Every time a new boy comes into the team, I'm telling him the score about the boots." He said that the more pieces that had to come out of the cake, the less you would get. I said, "I don't care. We're all out there together and we should all get exactly the same amount."'

When all three members of the Pontypool front-row trinity claimed the same amount in mileage expenses to play for one of the more distinguished invitation teams of the old amateur era, there was an unholy row which went on for weeks. Windsor, accompanied by his club props Charlie Faulkner and Graham Price, had been invited to play for Major Stanley's XV in their annual match against Oxford University at Iffley Road. They took time off from work to play the match, claimed £20 each for travel and food and thought nothing more of it until they were interrogated by the Welsh Rugby Union at the behest of Stanley's. They had been invited to play in the match by the former England and Harlequins scrum-half Nigel Starmer-Smith.

'Starmer-Smith gave the sheets out and I said to John Dawes, who was playing in the match, "How do you fill this in?" He gave us some advice and we put down 20 quid. We went training with Wales the next Sunday and Keith Rowlands, then the chairman of selectors, called us in. He didn't like us much. He said, "You've claimed money you are not entitled to. Unless you pay it back, you won't play rugby again." I said, "Oh yes. Why's that, then? You work the mileage out, up to Oxford and back, and stopping for a meal. Perhaps we are a pound short." Rowlands said, "With three of you in the same car?" I replied, "I went up on my own." Charlie twigged straight away. "Aye, we were on different shifts that day," he said. "Went up in different cars."

'Then it was put to us that because of what we'd done, the Barbarians might not pick another Welshman ever again. At that point Clive Rowlands, the team coach, intervened. "Hang on a minute," he said. "These boys haven't done anything wrong." He was good like that, Clive.'

The sequel to that particular episode turned out to be most unfortunate, especially so for the man who suffered from a severe case of mistaken identity, the former Scotland wing forward Mike Biggar. Another Scot, Alistair Biggar, had played in the Stanley's match, but he had the good luck not to be selected against Wales later that season because the Pontypool front row's intelligence – a comment on the accuracy of their information, not what was between their ears! – was not what it should have been.

'We tried to find out who nailed us and we were told the gentleman's name was Biggar,' Windsor said. 'When we played Scotland we decided to nail him. We gave him a good bump and he went off after half an hour. At the dinner that night he came over to us and obviously knew something of the background. "Thanks very much for that," he said. "But it was Alistair Biggar." My jaw dropped. There wasn't much to be said . . .'

Not surprisingly, Windsor had another run-in with the Establishment, this time with the Barbarians while on their Easter tour of South Wales. Sunday was always reserved for the golf championship which the Baa-baas' president Herbert Waddell, a devotee of the Royal and Ancient game, approached as if he were about to take part in the Ryder Cup.

Someone with a mischievous sense of humour had dropped a word in his ear to the effect that Windsor, on his first and what turned out to be his last Barbarians tour, could hit the ball a mile and played off a handicap of six, which made him appear to be the best golfer in the party. Tradition decreed that all the names went into a hat and the teams were then drawn out.

Waddell, no doubt eagerly anticipating Windsor's deft touch around the green and length off the tee, then discovered, no doubt by a huge coincidence, that the crafty Welshman was in his team. What the president did not realise was that his newly acquired team-mate could not have told the difference between a nine-iron and a three-wood.

'Herbert loved his golf and took it all very seriously. He obviously expected big things from me but after a couple of shots he got very short-tempered and said, "Stop fooling around, Windsor!"'

The hacking Baa-baa did not take kindly to being admonished.

'What are you on about? I've never played golf in my life.'

'But they told me you had a handicap of six.'

'What the hell is that supposed to mean?'

Waddell's team did not win the championship. Nobody could be too sure whether the two events were connected, but that evening Windsor and a few other players were in the bar of the Baa-baas' hotel in Penarth when Waddell joined them. 'He said to me, "Windsor, we have a game at Swansea tomorrow and you're playing. It's ten o'clock. Up to your room." When I asked him what he'd said, he repeated it, "Get up to your room."

'"Get stuffed," I said, "I'm on tour." And he said, "I'm telling you to go to bed." I said, "You wait there." I went up to my room, packed my suitcase, brought it down to the bar and told him I was off. He said, "You can't go." I said, "You watch me," and I went.

'Then the hooker who stood in for me got injured, so the next day the Baa-baas were on the phone to me, asking if I'd play for them against Newport. At first I refused, then I told Geoff Windsor-Lewis, the Baa-baas' secretary, that I'd play to help them out. He said, "We'll murder them." We lost 48–0.'

Windsor's Easter uprising explained why thereafter the Pontypool front row never appeared *en masse* or individually for the game's most exclusive touring club. 'They rang Pricey up a couple of years later and asked him to play against Australia. Fair dos to Pricey, he said that he wouldn't play unless the three of us were going to be asked. They said they would get back to him but I don't think they ever did. Good for Pricey. It was either all or nothing.'

From the end of one Lions tour to the start of the next, Wales had won 11 matches out of 13 and Windsor had played in every one, making him a certainty for the trip to New Zealand in 1977. Just as everything had gone right for him in South Africa, so it all went badly wrong even before he had to take his life in his hands and force himself to sit on an aeroplane.

This time Windsor went to great pains to avoid any food or alcohol poisoning but he was already in trouble. He pulled a calf muscle during pre-tour training at Pontypool Park with fellow Lions Terry Cobner and Graham Price. A lesser player would probably have been replaced there and then but Windsor's importance was such that the coach, his former Wales captain John Dawes, dismissed any notion of taking off without him.

Despite management assurances to the contrary, Windsor feared that the writing was already on the wall. Subsequent events proved that it had been put there in large, capital letters. 'As soon as I got to London, I said to Syd [Dawes], "I've got a real problem with this calf muscle." He said, "You'll be all right, don't worry." I wasn't all right. We went to a lot of towns in New Zealand on that tour and I saw the physio in every one of them but it didn't get any better. I couldn't go flat out. I just couldn't.'

Other, larger problems had loomed which would plague the tour from start to finish, not least Dawes's running feud with the press, British more than New Zealand. 'I don't think Syd could handle the pressure,' Windsor said. 'And that had a knock-on effect on Phil Bennett. Great player, lovely bloke, but too weak as a captain. We needed someone like Fran Cotton as captain. He'd have been the man. He wouldn't tell you to put your head anywhere that he wouldn't put his, and if you were in a bit of trouble on the field you could always count on Frannie. But that tour was lost because we didn't have a strong enough coach. At the start of the tour, Dawes would go to the training field and tell the forwards, "Get up there and do a bit." Then he'd go with the backs.

'We were a shambles. We had no set pattern. After two or three weeks of that, I went to see Syd one morning and told him we didn't know what was going on. The training for the forwards was so disorganised that there were English, Irish, Scottish and Welsh all over the place. I told Dawes we wanted to have one man in charge. I told him that whatever he said, we would do it, whether it was right or wrong. At least we would all be doing something together.

'Under Syd Millar in '74, training had been brilliant. He trained the players exactly the way Ray Prosser trained us at Pontypool. Same exercises, same sprints, same split of groups into hookers, props, locks, back row, half-backs, centres, wings and full-backs. I said to Syd one day, "Hey, you must have been on the phone to Pross!"

'Dawes and the manager, George Burrell, then asked me who I thought should be given the job of what was, basically, forwards coach. I told them I'd put Terry Cobner in charge because they'd listen to him and there would be a bit of discipline. Everyone seemed to get on well with Cob and he was also my club captain. We then got the scrum going so well that we blasted New Zealand teams all over the park. I even felt that if we'd had a scrum on the halfway line we could have pushed them over the try-line. We were flying.'

The Lions clearly decided that their hooker wasn't flying high enough. Windsor's crash-landing after the opening Test had been lost by the narrowest of margins provoked such a furious response that it ruined his close friendship with Cobner. Even now, more than 20 years later, their relationship is far from what it used to be. Windsor, dropped in favour of England's Peter Wheeler, refused to accept that he had an injury and blamed his old Pontypool colleague. 'I had a bitter argument with Cob because I thought he had kicked me where it hurts,' said Windsor. 'I thought he let me down. He could have warned me. I put him in charge of the forwards but he told me it was a decision taken by the selection committee.

'I found out years later through a very prominent member of the Lions party that that wasn't the case. Phil Bennett told me that whatever pack Cob wanted, he got. I wondered if he booted me out because he was jealous. I'm wrong in thinking that but that's the way I still feel about it. We played for Pontypool together, we went through all the muck and nettles together and we were 12,000 miles from home. If I'd been picking the forwards and Cob only had one leg, he'd have been in my pack. That's the way it should be.'

A winning second Test ensured there could be no way back for Windsor in the third. Another defeat raised speculation of changes for the final Test. 'Cob said that the same pack would play, which stuffed my chances,' Windsor said. 'And some of the boys were going out the night before to a nightclub in Auckland called the Grotto.' Windsor joined them, ignoring advice to the contrary from Bennett who, unlike the unhappy hooker, was not involved in the following day's match against Counties/Thames Valley at Pukekohe, just outside Auckland. Windsor was due to sit on the bench.

'We got in at half past five that morning, and the next thing "Benny" knew was that he was being woken up at nine o'clock to be told that John Bevan was sick and that he'd have to play. Half an hour later, the exact same thing happened to me. It was a good job the ref didn't have a breathalyser!'

His opposite number, Andy Dalton, went on to captain the All Blacks and never experienced a smell like it. 'Andy said that every time he went into the scrum it was like sticking his head into a brewery! All he could smell was the stench of stale beer. Totally embarrassing but, I'm afraid to say, totally true.

'At one stage there were 28 blokes fighting in that match. I was under the influence without a shadow of doubt. If I'd been in a car and they'd asked me to blow in the bag, I'd have been nicked. "Benny" was suffering too. Five minutes from time, he said to the ref, "If you don't blow that whistle, you could end up with a corpse on your hands!"'

Ironically, the occasion was the excuse for wild celebrations in Pontypool, which meant that Windsor, unwittingly, had merely been a trifle early with his. Windsor's unscheduled appearance meant that for the first time a complete club front row had represented the Lions: Faulkner, Windsor and Price, alias the Viet-Gwent.

After New Zealand, Windsor finally found a cure for his calf injury and went back to doing what he had been doing before the Lions tour, namely playing one of the leading roles in taking Wales to another Grand Slam. Their second title in three years culminated in another epic contest against France. Windsor, never one to couch his language in diplomatic terms, has his own controversial description for those around him.

'As a pack of forwards, we were a gang of thugs,' he said. 'That's what we were and that's the truth. We were not the biggest of packs so we had to go in and punch and boot like mad. That's the only way we could compete with some opponents because they were too big for us. All we had to beat them by was pure violence. We had no other way of matching their expertise.

'We'd do things the other home countries wouldn't do. We'd rip into them intent on causing injury. They say stamping on the head is dangerous, which it is. You stamp on someone's head, he goes off, has six stitches and comes back on. You stamp on someone's knee or ankle, he doesn't come back on. It was war. You were playing for your country and you wanted to win at all costs. You went out to physically intimidate them.

'You wore the longest studs you could find, then you went out and trampled them, booted them, punched them. The Irish boys would punch you, give you a bit of a nibble on the ear and a kiss afterwards. The French were different. They were mean and vicious. The French would rip your head off if they could and chuck it over the fence. I used to go down in the scrums and get a boot in my face. Every time I played against the French, I never came home without a busted nose and a stitched-up face. I used to bust a few myself, though, so it wasn't all one-way traffic. You had to be streetwise.

'Whenever I left the house to play against the French, I used to say to my wife, "Take a photograph of me now because I'm not going to look like this when I come back." And I tell you what, I loved it. Then they changed the rules and made the touch judges into linesmen who could flag against foul play. It finished Wales. They changed the rules so that cissies can play.'

Windsor survived a losing tour of Australia before giving the All Blacks a real going over, only for Wales to curse their luck at falling victim to the Andy Haden–Frank Oliver conspiracy to fake some barging at the line-out and hoodwink the English referee, Roger Quittenton.

At 30, Windsor would probably have been good for a third Lions tour in 1980 had his world not been shattered the previous year by the sudden death of his wife, Judy, from cancer at the tragically early age of

32. With three children to look after, Windsor then found himself out of work not long after leaving the steelworks for a job as a rep. By then his long run in the Wales team had been broken, not by any sudden dip in form but by the third-degree burns he suffered from lime which had been used by mistake to mark an area of touchline at Pontypool Park. He played on, but never for Wales.

Briefly out of work, Windsor refused to take unemployment benefit. 'I had too much pride to go on the dole,' he said. 'I did get as far as the dole office one day but I saw the people in there and walked out. I couldn't do it. My stupid pride wouldn't let me. I must have been daft but I was brought up to work. I didn't expect handouts.'

Typically, he came bouncing back, borrowing £1,000 from his father to set up a market stall in Pontypool. Now married to Lynne, the inimitable old Lion has two more children by his second wife and a thriving business, AquaRod, which specialises in cleaning drains. It may be a bit late for the late Herbert Waddell and the Barbarians but, at 50, he's even found time to play a bit of golf.

14

Game, Set and Match

On Tuesday, 23 April 1968, a teenaged medical student played a five-set match against the seasoned Australian Davis Cup player Bob Howe in the first round of the first open tournament in the history of tennis, the British Open at Dean Court in Bournemouth.

The young fellow had fought through three qualifying rounds to earn a place in the same men's singles as two of the most revered players in the game, Ken Rosewall and Pancho Gonzales. Howe's vast experience took him through in straight sets, 6–3, 6–3, 6–1, leaving his Welsh opponent with the consolation of a £20 cheque as a first-round loser.

He barely had time to pick it up. Within minutes of conceding match point, one of Britain's most promising young players was driving himself back home to Bridgend, hoping to make it in time for the local club's home match against Newport kicking off at 7.15 p.m. that evening. The most important five-setter of his highly promising career would have been more than sufficient excuse to have decided that a rugby match some 120 miles away on the same day was a bit too much. But for J.P.R. Williams nothing was ever too much. The match in question, far from a routine end-of-season affair, turned out to be a landmark in his sporting life of such significance that it swept him irresistibly down the road to rugby fame, if not fortune, at a time when he had been tempted to find both in the burgeoning world of professional tennis as the reigning champion of Junior Wimbledon.

His performance that night at the Brewery Field during a thumping 33–9 win, to which he contributed a great deal more than one conversion, convinced the Welsh selectors that the advent of a fearless new force in international rugby could be delayed no longer. On the evidence of what they saw that night, the Big Five picked him there and then as their full-back for the tour of Argentina at the end of the summer.

A fourth set at Bournemouth earlier in the day, therefore, could easily have left Wales none the wiser as to his readiness for the big stage. A winning fifth set might have been all the encouragement he needed to concentrate on tennis and build on his victory over David Lloyd the previous year in the final of Junior Wimbledon. Instead he became simply the finest full-back of his generation or, according to many high-profile observers the rugby world over, any other generation. He brought such a massive security to Wales and the Lions that it must have appeared to many an opponent that they had picked not merely a full-back but an entire Panzer division. There had never been anyone like him before and there hasn't been anyone like him since.

The most famous initials in sport were up and running as a direct result of that historic day at Bournemouth. Once he had chosen rugby ahead of tennis, nothing was ever going to stop him from becoming the most feared full-back in the world, if not always the most universally popular, given his ruthless readiness on one famous occasion to commit what was probably rugby's prototype professional foul to save a Welsh Triple Crown from disappearing before his very eyes.

His competitive ferocity was such that during their momentous march through New Zealand in the summer of 1971, the Lions banned him from training every Monday throughout the tour because in practice matches he proved too ferocious for the well-being of his own colleagues. The coach, Carwyn James, acutely aware that Williams never failed to do even the most menial chore as if his life depended on it, took the decision not merely to save his full-back's sledgehammer tackling for the All Blacks but to protect other Lions from being wounded by one of their own.

'He banned me from Monday training because I was injuring too many of our own players. I was phenomenally fit then and I used to do a lot of scrummaging against the front row. I remember once tackling John Spencer, then the England captain, when he came back inside and hurting him as a result. There were a few other heavy tackles and so for most of the tour I spent Mondays swimming. We had a Sunday school where the boys liked to have a few beers, so not having to get up as early as the rest on Mondays made it a very relaxed start to the week. But I'd sooner have been training.'

Unlike the majority of his contemporaries and the other great Lions of Wales, Williams did not come from a working-class environment. His parents, both doctors, gave him a relatively privileged upbringing which simply increased an already-burning desire to prove himself the best at whatever he did. 'Because I came from a middle-class family I was that much more determined to prove myself, to prove that I wasn't the boy with the silver spoon in his mouth. I think that's why I became so brave on the field. My father was a super tennis player but I got the competitive instinct more from my mother, a Lancashire lass from Rochdale.

'She gave me a will to succeed. I was brought up to take whatever I did in my stride. I did lots of things besides play sport. I played lots of musical instruments, I was a top chorister and I used to sing solos in the church choir. "Oh for the Wings of a Dove" was one and I still have a tape of it! So from an early age I was used to performing in front of people and I think that stood me in good stead later on when it came to developing a big-match temperament.'

Even in his early teens, Williams had such an unshakeable belief in his own ability that from the age of 14, when he first made the Welsh schoolboys' Under-15 team, he never had the slightest doubt that he would play rugby for Wales. 'I was very small for my age, so small that I was smaller even than Phil Bennett, who was in the same team. After that I had a huge growth spurt and shot up to over 6ft, whereas the rest of my family are no more than 5ft 9in.'

There was an aura of indestructibility about him almost from the beginning in Argentina in 1968. His impact on Wales over 12 years of Five Nations competition was such that in 45 championship matches, J.P.R. wound up on the losing side on a mere 7 occasions and never once against England. No Welsh team had ever been placed in safer hands.

For one who built his game on a flagrantly fearless disregard for his own safety, he suffered remarkably few injuries, which was probably just as well for his own peace of mind. J.P.R. hated having to make any concession to human frailty, an aversion which had nothing to do with the fact that he devoted his working life to putting all sorts of people back together again in his role as an orthopaedic surgeon. There was nothing of the Humpty Dumpty about him. On the rare occasions when he came out of a dangerous liaison in more than one piece, he invariably played on as though nothing had happened. Once against Scotland, for instance, he completed the final 25 minutes despite a fractured cheekbone. In his book there was only one thing worse than having to make a premature exit, and that was showing the opposition even the flicker of a grimace.

'I regarded it as a sign of weakness if you needed treatment, unless, of course, there was something seriously wrong. There were times when I was hurt but I would never show it. I felt that to do so was to give your opponent an advantage. I remember playing against New Zealand at the Arms Park in 1974 and being involved in quite a big collision with their famous wing, Bryan Williams. We both got up and walked back pretending we were not hurt, but we most certainly were. I had a depressed fracture of my right elbow when I ran into the back of Gareth Edwards's head during one match against England. I didn't know I'd done it until I went back to medical school the following Monday. It wasn't really painful. I didn't seem to suffer pain as much as the average person.'

The amount he inflicted on England was nobody's business, especially on the biennial visit to Twickenham. In four matches there during the '70s, Williams scored four tries, and it was somehow more than coincidence that the only two matches Wales lost to the old enemy over the period of J.P.R.'s reign were the two matches he missed.

His metamorphosis from ambitious tennis player to the world's number one full-back might never have happened had the law-makers not changed the concept of full-back play at a stroke by removing the soft option of kicking the ball into touch on the full from outside the 25-yard line. In that respect, Williams had timed his entry into the game to perfection.

'I was very lucky in that respect. If they hadn't changed the law, I would have found the game too boring. Just whacking the ball straight back into touch would have bored me stiff. I was really a flanker playing full-back. I didn't like to kick the ball and I'm very glad I wasn't given much talent as a kicker because it meant I had to run it.'

Never one to suffer fools, gladly or not, J.P.R. came to expect of others the same demanding standards he imposed upon himself. When they failed to measure up, as they invariably did, he would often view their shortcomings with palpable intolerance. 'Yes, listening to the people around me at London Welsh at the time, I was very intolerant of other people's mistakes. I'd give them a rollicking, even in training. I believed that if you made mistakes in training, then you'd make them in the game. I think I could have been a bit more tolerant but that was part of my make-up. I've changed a lot since my playing days. Veterans' rugby has taught me to be more tolerant, to concentrate on my own game and not to worry about anyone else's.'

Not even Gareth Edwards could escape a rollicking from J.P.R. It happened towards the end of a runaway Wales win over Ireland at the

Arms Park in March 1975, a match notable for two reasons: it brought both the first international season of the Pontypool front row to a rousing end and Willie John McBride's marathon career to a sad end. Wales had scored five tries when Ireland grabbed a late consolation try through Willie Duggan. J.P.R. blamed Edwards for throwing it away and promptly let him have both barrels. 'Gareth will openly admit he threw out a wild pass in the last minutes of the game which Willie intercepted to score. I gave him a real rollicking along the lines of: "How dare you let them cross *my* line!" That was typical of me. We'd won the game 32–4 but that wasn't the point. I can laugh about it now but, believe me, I was upset at the time.'

There were times when he was too busy to have time to be upset, and never more so than during his first exposure to the All Blacks, a distinctly one-sided affair at Christchurch during the Welsh tour when a New Zealand team under Brian Lochore ran in four tries without reply. In the course of winning 19–0 – positively respectable judging by recent Welsh standards but quite a beating at the time, especially as the try was worth only three points – they exposed Williams to a severe test of his courage. He came through it, of course, with flying colours.

'My abiding impression of that match is of hundreds of All Black jerseys coming towards me. I still have nightmares about it. I remember telling myself, "Don't panic." And then I remembered what my old teacher used to say: "Whatever you do, tackle the man with the ball." I kept doing that because it seemed as if there was a continuous avalanche of black jerseys.'

Williams learnt so much from the experience that by the age of 25 he had done it all: Triple Crown, Grand Slam and two winning Lions series in countries where they had never won before. During the previous half-century, the Lions had never won a Test series in New Zealand or South Africa. With J.P.R. at the rear, they beat both in their own backyards within three years. He clinched the 1971 series against the All Blacks precisely as he said he would, by doing something he had hardly done before or since. The Lions, 2–1 up going into the last Test in Auckland, were on their way by coach to Eden Park when Williams told anyone who cared to listen what he was going to do.

'In the bus on the way to the ground, everyone was very, very nervous. I said, "I'm going to drop a goal today," and everyone burst out laughing. I'd only ever dropped two goals in my life. I'd dropped one in my first match for Bridgend, against Bristol in 1967, and another for Wales against Fiji two years later. Not surprising, really, because if I was given the ball, I always preferred to run with it.'

He had done that to devastating effect throughout the series, barely missing the opportunity to launch a counter-attack from the rock-like base built by a full-back whose tackling, catching and acute positional sense enabled him to complete a full set of masterful performances. On top of all that, he had the presence of mind and self-discipline to curb his natural instinct and drop the goal of a lifetime.

It came with the match – and the series – hanging in the balance at 11–11. David Duckham's pass left Williams in a position 50 yards out, which would hardly have encouraged an expert goalkicker, never mind one who would only kick the ball as a last resort. Typically, he had spent time on the training field practising on the off chance that such an opportunity might present itself.

'I'd stay behind after every training session and field the ball for Barry John while he practised his kicks. One day he said, "Why don't you come over here and try some drop goals?" He gave me the confidence to have a go. So when the ball went out to the left wing during that last Test and David Duckham chucked it inside, we were going backwards. I was back on their ten-yard line when I let fly. It was still climbing as it went through the posts. I'd hit it perfectly.'

With New Zealand unable to manage anything more than an equalising goal, the Lions were home and dry. They had achieved their major objective, to produce the 'bottle' and succeed where too many Lions teams down the decades had bottled out. 'Bottle' was dressing-room slang for having the nerve, skill and sheer bloody-mindedness to deliver victory against all the odds. In that respect, nobody had more of the stuff than J.P.R.

'There was no doubt that some earlier Lions teams had bottled out in New Zealand and South Africa. They were unquestionably as talented, probably more so, but they lost the series. We had the right players and undoubtedly the best coach I have ever come across in Carwyn James, a real psychologist. He was an original thinker on the game but he was also practical. It was Carwyn who said before the '71 tour, "Get your retaliation in first."

'I knew we had the bottle after the first Test in Dunedin. We were up against it in a way which meant we had to tackle as if our lives depended on it. They kept coming at us but we kept knocking them over and won 9–3. They were no longer supermen.'

Not only did the Lions achieve something that had never been achieved before, they did so in style, baffling teams all over New Zealand with the sheer breathtaking audacity of their tries. The vast majority had a made-in-Wales stamp all over them, the Grand Slam winners having provided the lion's share of the backs whose wit and daring proved the decisive factor – which was just as well, given the pack's struggle to secure much in the way of ammunition.

'We knew we had to be unorthodox to beat them. Their planning was so good that we had to do something out of the ordinary, which meant moving what ball we had. It would take exceptionally good players, especially when you were never going to get more than 40 per cent of the ball. There's no better place to attack than from your own twenty-two, and we scored a lot of tries from that part of the field.

'You could see the sheer look of disbelief on the faces of the spectators. The tour was a turning point for British rugby. There was also quite a high IQ in that team. One of the problems with Welsh rugby today is that there are not too many bright guys. In '71 we had Ray McLoughlin, who was a very bright guy despite being a prop! There were plenty of others, John Taylor, John Dawes, Mike Gibson, myself, Gerald Davies, all bright.

'The success made it easier for the Lions to succeed again in South Africa three years later. In '74 we totally dominated their forwards so that we didn't have to play as well behind as we had done in New Zealand. The dream team would have been the '74 pack and the '71 backs.'

The distribution of the 'bottle' factor throughout the Lions' clean sweep of southern Africa can never have been more uneven. The tourists had gallons of the stuff, the Springboks precious little, and yet, for all their invincibility, Willie John McBride and his troops did not complete their unbeaten business without acquiring more than a whiff of notoriety.

The infamous '99' emergency call had been devised before the first ball had been belted, never mind the first opponent. 'Willie John coined the name and it was part of the tour strategy. If we called "99", you all got stuck in. It was really to prevent any player being sent off, the theory being that if everyone got involved it would make it difficult for the referee to single anyone out. He could hardly send the whole team off. I'm not very proud of it but we felt it was a case of one in, all in.'

He was not particularly proud either of being at the centre of an ugly incident which caused a near riot during the match against Natal in Durban towards the end of the tour. Williams has been accused of 'going berserk' in attacking Tommy Bedford after the Natal captain had tackled him into touch, a fracas which ended only after the police had intervened, while McBride and his men waited in the middle of the pitch. It took them fully ten minutes to restore law and order.

'I was wearing a headband and after the tackle he pulled my hair. So I punched him. The crowd went mad. Even after the incident, I had lots of letters from people saying "well done".' His wife, Scilla, gave him a piece of her mind after witnessing the whole sorry episode from the stand.

On the previous Lions tour, Carwyn James's only concern about J.P.R. – once he had kept him a safe distance from the training ground on Mondays – had been to calm him down as opposed to winding him up. 'He used to try to calm me down. He'd say, "Take it easy."

'Playing for Wales at Cardiff Arms Park in the '70s was a hell of an experience. I suppose it must have been like being on a drug. It had such a great buzz and atmosphere that we knew we were going to win. Before going out on to the field, I would look at myself in the mirror. The eyeballs would be up and I'd have to tell myself, "Calm down. Be in control of the atmosphere. Don't let the atmosphere control you." It wasn't easy.'

His Lions duty done, J.P.R. reverted to the normal Welsh business of the time, churning out Triple Crowns. They had produced three in a row and were in imminent danger of losing the fourth at Lansdowne Road on 4 March 1978 when their full-back averted the crisis in a way that resulted in his perceived good sportsmanship reeling from a self-imposed pounding.

When Mike Gibson chipped over his fellow Lion and looked as if he was going to score a certain try, J.P.R. calculated the potential damage and came up with a prognosis which, as he saw it in the heat of the moment, demanded drastic action. He took it, without compunction. He flattened Gibson, conceded a penalty and probably reckoned that the barracking of an angry crowd was a small price to pay for ensuring another Welsh crown.

Williams called it a 'professional foul'. 'I was a "professional" rugby player, in terms of attitude, playing in a non-professional era. Gibson kicked over my head, which was the only way to beat me. I'm not proud of what I did but you do what's best for the team and we never had a problem with it. Afterwards I went straight into the Irish dressing-room and apologised to Gibson. I wouldn't do it today because it would be a penalty try and I'd be sent off as well.'

There was nothing in the laws at the time, though, to prevent the French referee, Georges Domercq, from deciding that the spirit of the game had been assaulted and that therefore Wales would be docked six points, then the value of a converted try. Instead J.P.R. got away with it and Wales won an epic match by four points, 20–16.

By then he had turned down a third successive Lions tour for professional reasons. More intriguingly, he had also turned down an offer from Hull to play rugby league. If he has one regret about his rugby life, J.P.R. in reflective mood will confess that he regrets not having tested himself in the 13-a-side code.

'Hull offered me a £10,000 signing-on fee, a car, a house, a job as a registrar in Hull Infirmary and £100 a game, plus win bonuses. It was a lot of money and a very attractive package. I must say I was tempted. My father, though, told me that if I went, he would never speak to me again. He felt that strongly about it.

'He said, "You are an all-round sportsman. You don't need to be paid to play any sport. You have a career for the rest of your life. So enjoy your sport. If you are paid to play it, you will enjoy it less." If my father's attitude had been different, I might well have gone. He felt there was a stigma attached to union players going to league, and I think that lasted until when Jonathan Davies went north ten years later.

'One of my very few regrets is that I'd like to have had a go at league. The essence of the game, confrontational, straight running, hard tackling, would have suited me. I've been up to Wigan quite a few times on medical matters and I have been hugely admired up there.'

He won a third Grand Slam with Wales in 1978 and applied his own inimitably shuddering finish to the campaign, barging Jean-François Gourdon into touch perilously close to the line when a try might easily have resulted in the hitherto unbeaten French winning the Slam, instead of having it jolted from their grasp by the slamming J.P.R.

'If he had scored, they would have won. I remember thinking as he came running down the touchline, "If I tackle him round the legs, he'll probably still score." It was too close to take any chances. I had to take him out. I shoulder-barged him into touch and I knew the importance of what I'd done. It was a Grand Slam tackle.'

The following season, by which time the three previous Welsh captains, Phil Bennett, Terry Cobner and Gerald Davies, had all retired, J.P.R. assumed command and very nearly started his captaincy with another win over the All Blacks. Wales, 12–10 ahead, lost to a late Brian McKechnie penalty, and nobody will ever convince their captain that the decisive kick was anything other than the result of a line-out plot deliberately engineered to deceive the English referee, Roger Quitten-ton.

J.P.R. is adamant. 'He was definitely conned. I heard after the match that a friend of my father's had been down to watch them training and they were practising the trick of falling out of the line-out to make it appear that they had been barged by an opponent. I wish we had known that at the time. We were the better side that day, even if we made the mistake of sitting on our lead when we should have been putting more points on the board.'

J.P.R. signed off the following March in suitable style, the annual win over England delivering another Triple Crown, although the match turned out to be a collector's item for a different reason. A gash in his leg was so deep that he had no alternative but to leave his post and make the only premature exit of his Wales career. The match was as good as won before he departed, later to announce his retirement from international competition.

The Lions made one final attempt to bring him back, as a reinforcement for their accident-ridden tour of South Africa in 1980. 'I had a phone call from Syd Millar, the manager, asking whether I would be able to go out because they didn't have any full-backs left. I was tempted, but I felt it was a time when work had to come first.'

The temptation to give it one more go proved too strong the following season. J.P.R. made the customary winning return against England but the next game, Scotland at Murrayfield, was to prove one too many. Wales, lucky to have escaped a far worse beating than 15–6, made wholesale changes, and the player who once told me he would never make the mistake of playing on for too long, thus allowing the selectors to drop him, had become the biggest casualty.

'They told me at the training session for the next game, against Ireland. Steve Fenwick, the skipper, had been dropped as well. He went off home. I trained with the team and hit shit out of the rest of the team, which was a fairly typical reaction! Maybe the desire for international rugby had waned, plus the fact that I didn't have as many outstanding players around me. That's why it was so much easier playing for the Lions.'

Just as they had beaten the Springboks with one Welshman at full-back, the Lions did so again almost a quarter of a century later, Neil Jenkins emerging, albeit out of position, to make a huge contribution in a way that the initialled one could never have done. The 1997 Lions would never have made it without Jenkins's priceless knack of kicking high-pressure goals.

While J.P.R. is still playing at almost 50, for village club Tondu whenever his duties at Bridgend permit, he is in despair over the state of the Welsh game. 'The Welsh decline is multi-factorial: the loss of the grammar schools, the closure of traditional industries and a quite dreadful administration by the Welsh Rugby Union. It was never very good even in my playing days. It's an absolute farce, for example, to set up a committee to appoint a coach, as they did, and then make him report back to the main committee.

'I don't think Wales will ever get back to where we were in the '70s. I'm afraid I am resigned to seeing the sort of results we've seen recently. Watching South Africa score 96 points against us in Pretoria, you were almost hoping for the 100, but the decline started a long time ago, in the mid-'80s.

'A lot of players today just play for the money. Too many are happy to be sitting on the bench, and at Cardiff they're being paid £45,000 a year to do that. It's nonsense. There isn't enough money in the game to support a fully professional operation. It should be part-time. You can only train so much.'

Had he been around to take advantage of today's over-inflated market, the mind boggles at what J.P.R. would have been worth, on the tennis court as well as the rugby field.

15

A Win Bonus from Robben Island

Only one player in the history of the Lions has scored four tries in consecutive Test matches. In doing so he won the unstinting admiration of inmates of a prison whose name would become as notorious as Alcatraz. Their gratitude for what he had accomplished resulted in J.J. Williams receiving the first bonus of his career, the original brown envelope. His deeds in securing the rout of South Africa during the summer of 1964 prompted certain political prisoners at Robben Island to send a small token of their appreciation which extended to more than a few congratulatory postcards.

The combined British and Irish team were not content with merely beating the Afrikaner but wiped the floor with his team, scoring eight tries without a solitary reply during thumping victories in the second and third Tests, half of them scored by a speed merchant from Nantyffyllon who had made his first major appearance for Wales four years earlier at the Commonwealth Games in Edinburgh.

J.J. was the Lions' executioner-in-chief, his deadly finishing ensuring that the 'Boks paid the full price for their bludgeoning up front. The two tries he delivered in the 28–9 win in Pretoria were followed by two more in an almost identical victory in Port Elizabeth, where the unbeaten Lions clinched the series. Altitude or sea level, it was all the same to J.J.

When the Lions ran out for that decisive match at the Boet Erasmus Stadium they made a point of waving to the only black spectators, a group corralled into a corner of the ground. As if to acknowledge their presence, J.J. duly touched down for both his tries in the same corner and the cheering extended far beyond Port Elizabeth to Robben Island itself, where Nelson Mandela had been incarcerated since the early '60s.

The following week J.J. had a fair idea of how much pleasure the prisoners took from the Lions embarrassing what they saw as the representatives of the reviled apartheid regime. 'I had all sorts of messages from people in jails and one of them said they had clubbed together to send a small token of their appreciation. They sent me two rand notes, which was a fantastic gesture.'

His supporters on the inside, so to speak, included Steve Tshwete, Minister for Sport in President Mandela's government. Returning to South Africa almost a quarter of a century later as part of the BBC Wales commentary team covering his country's ill-fated tour of the Republic during the summer of 1998, Williams was staggered to discover that people still wanted his autograph.

The trip also brought a poignant reminder that he and the invincible Lions had certainly not been forgotten. 'I was in the hotel in Pretoria chatting to a few people one night when I became aware of this black gentleman crying. I went up to him and said, "I'm sorry to see that you're upset. I hope I haven't said anything to cause offence."

'"No, no, not at all," he said. "It's just that the last time I saw you was in 1974 at the Test match and after that the authorities put some of us in a cage and kept us there for two days. Seeing you again brought all those memories flooding back."'

That J.J. ought to have been singled out during the tour as the recipient of a small but touching reward was not entirely inappropriate considering his own financial plight. If the definition of a true-blue amateur is someone who loses money hand over fist through representing his country overseas, then they didn't come any truer or bluer than J.J.

The Labour-controlled local education authority refused to grant him paid leave from his position as a PE teacher at Maesteg Comprehensive School, a decision which meant he stood to suffer more than anyone because the Lions were defying political pressures in refusing to abort the tour. 'This was my big chance to play in what I saw as a rugby version of the Olympics. I had no qualms about going. I wasn't going to miss it for anything.'

How ironic, therefore, that his deeds should have had such an enthusiastic impact in the kind of places which were definitely not to be found on the Lions' itinerary. 'I was told that Steve Tshwete was among those listening on the radio and cheering every time we scored and that

I was supposed to be one of President Mandela's favourite players. I don't think anyone could ask for a bigger compliment than that.'

Williams's matchwinning role for the Lions inevitably drew comparisons with another matchwinner that summer, the Dutch footballer Johann Cruyff, whose country lost to West Germany in the World Cup final. 'We both ran about on the football field but the similarities ended there. As one newspaper pointed out, "One of these men earns millions, the other doesn't get a penny and ends up out of pocket."'

The profit and loss account would have been seriously lopsided had Williams and his wife Jane, then also a schoolteacher, not been invited to meet a South African businessman living in Bridgend. 'He invited us round to tea one afternoon. He'd obviously read about my difficulty with the local authority and insisted on putting some money into my bank account. The only condition he made was that nothing was to be said because he didn't want any publicity. It was a lovely gesture which helped Jane pay the mortgage for the four months while I was away.'

At a time when some players in England are paid £200,000 for a season's work by their clubs, it is an absurd fact of rugby life that in return for scoring a record number of tries in a single Lions series, the finest left wing in Europe if not the world should have been punished financially. Incredibly, the punishment went on after he had been fêted as a conquering hero upon his return.

'There were other teachers in the Lions party but I suffered more than most. As far as I was concerned, the local authority broke my contract. I'd just bought a house but they wouldn't pay my wages during the school holidays either, which meant I'd gone five months without any pay. The Labour people used the tour as propaganda for the party and a chance to win some votes. Of course, when we got home we were all treated like gods. They were all slapping my back, no doubt the same people who had voted not to pay me while I was away. I was hurt by the hypocrisy of it all.'

Within weeks he had been hit by more hypocrisy, a real double whammy which served only to deepen his suspicion – if that were possible – of those professing to administer the game. Two months after the Lions tour, the Welsh Rugby Union attempted to ban J.J. Williams from the game. His crime? Being honest enough to admit that he had considered an offer from Widnes rugby league club.

Widnes had offered him so much money that nobody in his right mind would have turned it down without taking a little time to think about it. For generations, players had been scared to make any public admission of as much as an approach from rugby league for fear of being branded a professional on the spot and hounded out of the game, as poor old George Parsons had been, as if he were some sort of leper in a jockstrap.

On 15 September 1974 I reported in the *Daily Mail* that J.J. Williams had been offered a sum of £15,000, then a world record for a rugby union player, to turn professional. I advised him that it would be prudent for political reasons if I did not quote him directly on the subject in case of reprisals from the Union. He was happy to be quoted as saying that he had to give due consideration to such a good offer.

The real story of the WRU's ham-fisted reaction has never been told until now. 'Vince Karalius, the Widnes coach, turned up one morning and parked his massive Mercedes outside my little house in Maesteg. They didn't have massive Mercedes in Maesteg in those days. Anyway, he wrote out a cheque for £12,000. I then had to dash off to go to school. When I got back home later in the day, he wrote out another cheque, this time for £15,000.

'That Saturday, I turned up at Stradey for Llanelli's match against Bridgend. When I walked in, I had a message to go and see Ken Jones, the club secretary. He said, "I'm sorry to have to tell you this, John, but you can't play. Bill Clement [the WRU secretary] has been in touch and the Union say that because you've been considering this league offer, you have professionalised yourself."

J.J., being a man of independent mind, told the Union, via Ken Jones, where to go. 'You tell Bill Clement,' he told Jones. 'You tell him that if someone offered him 15 grand in his hand, he would consider it, too.' With that he stormed out of the office, went to the dressing-room and played the match as if nothing had happened. In terms of Union-bashing, J.J. was ahead of his time!

In doing so, he saved the WRU from themselves. Imagine what would have happened had he kowtowed to the Union demand, taken his boots home and gone into a state of indefinite suspension. Imagine the furore! Fortunately, J.J. responded to being shoved into a corner with considerably more savvy than those who tried to shove him there. He was also aware of his worth and his special status as a Lion *par excellence*. The WRU may have been able to chuck poor old George Parsons off the train taking the team to Paris in 1947, but J.J. was never one to be messed around.

'The issue rumbled on for a week or two, then died a death. Once I'd decided to ignore the instruction, I never really heard anything more about it. If they had pressed the point, I'd have told them straight:

"Come off it!" It was typical of the tin gods on the WRU to act like that but at that time, straight after the Lions tour, the six Welsh players involved were on top of the world. We could do no wrong.'

The same could be said of virtually his entire Wales career, from its beginning as a replacement against France in Paris in 1973 to the Triple Crown finale against England at Cardiff six years later. The smartest decision J.J. ever made was based on his early appreciation of the fact that he was unlikely to win the 100 metres in the Olympic Games. After the 1970 Commonwealth Games, he decided to use his speed in a different direction.

'I knew I was never going to be a world-class sprinter. I would always have been British-class but nothing more. Being brought up in a rugby background meant it was no problem to switch sports. Rugby came naturally to me and I had the added advantage of being in a game where not everyone could do 10.4 or 10.5 for the 100 metres.'

There was a great deal more to J.J. than a lot of gas. A sharp brain and footballing skills performed at high velocity invariably to pinpoint accuracy made him a lethal finisher despite the fact that he spent almost his entire career on the 'wrong' wing. A natural right-footer, the presence of Gerald Davies dictated that he would have to become the best left wing in the world instead.

He found it more of a help than a hindrance in perfecting his trademark, the chip over the last man and chase when, more often than not, there would only be one winner. 'Running down the left wing meant that I'd be kicking the ball ahead with the wrong foot. Kicking with the foot furthest away from the touchline meant you could kick it straighter and there would be far less chance of the ball bouncing into touch.

'Whenever there was one man left to beat, I could always do the kick over his head without ever slowing up. A lot of players can't do that but I always found it very easy. It's always been a good attacking ploy but there's even more need for it nowadays with defences often spread out across the field just like in rugby league. If you can break that line with a chip and you've got a bit of pace, you're in before the opposition can get anywhere near.'

When Gerald's rare absence first allowed J.J. one of the very few opportunities to appear on his more favoured right wing, against Australia in December 1975, he scored a hat-trick, something no Welsh wing has done at the Arms Park since. By then he had sprinted through one full season of Five Nations competition clean into the Lions party for the tour of tours, proving along the way that there was more than one John Williams, hence the initialled reference to both as coined by John Taylor.

He scored 12 tries in 12 matches, half of them in one afternoon of uninterrupted mayhem at Mossel Bay where the Lions outclassed South-Western Districts to the tune of 97–0, a final score which under current scoring values would have worked out at 113–0. J.J. accounted for six of the sixteen tries, equalling a Lions feat achieved only once before, by David Duckham in New Zealand three years earlier. From then on, the Lions' battle hymn 'Flower of Scotland', as chosen by the choirmaster, Scottish wing Billy Steele, was belted out with an ever-increasing fervour.

When the Lions came closest to losing during that unbeaten trek all over South Africa, it was J.J. who saved them, his desperately late try against the Orange Free State in Bloemfontein turning a 9–7 defeat into an 11–9 win. He has never forgotten that match for another reason, which explained why blood was still being spilt when the protagonists filed into a church hall for the after-match reception and the obligatory platitudes.

'It was a brutal match with a lot of punch-ups. We'd win them, it would calm down and then it would erupt again when people like J.P.R. would go steaming in. We'd sort them out up front and get on with playing a bit of rugby. Some of the players were in a state by the end, including their captain. He had a big bandage around his head when he got up to speak at the reception. He said, "I'd like to thank you for a good, clean, hard game." He went on in that vein for a few minutes with blood seeping out of his nose. Every so often you could hear it dripping on to the floor. They were dirty, horrible, b*******. "A good, clean, hard game!" I'd hate to have played in his version of a nasty one!'

A couple of weeks later, before another critical match, Willie John McBride summoned the troops to a meeting in his room. 'We filed in, the fifteen players, six subs and Syd Millar, the coach. McBride just sat there. For what must have been a good half-hour, nobody said a word. Then McBride got up. "Right, lads," he said. "I think the atmosphere's great." And we all filed out. Only Willie could do that.

'I don't think he was the greatest player in the world but he and Syd had been there in 1968 with the Lions and they'd been smashed. Those two boys from Ballymena hammered it into us from the outset that the Springboks were bullies and like all bullies they didn't like it when anyone stood up to them. There were some violent scenes because we never took a backward step.'

There were also scenes of dazzling beauty, none more so than the chessboard choreography which ended with J.J. touching down under the posts during the Port Elizabeth Test. 'The crowd stood and applauded us all the way back to the halfway line. We realised then we were a special team on a special mission. We had to be bloody good for a South African crowd to do that.'

Throughout the series the Lions used only 17 players. The Springboks went through twice as many, much to the chagrin of their president, the formidable Dr Danie Craven, then at the height of his long reign as the most powerful autocrat in the game. The Doc was not one to spare the rod. When the Lions had flown into Jan Smuts Airport a few months earlier, he had told them, perhaps with tongue only partially in cheek, 'Welcome, and please don't wreck the place like the last Lions.' The wreckage wrought by McBride and his troops was infinitely more serious in that it was almost all done on the field.

When they had finished with the best his country could find, Craven was not amused at being forced to preside over a series where the 'Boks failed to win a single Test. When it was all over, even the hard-nosed Brits felt that Danie had gone a bit over the top. J.J. almost began to feel sorry for the opposition. Almost.

'Dr Craven presented the blazers to the new Springboks after the last Test and said something to the effect that he doubted if they were fit to wear them. I thought that was below the belt. Those boys had put their bodies on the line. They never said anything to us at the receptions. They weren't a friendly bunch but they'd done their best for their country. They're a vain rugby nation, like Australia. You beat them and they can't take it.'

Despite that, the Lions left their hotels intact – well, most of them. J.J. recalls the 'mad moments', and one of them happened in East London during the final month of the epic. 'I remember leaving the hotel there on the Monday morning and seeing Tommy David's bed hanging over the balcony above the entrance. There was a lot of fun but it wasn't a wrecking tour like '68 had been.

'The '74 Lions had a very professional attitude but without the professional back-up which they get today. I always thought we were sent away to get the results without any back-up. We were given 50p a day, £3.50 a week, which meant that people from a hard background, like Bobby Windsor, suffered. We made sacrifices but it made us hungry and rugby was the only thing on our mind. Nothing else mattered, even when they put us in some second-rate hotels. We left one of them, in the centre of Johannesburg, because it wasn't good enough, but we still had a lot of fun. There was some drinking but not an enormous amount.'

There were plenty of sorrows to be drowned during that soggy New Zealand winter when the Lions went down the Swanee 3–1. J.J. is in no doubt where the blame for the failure of the New Zealand expedition lay: 'Bad management. All that bickering with the press wasn't on. The senior players, and that included me, should have pulled it together. John Dawes was pouting with the press all the time. We should have told him we were going about it the wrong way. You're always liable to get bad publicity on a tour if things aren't going well. That's part of top international sport and people like Carwyn James and Willie John McBride could handle that.

'We were the better team but we were our own worst enemies. The All Blacks were in disarray and we still weren't good enough to beat them. We blew that tour. I would have taken Mighty Mouse [Ian McLauchlan] as captain instead of Phil Bennett. The tour affected Phil greatly. He was under so much pressure that it affected his game and John Bevan, the number two outside-half, was possibly playing better rugby at the time.

'Terry Cobner more or less took over the captaincy towards the end as pack leader but he was very homesick. We had a very strong pack but we were a bit weak at scrum-half. If J.P.R. or Gareth had been there, we would have won the series.'

Williams at least had the satisfaction of beating the All Blacks, albeit just the once, his try making all the difference at Christchurch in the second of the four matches before injury forced him to miss the finale in Auckland. It brought his Lions try record to five in seven matches, a strike rate fractionally superior even to Tony O'Reilly's six in ten.

As good as ever the following season, J.J. assumed personal responsibility for delivering the first triple Triple Crown in the history of the International Championship. As a demonstration of his priceless knack for winning tight matches, there was nothing to beat the try he scored to win the tightest match of all, against Ireland at Lansdowne Road on 4 March 1978, when he found himself pitched into direct opposition to a temporary but famous Irish right wing, Mike Gibson.

At 13–13, with the Triple Crown hat-trick and history hanging in the balance, Gareth Edwards and Steve Fenwick created just enough space for their left wing to break the thunderous deadlock with a streak to the corner for the decisive try. It was truly the stuff of legends, but not even J.J.'s devastating finish might have been enough had his namesake not played that dirty trick to prevent Gibson from scoring.

'J.P.R. gave him a whack that day. He and Gibson were not exactly soulmates. I got on well with Mike. He wasn't a typical rugby man in that he didn't indulge in any kind of carousing. He was a very professional man in every sense but he wasn't J.P.R.'s cup of tea. J.P.R. would train like a nutter and do things other players would never think of.

'Against Natal on the '74 tour, he flattened the local hero, Tommy Bedford, in front of the grandstand at King's Park. It caused such an uproar that when the Coke cans and the oranges started flying, we all fled to the middle of the pitch because it was the only place where we could get out of range. After that J.P.R. was despised in Durban. After the tour he stayed on to further his medical career, and where did he go? Durban!

'He was the most competitive player I ever played with or against, although not the most talented. He was totally unselfish, a terrific team player. J.P.R. would always give you the ball, whereas other players, like Andy Irvine, wouldn't.'

Since retiring after the fourth Triple Crown in 1979, J.J. went into business the following year. His company, J.J. Williams Painting Services Ltd, is an expanding concern employing 25 people. He may not quite have reached millionaire status but the lawns at his luxury home near Bridgend extend far enough to have demanded the investment of £10,000 in a motor-mower capable of tackling the job. Speed, though, is still a family speciality. His daughter Kathryn is a British Under-20 international hurdler, elder son James (16) has represented Welsh schools in the 1,500 metres and younger son Rhys (14) is the Welsh junior backstroke champion.

Williams was the middle man in a trinity of Welsh wings responsible for causing unholy trouble on behalf of the Lions. Their stirring deeds spanned a period of four decades, beginning with the late Dewi Bebb in the '60s and ending with Ieuan Evans in the '90s. By then the triumvirate's aggregate collection of international tries totalled 63, Bebb with 12 from 42 matches, J.J. 17 from 36 and Evans 34 from 78.

Bebb's total does him less than justice. Arguably the outstanding wing of his generation, he played at a time when international rugby was played almost in a strait-jacket, when opportunities for wings to score tries were so limited that matches were often won by a penalty goal to nothing. In four successive international seasons, 1960, 1961, 1962 and 1963, Welsh three-quarters managed a collective total of four tries – and Bebb scored them all.

A predilection for producing the majority of those tries against England guaranteed his popularity from the outset, a try on his debut at Cardiff in January 1959 ensuring Wales, under the captaincy of Clem Thomas, a 5–0 win over the old enemy.

A double Lion who appeared in more Tests, eight, than either of his celebrated successors, Bebb retired in 1967 to concentrate on a career in television, where his success exploded one of the great sporting myths: that nice guys always come second. The great multitude at his funeral after his death at the age of 57 following a short illness bore silent testament to the passing of a lovely man.

Evans, born on the very Saturday in March 1964 when Bebb helped Wales to a share of the Five Nations title on the strength of drawing with France in Paris, went one better than his predecessors and became a triple Lion, touring Australia, New Zealand and South Africa over a period of eight years, winning Tests in all three countries.

By the time he retired from international competition, his career with Wales had assumed record-breaking proportions. Over a period of ten years he played more matches (71) and scored more tries (33) for his country than anyone else, figures which would have been even more imposing had some serious injuries not taken a large chunk out of the early years in particular. Five dislocations of the right shoulder, between October 1985 and October 1989, made his subsequent success all the more satisfying.

As if fate had not dealt him enough adversity, the most savage blow came during his 28-match run as captain in the grotesque shape of a dislocated ankle. Miraculously, he was playing for Wales again five months later thanks to his medical care, his courageous refusal to be beaten and, most significantly of all, the prompt attention of the prominent orthopaedic specialist John Fairclough. He had been at the Cardiff–Llanelli match in case of precisely the sort of emergency which unfolded before his eyes after a routine tackle. 'This was no ordinary dislocation,' said Evans. 'My left foot was at a right angle to my left leg. It was literally hanging off. If John Fairclough had not been at the match quite by chance, I would never have played again. When it happened, someone said to John, "Ieuan's gone down. Looks as though his boot's come off."

'"Yes," came the reply. 'But his foot's still in it.'"

Nobody can ever say he had it easy. As well as his struggles against a series of bad breaks, Evans spent most of his time in a struggling Welsh team and still came up trumps. Nicknamed 'Merlin the Magician' after cutting a swathe through Scotland for a famous solo try at Cardiff in February 1988, he revelled in the rarefied atmosphere of the Lions, and never more so than at the Sydney Football Stadium on 15 July 1989.

With the rubber level at one win each, Evans clinched the series for the Lions and David Campese lost it for Australia in what became known as 'Campo's clanger'. As he attempted to run the ball out from his own in-goal area in typical Campese style, Evans forced him to commit hara-kiri instead by chucking a pass in the general direction of the Wallaby full-back Greg Martin. It landed so obligingly at Evans's feet that he only had to fall on it to claim the try and the Lions won 19–18.

Eight years later in South Africa, he finished as he had started: a winning Lion, albeit a wounded one, during a series when Scott Gibbs, having elbowed Will Carling out of the Test team in New Zealand four years earlier, made such a shuddering impact in midfield that he emerged with the ultimate accolade of 'The Lion of the Lions'. He will surely emulate Evans by embarking on a third successive tour, to Australia and New Zealand in 2001, and make an even greater contribution.

Still peerless on the right wing, Evans was in the throes of a fitness test in Durban for the second match at King's Park when he tore a groin muscle. 'Merlin' had played his last international. He retired from Welsh duty a few months later and stayed retired when new coach Graham Henry invited him to make himself available shortly after starting his final season at Bath.

Rumours that he has asked J.J. Williams to reappear on the left wing have yet to be confirmed . . .

16

The Warrior Prince

When Ray Gravell opened the last of the five telegrams waiting for him in the visitors' dressing-room at the Parc des Princes that momentous Saturday in Paris, he burst into a flood of tears. The message from home in Mynydd-y-Garreg contained no more than 12 words of stark simplicity: 'To my dear Raymond, best wishes Stop. All our love Stop. Mammy and Toodles.'

The rest of the team had no way of knowing that the snivelling new boy was destined to become the warrior prince of Welsh centres. Nor had they any way of knowing that he had endured a personal tragedy of terrible magnitude, that nine years earlier Jack Gravell had committed suicide by shotgun and that his son, his only child, had made the gruesome discovery.

Wales, having chosen a team stuffed with six new caps, fore and aft, had been in a state of mounting anxiety about their chances, and one look round the dressing-room after Gravell had read his last telegram would have suggested that the match would be nothing less than a crying shame. Any minute and the team would be called outside into the cold red-bricked corridor leading along the tunnel, through the large, automatically operated glass doors and out into the stadium. Gravell, by his own admission, had reduced himself to 'a nervous wreck'. Yet when the call came, he felt an inspiration pumping up inside him, an irresistible supply of power as a direct result of the telegram from his mother and Toodles the cat.

'We lined up side by side in the tunnel, waiting for the go-ahead to take the field,' he said. 'I don't know who he was but he was a big French forward. I didn't hit him in anger. It was a punch on the shoulder and I remember him looking at me as if I was mad, shaking his head and saying, "Crazy Welshman. You crazy Welshman."

'Out on the field, I deliberately stood beside Gareth Edwards for the anthems. To watch your heroes is one thing, but to stand and play alongside your heroes . . .

'Standing there, I felt something I had never felt before or since. I felt a presence. I had never heard such noise before, the firecrackers, the Dax band, and yet I felt this amazing presence, a surge of energy. I felt so strong. I don't know what it was but I was damned sure that somewhere, somehow, my father's influence was there. His spirit took over that day. I never felt as strong as I did then. I felt emotionally charged. Physically, I felt fearless. Totally fearless. Nothing afterwards was ever quite like that first game in Paris. Nothing could ever quite compare with how I felt that day.

'It's hard to explain, but one thing in particular had a lot to do with it. I was fulfilling my father's dream. It was beyond the wildest of my wildest dreams that one day I would play for Wales, but what mattered that day was that I had fulfilled his dream. It was as if his spirit had made me twice the man.

'He had wanted me to be an outside-half and a champion 100-yard sprinter. He adored Cliff Morgan and idolised Bleddyn Williams. My father was such a huge influence on me. He had a crop of red hair, a 50-inch chest and I adored him. He was my hero, my god, my friend. He showed me things not known to kings. He taught me to shoot rabbits and to skin them. He taught me about life.

'My father was obviously under huge stress. He had slipped a disc in his back whilst underground. He'd go to work for a month, then the pain would get the better of him and he couldn't work. His pride took one hell of a blow and he committed suicide.

'I had been playing in an Under-15 Carmarthenshire trial match at Ammanford. When I got home, he'd gone for a walk with the dog and his gun. When it got dark and he hadn't come back, my mother began to worry. I found him on top of the mountain, in the middle of the night. He was 42 years of age. I was 14.

'For years I didn't accept that he had committed suicide. I do have a pang of guilt about it which comes back now and again to haunt me. I remember as a boy of 13 or 14 being very proud of my family but, on occasions, slightly embarrassed by them as well, which I suppose is a fairly natural experience for kids the world over. You're entering your teens and keen to make an impression on your own.

'I remember playing in the Under-15s for Carmarthen in September 1965. I saw him there watching me play and I was embarrassed that he was there. Why, I don't know. After the game, he was waiting outside and I showed my embarrassment. He said, "Right. I won't come and see you again."

'I didn't think anything of it. But that still hurts me to this day. I have my own little daughter now. She's three, and if she's at a little disco they put on for the kids, she'll say, "Go away, Dad." So long as Dad's dancing about five yards behind her, she's happy. I understand that, but I didn't understand it back then.

'My father faced danger, as every coalminer did whenever he put on his working kit and went below. To me, they were real men. Fearless men. My first recollection is of the lovely leathery smell of a rugby ball which my father gave me as a present when I was a kid of four or five, along with a pair of boots. I can still smell that ball to this day.

'Rugby, and I firmly believe this, was my salvation, otherwise I would have gone completely off the rails, especially after my father's death. I saw what it did to my mother and I'm lucky that rugby gave me some kind of discipline. Mind you, it gave me acres of fear as well.'

All the fearing that Saturday afternoon in Paris had been done by the French, from the start, when a miscued drop kick from Gareth Edwards bounced perfectly for an unmarked Steve Fenwick to score with the first touch of his international career, to the very end, when another new cap, Graham Price, ran some 70 yards to apply a thunderous finish, the ultimate *coup de grâce*. The new centre with the fiery Celtic beard had made it possible with what was to become his trademark, the bone-crunching tackle. 'We scared the French,' he said. 'We frightened them, and that takes some doing.'

The match ended France 10 Wales 25, five tries to one, with one for almost every new cap. An unfancied Welsh team had achieved more than a stunning victory. They had given the rest of northern-hemisphere rugby early notice that the only issue to be resolved in seasons to come would be who finished second.

That first season ended with the title returning to Wales on the strength of a crushing victory over Ireland at the Arms Park which Gravell will never forget, not for the sheer size of the win, 32–4, but for the funniest thing he ever heard anyone utter on a rugby field. That it centred around Willie John McBride, the legendary Irish Lion in his last match, made it all the better.

'There were only about five minutes to go when Phil Bennett chipped through. Sometimes, even in the hullabaloo of an international, you can hear a distinctive voice, and as we all chased this kick, I could hear this gasping voice very distinctly. It was McBride. "Kick ahead, Ireland. Kick ahead, Ireland. Any ******* head!"

'I still find that funny. As you get older, you realise it is only a game after all, and even I sometimes begin to think like that. There was McBride, his team down the pan, but refusing to give up. All was lost and yet all was not lost. McBride had put it all into context.'

As seminal victories go, history will surely put Paris on 18 January 1975 in a league of its own. In five seasons of Five Nations competition, Wales won two Grand Slams, four championship titles and four Triple Crowns on the trot. Gravell, a permanent fixture for the next four seasons, had timed his arrival to perfection.

More than anyone else of his generation, he raised Welsh pride to an almost unbeatable level. Even the All Blacks wondered how they had survived at Cardiff in 1978 until Andy Haden's unashamed revelation that he and his second-row sparring partner Frank Oliver had conspired to create a diversion from the very line-out which led to Brian McKechnie's winning penalty.

Gravell played with such a buccaneering spirit that it was never difficult to imagine him as a latter-day Owain Glyndwr in size ten boots, a hard man every bit as ferocious as he looked, a man who launched a thousand or so crash-balls, each one designed to explode a hole in the opposition midfield. And yet for all his undoubted bravado, Gravell the man felt such a deep sense of insecurity that he was – indeed, still is – in constant need of reassurance.

J.J. Williams, his room-mate on that first occasion in Paris, suffered from an early exposure to the newcomer's innate uncertainty. 'I didn't sleep at all on the Friday night, not a wink. It wasn't fair on John. I kept him awake all night and then, blow me, the first pass I gave him went about two feet above his head!

'But the joy after the game! The champagne corks, the realisation that we had beaten France against all the odds and Cliff Jones, the chairman of selectors, presenting me with my cap and saying, "Ray, by the time you've finished playing, you will have a drawerful of caps." It was a great day all round.'

For one who believed passionately in Welsh nationalism, there was only one thing better than beating the French and that was beating the English, something he managed three times in four attempts between 1975 and 1982. The innate sense of injustice he felt at the hand Wales had been dealt by their neighbours gave him a perception of the 'old enemy' which extended beyond the annual rivalry on the rugby field.

Gravell's emergence as an international player of growing repute coincided with the rise of Dafydd Iwan as a folk-singer-cum-political activist, a strident voice of the Welsh Language Society. Tradition decreed that on Friday nights before an international the Welsh team would go *en masse* to the cinema. On one occasion before a Scottish match, Gravell was given permission to go to a Cardiff theatre instead and see one of his heroes in concert.

'I stood at the back of the hall and when Dafydd saw me he called me on to the stage and we sang a duet. His songs aroused in me a Welshness which I suppose was always there but which I wasn't conscious of. He made me aware of it. He gave me a lot of the Welsh history which I didn't get at school because all we had been given was British history.

'He made me more aware of the Welsh language. It is ours, ours to keep and nurture, not to impose on anyone, but we do have a responsibility as Welsh people to maintain it and strengthen it. I am indebted to many people in my life and Dafydd is one of them.

'His songs inspired me. At Llanelli I used to sing them in the dressing-room. I'd sit there and sing out loud, loud enough for it to have a psychological effect on the opposition, because they could hear it all right. Players who had never been to Stradey before must have wondered what they were letting themselves in for. I know it made some of them uneasy.'

Gravell saw the English as 'the oppressor', and still does. 'England was *the* game. It went beyond that because, to me and most of the Welsh players, it was more than a game. To beat England was a small way of redressing the balance of injustice over the centuries. It goes back to 1536 and the Act of Union. This rule was imposed on us in such a way that Welsh children were not allowed to speak Welsh. Having said that, one realised it was only a game of rugby, but those feelings were there in the subconscious and from time to time they bubbled to the surface.

'The England match, therefore, was a challenge to the pride of our nation. It gave me immense satisfaction to beat them, especially to beat them at Twickenham. To march into the lions' den, so to speak, and come out victorious was a re-enactment of something our forefathers would love to have done: righting an old wrong.'

The notion, therefore, of a Welshman playing alongside an English-man, never mind taking orders from him, would have been little short of anathema to someone steeped in the culture surrounding Mynydd-y-Garreg, his beloved Rocky Mountain of West Wales. In the spring of 1980 the Lions offered him precisely such a scenario, another glorious reminder of their enduring appeal as a unifying force unique in rugby.

When the Lions selectors congregated in Dublin at the end of the Five Nations championship to finalise the chosen few, Gravell feared that he may have drowned his chances in a bottle of Captain Morgan's rum. Denied a place among the 1977 Lions by injury, he had spent the entire 1980 championship among the Welsh replacements.

Wales were finishing their season in Ireland and another Welsh reserve, Derek Quinnell, had arranged to meet his employer on the Friday night at his suite in the Shelbourne Hotel. He invited 'Grav' to join him. 'There was a bar in the corner and before I knew it I'd knocked back a lot of rum,' said Gravell. 'We had a bite to eat and then it was off to the pictures with the rest of the squad.

'I was conscious that I'd had a fair bit to drink and I was even more conscious when I found myself sitting in the cinema next to Keith Rowlands, the chairman of selectors. I was reeking of rum but I was coherent – at least, I thought I was coherent. The next thing I knew, I got a nudge and this voice said, "Come on, Grav, we're off."

'It was Keith. I'd slept through the entire picture with my head on his shoulder. Keith was the Welsh selector on the Lions panel and it dawned on me the next day that I might not have done my chances much good. I could imagine them ruling me out by saying, "He's no good. Can't hold his rum!"

'Well, when I joined the Lions a few weeks later, the coach, Noel Murphy, said, "Your man gave you the vote." Keith had not held it against me. "Carrots", which is what I called him because of his ginger hair, had stood by me, which was great.'

Gravell's selection, at a time when he had achieved just about everything there was to achieve with his country, presented him with the chance to broaden his horizons in every sense. As well as giving him the opportunity to prove himself not merely the best in Wales but the best in Great Britain and Ireland, the trip would also give him the opportunity to get to know a few English foes, chief among them William Blackledge Beaumont.

The Lions may have lost the series 3–1, but whatever they may have lacked, it certainly had nothing to do with disunity. 'We were all for one and one for all,' said Gravell. 'Barry John had told me years before that if I ever got the chance to go on a Lions tour I had to take it because I would remember it for the rest of my life. He was right. It *was* different, if only because you forgot differences.

'Billy Beaumont was tremendous. I never thought I would respond to and respect an Englishman so much, and I am glad I did. I respect him so much. What he did more than anything was lead by example. He took all the blows, including the criticism after we'd lost the series. I nicknamed him "Bobo" and he mimicked my accent. I used to smoke like a trooper in those days and every so often he'd be asking me for a fag. With people like Billy, Paul Dodge, Peter Wheeler and Clive Woodward, I got a different impression of English players from the one I had been given. Those guys broke the barrier of bigotry which I had in my mind. They were great to tour with, but once South Africa was over and Wales had to go back to Twickenham, I wanted to beat them all the more, if that was possible!'

There are two untold anecdotes from the Lions' African safari which say everything about Gravell and his new English friends. The first underlined his readiness to go to any lengths in support of the team cause, even if it brought the wrath of the crowd howling around his ears. The second, at the end of the tour, illustrated how one English player turned the tables on the 'home fires' controversy raging at the time.

The fifth match of the tour brought the Lions into collision with Orange Free State in the rarefied atmosphere of Bloemfontein and a fly-half of rare goalkicking quality in De Wet Ras. The Lions, seven points down, were in some danger of being left high and dry by De Wet's strategic bombardment when the tourists decided to make use of Gravell's capacity as a hit-man *par excellence*.

'The way De Wet Ras kicked the ball out there in the thin air, it could travel for days! We were under immense pressure in the first ten minutes and Peter Morgan, another Llanelli man but playing out of position at full-back, was being pulled all over the place.

'After a short while Billy came up to me and said, "Grav, do something about their number ten." Ollie Campbell was playing outside-half for the Lions and I said to Ollie, "Next line-out, you go for my man and leave the outside-half to me." The ball duly came back on their side from the line-out and De Wet Ras hammered it downfield. He was standing there admiring his kick when I charged up at a hundred miles an hour. I could have stopped. I could have avoided the tackle, but there was only one thing going through my mind at the time and that was, "Ah, to hell with it, I'm going in."

'I carried on, laid him out, broke his shoulder. It was a bad tackle, a sending-off offence, but it had the desired effect. The crowd went mad. Billy said, "Grav, what have you done?" I said, "Billy, I've got him a late one, early!" The ref didn't see it but I don't think it would have made any difference if he had. They were quite lenient in those days.'

De Wet Ras took no further part in that match, nor for a good many more. The Lions scored four second-half tries and squeezed home with four points to spare. Almost as significantly, their *agent provocateur* lived to tell the tale.

By the time the tour ended in Cape Town with the Lions winning the last Test, Gravell had become the only three-quarter to appear in the entire series, having started as a replacement wing for an injured John Carleton in the opening Test when the sheer power of his performance forced the selectors to make room for him in midfield.

If the 'Boks had not got the message about Gravell after the Free State match, they certainly got it when he made his presence felt at the expense of South Africa's match-winning wing Gerrie Germishuys. Not to put too fine a point on it, the former electricity-board lineman from way out west had splattered him at the first opportunity.

'I ran at him and smashed him down. I said, "You're not going to score against me, Germishuys, you 'Bok b******." There were a lot of verbals in that series, as you'd expect. He didn't score against me but he did score twice on the other wing, and although we lost, the Lions seemed pretty pleased with me. Syd Millar, the manager, came up and said, "Grav, I'm only going to tell you one thing: you're in the next Test," which surprised me, because the next Test wasn't for a fortnight.'

The second tale of Gravell's developing relationship with an English colleague revolved around an incident which took place on the last weekend of the tour in the room he shared with Wheeler. The celebrations had gone on long into the night before a jubilant Welshman finally made it back to his room.

'Peter and I got on so well that during that last week it had been arranged that he and I would finish off the tour together. Well, when I got back to the room there was smoke coming from the bathroom. It seemed as if something was on fire but Peter was laughing and joking. "Grav," he said, "I'm burning off a bit of excess baggage – your T-shirts." I began to protest, but then he said, "I'm getting my own back."

'"For what?"

'"All those holiday homes you've burnt in Wales."'

The late Carwyn James would have liked that. Nine years earlier the Lions had beaten the All Blacks under the direction of Gravell's celebrated mentor at Llanelli at a time when they were so good that not even Ian Kirkpatrick's New Zealanders could hold them. When the tidal wave of public support demanded that he be swept into control of the Welsh team, James, not unreasonably, asked to be allowed to do the job his way or not at all.

His head would be on the block so, naturally enough, he wanted to pick the team, which would mean dispensing with the selection committee, alias the Big Five – or, more often than not in times of trouble, the Little Five. James had truly been a man ahead of his time. How foolish, and how petty, of the Welsh Rugby Union not to have granted him his wish.

'Carwyn was a very complex character, a lovely, delightful man who understood people while perhaps not understanding himself,' said Gravell. 'We loved him at Stradey, even the toughest of the tough. He knew how to get the best out of every individual, and this is a true story. Llanelli were playing up at Coventry in the early '70s, and I was marking David Duckham. Now Carwyn knew more about psychology 30-odd years ago than modern-day psychologists know. I'm convinced of that. He could make you believe that you were actually better than you were.

'He was a preacher. He'd stand there, always immaculately dressed, hair back and always the cigarette. He'd go round each player one by one, and he always spoke to me in Welsh. As he stood there in front of me, this is what he said. "Raymond [only Carwyn and my mother always called me Raymond, never Grav or Ray], today you are playing against arguably one of the greatest three-quarters in the world, David Duckham of England and the Lions." His words physically moved me, back a few inches. Then he went on, "I'll tell you this, Raymond. You are a *better* centre than David Duckham."

'Now I knew he was being economical with the truth. I knew he was lying, but this is the strange thing which I cannot describe. I believed him. Call that blind faith if you like, but I believed him. I scored a try against David which won the game. I think David had an off-day, but it was still quite uncanny. Carwyn had this inexplicable, magical charisma about him.'

James, his Wales ambitions unfulfilled, had moved into journalism by the time Gravell had been offered a fortune to turn professional by Hull rugby league club. They made their approach immediately after Llanelli had beaten Bridgend in the 1976 Welsh Cup semi-final at Swansea.

'I was walking across the field to the clubhouse when I was approached by Mike Page, a director of Hull, and Arthur Bunting, the coach. They said they'd liked the way I'd played and asked if I would be interested in signing for them. The upshot of all that was that my phone hardly stopped ringing for the next month.

'The final offer was £25,000, £15,000 of it as a signing-on fee, tax-free, and £10,000 over a two-year period. In 1976 that was really big money. But I say this quite unashamedly: I was afraid to go. I didn't want to leave West Wales. I was afraid of the unknown. They said rugby league would suit me, which it probably would have. I wasn't afraid of the physical confrontation. Far from it, I thrived on all that, but I don't mind admitting I was afraid of leaving Wales. I have admired many rugby league players for their professionalism over the years but I never had any regrets about turning the Hull offer down.'

His international career over in 1982, Gravell played on for his beloved Llanelli, smashing every appearance record before calling it a day. Even then, after almost 500 matches for the Scarlets, he could still be found in the entertainment business, whether it was behind a microphone for Radio Wales, in front of the television camera or on location with the odd Oscar-winning actor. By then Gravell had become a card-carrying member of Equity, although he needed a great deal more than that to land parts in such dramas as *Rebecca's Daughter* with Peter O'Toole and, more recently, with Jeremy Irons and Miranda Richardson in *Damage*, for which he was cast by none other than the famous Louis Malle himself.

It had all begun as a bit of fun ten years earlier when John Hefin, head of drama at BBC Wales, invited Gravell to make a guest appearance on the long-running soap opera *Pobol y Cwm*. All he had to do was walk into the pub and ask for a packet of cigarettes. It may not be the politically correct thing for an athlete to do now but, as a smoker himself, he saw nothing wrong with it then.

He played one of the leading roles in another film, *Filipina Dream Girl*, starring Bill Maynard and Charlie Drake, which happened to catch the attention of one of Hollywood's finest. 'This call came out of the blue one day saying that Louis Malle wanted to see me and could I get to London,' he said. 'I thought it was a wind-up but then, to my amazement, I began to realise that they were being serious. I broke out in a cold sweat. Louis Malle wanted to see me? About a film? This was one of the great film directors of our time, who had had an apprenticeship as a director with Jacques Cousteau.

'Anyway, I went to see him and it turned out to be more of a chat than an interview. He told me in that French-American accent of his that he was interested in rugby and that he had once been to the Arms Park. I said, "Mr Malle, I am not an actor. I mean, I am not a trained actor."

'"Ah," he said. "But I saw you in *Filipina Dream Girl*."

'"Yes," I said. "But in that I was just being myself."

'And then he said something to me which I will never, ever forget. "My friend" – and he lifted his little finger to emphasise the point – "being yourself is the most difficult thing for any actor to portray."

'I caught the train home. When I got back to Mynydd-y-Garreg, my wife Mari asked me how I'd got on, whether I'd got a part. I said I didn't think so and asked her to get some milk from the fridge. She opened it and there were two bottles of champagne inside. They had phoned to say I'd got the part!'

On location in London, Malle discovered that the brawny Welshman who had begun his working life labouring on the roads around Llanelli could do more than act. 'Louis said one day, "Ray, can you whistle?" I started whistling a tune and he said, "Stop. What is that called?"'

Gravell had given him a burst of an old Welsh love song, 'Ar lan y mor' ('on the seashore'). Malle liked it so much that he altered the script to include it in the film, so that Ray, playing the part of Jeremy Irons's chauffeur, could whistle while he worked on cleaning the car.

'I spent three weeks filming in London and they invited me to the première in the West End. It was all, "Hello, Louis, baby!" as if I'd been going to those sorts of things all my life. I only had a small part but when they rolled the names up on the screen, there it was in big capital letters: Raymond Gravell. Very intoxicating.'

His dad would have loved it . . .

Appendix 1

The Test Lions of Wales

Player	Birthplace	Club	Tests	Tours
Ackerman, Robert *born 2 March 1961*	Ebbw Vale	Newport	2	NZ 1983
Bassett, Jack *born 11 July 1905* *died 19 February 1989*	Trebanog	Penarth	5	NZ, Aus 1930
Bateman, Allan *born 6 March 1965*	Maesteg	Richmond	1	SA 1997
Bebb, Dewi *born 7 August 1938* *died 14 March 1996*	Bangor	Swansea	8	SA 1962; NZ, Aus 1966
Bennett, Phil *born 24 October 1948*	Felinfoel	Llanelli	8	SA 1974; NZ 1977
Bevan, John *born 28 October 1950*	Tylorstown	Cardiff	1	NZ 1971
Bowcott, Harry *born 30 April 1907*	Cardiff	Cardiff	5	NZ, Aus 1930
Burcher, David *born 26 October 1950*	Newport	Newport	1	NZ 1977

Player	Birthplace	Club	Tests	Tours
Cleaver, Billy *born 15 September 1921*	Treorchy	Cardiff	3	NZ, Aus 1950
Cobner, Terry *born 10 January 1946*	Blaenavon	Pontypool	3	NZ 1977
Davies, Cliff *born 12 December 1919* *died 28 January 1967*	Kenfig Hill	Cardiff	1	NZ, Aus 1950
Davies, Dai *born 2 May 1925*	Penygraig	Somerset Police	3	NZ, Aus 1950
Davies, Gareth *born 29 September 1956*	Carmarthen	Cardiff	1	SA 1980
Davies, Gerald *born 7 February 1945*	Llansaint	London Welsh	5	SA 1968; NZ 1971
Davies, Harold *born 5 December 1898* *died 29 March 1976*	Newport	Newport	1	SA 1924
Davies, Mervyn *born 9 December 1946*	Gorseinon	Swansea	8	NZ 1971; SA 1974
Davies, Terry *born 24 September 1933*	Llwynhendy	Llanelli	2	NZ, Aus 1959
Dawes, John *born 29 June 1940*	Chapel of Ease	London Welsh	4	NZ 1971
Edwards, Gareth *born 12 July 1947*	Gwaun-cae-Gurwen	Cardiff	10	SA 1968; NZ 1971; SA 1974
Evans, Gareth *born 2 November 1953*	Newport	Newport	3	NZ 1977
Evans, Gwyn *born 6 September 1957*	Maesteg	Maesteg	2	NZ 1983

Player	Birthplace	Club	Tests	Tours
Evans, Ieuan *born 21 March 1964*	Capel Dewi	Llanelli	7	Aus 1989; NZ 1993; SA 1997
Evans, Robert (Bob) *born 16 February 1921*	Rhymney	Newport	6	NZ, Aus 1950
Evans, Roddy *born 19 December 1934*	Cowbridge	Cardiff	4	NZ, Aus 1959
Evans, Trefor *born 26 November 1947*	Chorley	Swansea	1	NZ 1977
Faull, John *born 30 June 1933*	Swansea	Swansea	4	NZ, Aus 1959
Fenwick, Steve *born 23 July 1951*	Nantgarw	Bridgend	4	NZ 1977
Gibbs, Scott *born 23 January 1971*	Bridgend	Swansea	5	NZ 1993; SA 1997
Gravell, Ray *born 12 September 1951*	Kidwelly	Llanelli	4	SA 1980
Griffiths, Gareth *born 27 November 1931*	Penygraig	Cardiff	3	SA 1955
Griffiths, Vince *born 29 May 1901* *died 7 January 1967*	Pontypridd	Newport	2	SA 1924
Hall, Mike *born 13 October 1965*	Bridgend	Bridgend	1	Aus 1989
Harding, Rowe *born 10 September 1901* *died 10 February 1991*	Swansea	Swansea	3	SA 1924
Hayward, Don *born 30 June 1925*	Pontypool	Newbridge	3	NZ, Aus 1950
Holmes, Terry *born 10 March 1957*	Cardiff	Cardiff	1	SA 1980; NZ 1983

Player	Birthplace	Club	Tests	Tours
Hopkins, Ray 'Chico' *born 8 July 1946*	Maesteg	Maesteg	1	NZ 1971
Jenkins, Neil *born 8 July 1971*	Church Village	Pontypridd	3	SA 1997
Jenkins, Vivian *born 2 November 1911*	Port Talbot	London Welsh	1	SA 1938
John, Barry *born 6 January 1945*	Cefneithin	Llanelli/Cardiff	5	SA 1968; NZ 1971
John, Roy *born 3 December 1925 died 30 September 1980*	Neath	Neath	6	NZ, Aus 1950
Jones, David Kenneth *born 7 August 1941*	Cross Hands	Llanelli/Cardiff	6	SA 1962; NZ, Aus 1966
Jones, Elfet *born 29 April 1912 died 5 October 1989*	Llanelli	Llanelli	2	SA 1938
Jones, Ivor *born 10 December 1901 died 16 November 1982*	Loughor	Llanelli	5	NZ, Aus 1930
Jones, Ken *born 30 December 1921*	Blaenavon	Newport	3	NZ, Aus 1950
Jones, Kingsley *born 5 August 1935*	Pontypridd	Cardiff	4	SA 1962
Jones, Lewis *born 11 April 1931*	Gorseinon	Devonport Services	3	NZ, Aus 1950
Jones, Marsden *born 1893 died 5 January 1955*	Swansea	London Welsh	2	SA 1924
Jones, Robert *born 10 November 1965*	Trebanos	Swansea	3	Aus 1989; NZ 1993

Player	Birthplace	Club	Tests	Tours
Jones, Staff *born 4 January 1959*	Ynysybwl	Pontypool	3	NZ 1983
Lewis, Allan *born 26 September 1941*	Crumlin	Abertillery	3	NZ, Aus 1966
Martin, Allan *born 11 December 1948*	Port Talbot	Aberavon	1	NZ 1977; SA 1980
Matthews, Jack *born 21 June 1920*	Bridgend	Cardiff	6	NZ, Aus 1950
Meredith, Bryn *born 21 November 1930*	Cwmbran	Newport	8	SA 1955; NZ, Aus 1959; SA 1962
Meredith, Courtenay *born 23 September 1926*	Pontypridd	Neath	4	SA 1955
Morgan, Cliff *born 7 April 1930*	Trebanog	Cardiff	4	SA 1955
Morgan, Eddie *born 18 December 1913* *died 16 April 1978*	Pontardawe	Swansea	2	SA 1938
Morgan, Haydn *born 30 July 1936*	Oakdale	Abertillery	4	NZ, Aus 1959; SA 1962
Morley, Jack *born 28 July 1909* *died 3 March 1972*	Newport	Newport	3	NZ, Aus 1930
Morris, Dewi *born 9 February 1964*	Crickhowell	Orrell	3	NZ 1993
Norris, Howard *born 11 June 1934*	Porth	Cardiff	3	NZ, Aus 1966
Norster, Robert *born 23 June 1957*	Blaina	Cardiff	3	NZ 1983; Aus 1989
O'Shea, John *born 2 June 1940*	Weston-super-Mare	Cardiff	1	SA 1968

Player	Birthplace	Club	Tests	Tours
Parker, Dai *born 8 August 1904* *died 16 June 1965*	Llansamlet	Swansea	5	NZ, Aus 1930
Pask, Alun *born 10 September 1937* *died 1 November 1995*	Blackwood	Abertillery	8	SA 1962; NZ, Aus 1966
Poole, Howard *born September 1906*	Cardiff	Cardiff	1	NZ, Aus 1930
Price, Brian *born 30 October 1937*	Bargoed	Newport	4	NZ, Aus 1966
Price, Graham *born 24 November 1951*	Alexandria	Pontypool	12	NZ 1977; SA 1980; NZ 1983
Price, Malcolm *born 8 December 1937*	Pontypool	Pontypool	5	NZ, Aus 1959
Prosser, Ray *born 2 March 1927*	Pontypool	Pontypool	1	NZ, Aus 1959
Quinnell, Derek *born 22 May 1949*	Llanelli	Llanelli	5	NZ 1971; NZ 1977; SA 1980
Rees, Elgan *born 5 January 1954*	Clydach	Neath	1	NZ 1977; SA 1980
Richards, David *born 23 May 1954*	Cwmgwrach	Swansea	1	SA 1980
Richards, Maurice *born 2 February 1945*	Ystrad, Rhondda	Cardiff	3	SA 1968
Robins, John *born 17 May 1926*	Cardiff	Birkenhead Park	5	NZ, Aus 1950
Robins, Russell *born 21 February 1932*	Pontypridd	Pontypridd	4	SA 1955

Player	Birthplace	Club	Tests	Tours
Rowlands, Keith *born 7 February 1936*	Brithdir	Cardiff	3	SA 1962
Squire, Jeff *born 23 September 1951*	Pontywaun	Newport/ Pontypool	6	NZ 1977; SA 1980; NZ 1983
Stephens, Ian *born 22 May 1952*	Tongwynlais	Bridgend	1	SA 1980; NZ 1983
Stephens, Rees *born 16 April 1922* *died 4 February 1998*	Neath	Neath	2	NZ, Aus 1950
Tanner, Haydn *born 9 January 1917*	Gowerton	Swansea	1	SA 1938
Taylor, John *born 21 July 1945*	Watford	London Welsh	4	SA 1968; NZ 1971
Taylor, Russell *born 2 December 1914* *died 9 October 1965*	Risca	Cross Keys	2	SA 1938
Thomas, Clem *born 28 January 1929* *died 5 September 1996*	Cardiff	Swansea	2	SA 1955
Thomas, Delme *born 12 September 1942*	Bancyfelin	Llanelli	7	NZ, Aus 1966; SA 1968; NZ 1971
Thomas, Malcolm *born 25 April 1929*	Machen	Devonport Services/Newport	4	NZ Aus 1950; NZ Aus 1959
Travers, William 'Bunner' *born 2 December 1913* *died 4 June 1998*	Newport	Newport	2	SA 1938
Watkins, David *born 5 March 1942*	Blaina	Newport	6	NZ, Aus 1966
Watkins, Stuart *born 5 June 1941*	Newport	Newport	3	NZ, Aus 1966

Player	Birthplace	Club	Tests	Tours
Williams, Bleddyn *born 22 February 1923*	Taff's Well	Cardiff	5	NZ, Aus 1950
Williams, Brynmor *born 29 October 1951*	Cardigan	Cardiff	3	NZ 1977
Williams, Clive *born 2 November 1948*	Porthcawl	Swansea	4	NZ 1977; SA 1980
Williams, Denzil *born 17 October 1938*	Trefil	Ebbw Vale	5	NZ, Aus 1966
Williams, J.J. *born 1 April 1948*	Nantyffyllon	Llanelli	7	SA 1974; NZ 1977
Williams, J.P.R. *born 2 March 1949*	Cardiff	London Welsh/ Bridgend	8	NZ 1971; SA 1974
Williams, Rhys *born 14 July 1930* *died 27 January 1993*	Cwmllynfell	Llanelli	10	SA 1955; NZ, Aus 1959
Williams, Billy 'Stoker' *born 19 November 1929*	Gower	Swansea	4	SA 1955
Willis, Rex *born 25 October 1924*	Ystrad, Rhondda	Cardiff	3	NZ, Aus 1950
Windsor, Bobby *born 31 January 1946*	Newport	Pontypool	5	SA 1974; NZ 1977
Young, David *born 27 June 1967*	Aberdare	Cardiff	3	Aus 1989; SA 1997
Young, Jeff *born 16 September 1942*	Blaengarw	Harrogate/ RAF	1	SA 1968

Appendix 2

Lions Records

MOST TEST APPEARANCES

17	Willie John McBride (Ireland)	Tours 5 – 1962, '66, '68, '71, '74
13	Dickie Jeeps (England)	Tours 3 – 1955, '59, '62
12	Mike Gibson (Ireland)	Tours 3 – 1966, '68, '71
12	Graham Price (Wales)	Tours 3 – 1977, '80, '83
10	Tony O'Reilly (Ireland)	Tours 2 – 1955, '59
10	Rhys Williams (Wales)	Tours 2 – 1955, '59
10	Gareth Edwards (Wales)	Tours 3 – 1968, '71, '74
9	Syd Millar (Ireland)	Tours 3 – 1959, '62, '68
9	Andy Irvine (Scotland)	Tours 3 – 1974, '77, '80
8	Bryn Meredith (Wales)	Tours 2 – 1955, '62
8	Dewi Bebb (Wales)	Tours 2 – 1962, '66
8	Mike Campbell-Lamerton (Scotland)	Tours 2 – 1962, '66
8	Alun Pask (Wales)	Tours 2 – 1962, '66
8	Jim Telfer (Scotland)	Tours 2 – 1966, '68
8	Mervyn Davies (Wales)	Tours 2 – 1971, '74
8	Ian McLauchlan (Scotland)	Tours 2 – 1971, '74
8	J.P.R. Williams (Wales)	Tours 2 – 1971, '74
8	Gordon Brown (Scotland)	Tours 3 – 1971, '74, '77
8	Ian McGeechan (Scotland)	Tours 2 – 1974, '77
8	Phil Bennett (Wales)	Tours 2 – 1974, '77
8	Maurice Colclough (England)	Tours 2 – 1980, '83
8	Jeremy Guscott (England)	Tours 3 – 1989, '93, '97

MOST APPEARANCES IN ALL LIONS MATCHES

65 Willie John McBride
64 Mike Gibson
45 Derek Quinnell (Wales)
43 Syd Millar
43 Delme Thomas (Wales)
42 Dickie Jeeps
41 Andy Irvine
40 Gordon Brown
40 Mike Campbell-Lamerton
40 Bryn Meredith
39 Gareth Edwards
38 Tony O'Reilly
37 Noel Murphy (Ireland)
37 Rhys Williams
36 Alun Pask
36 Graham Price
34 Fran Cotton (England)
34 Hugh McLeod (Scotland)
34 Haydn Morgan (Wales)
32 Bill Mulcahy (Ireland)
32 Jim Telfer
31 Jeff Squire (Wales)
30 J.P.R. Williams

MOST TRIES IN TESTS

6 Tony O'Reilly
5 J.J. Williams (Wales)
4 Malcolm Price (Wales)
3 Carl Aarvold (England)
3 Jeff Butterfield (England)
3 Gerald Davies (Wales)
3 David Kenneth Jones (Wales)
2 Gordon Brown
2 Matthew Dawson (England)
2 Laurie Duff (Scotland)
2 Jim Greenwood (Scotland)
2 Andy Irvine
2 Peter Jackson (England)
2 Ken Jones (Wales)
2 Jack Kyle (Ireland)

2 Jimmy Nelson (Ireland)
2 John O'Driscoll (Ireland)
2 Bev Risman (England)
2 David Watkins (Wales)

MOST TRIES FOR THE LIONS IN ALL MATCHES

38 Tony O'Reilly
22 Mike Gibson
22 J.J. Williams
20 Andy Irvine
20 Peter Jackson
17 John C. Bevan (Wales)
16 Ken Jones
16 Tony Novis (England)
14 Malcolm Price
14 John Young (England)
13 Gerald Davies
13 Tom Grace (Ireland)
13 Bleddyn Williams (Wales)
12 John Carleton (England)
12 Noel Murphy
12 Ken Scotland (Scotland)

MOST POINTS IN A LIONS TEST

18 Tony Ward (Ireland) v. South Africa, Cape Town, 1980
18 Gavin Hastings (Scotland) v. New Zealand, Christchurch, 1993
17 Tom Kiernan (Ireland) v. South Africa, Pretoria, 1968
16 Lewis Jones (Wales) v. Australia, Brisbane, 1950
15 Gavin Hastings v. Australia, Sydney, 1989
15 Neil Jenkins (Wales) v. South Africa, Cape Town, 1997
15 Neil Jenkins v. South Africa, Durban, 1997
13 Stewart Wilson (Scotland) v. Australia, Brisbane, 1966
12 Ollie Campbell (Ireland) v. New Zealand, Christchurch, 1983
12 Gavin Hastings v. New Zealand, Wellington, 1993

MOST APPEARANCES ON ONE LIONS TOUR

22 Alun Pask   Australia, New Zealand 1966
21 George Beamish (Ireland)   New Zealand 1930
21 Roy John (Wales)   Australia, New Zealand 1950

21	Tony O'Reilly	Australia, New Zealand 1959
21	Ken Scotland	Australia, New Zealand 1959
21	Rhys Williams	Australia, New Zealand 1959
21	Dewi Bebb	Australia, New Zealand 1966
21	Mike Campbell-Lamerton	Australia, New Zealand 1966
21	Jim Telfer	Australia, New Zealand 1966
20	Blair Mayne (Ireland)	South Africa 1938
20	Bunner Travers (Wales)	South Africa 1938
20	Sammy Walker (Ireland)	South Africa 1938
20	Jack Matthews (Wales)	Australia, New Zealand 1950
20	Bleddyn Williams	Australia, New Zealand 1950
20	Colin McFadyean (England)	Australia, New Zealand 1966
20	David Watkins	Australia, New Zealand 1966

MOST POINTS IN A TEST SERIES

41	Neil Jenkins	South Africa 1997 (3 matches)
38	Gavin Hastings	New Zealand 1993 (3 matches)
35	Tom Kiernan	South Africa 1968 (4 matches)
30	Barry John (Wales)	New Zealand 1971 (4 matches)
28	Gavin Hastings	Australia 1989 (3 matches)
26	Phil Bennett	South Africa 1974 (4 matches)
21	Lewis Jones	Australia 1950 (2 matches)

MOST POINTS IN ALL LIONS MATCHES

274	Andy Irvine
215	Phil Bennett
214	Bob Hiller (England)
188	Barry John
184	Ollie Campbell
167	Gavin Hastings
114	Mike Gibson
112	David Hewitt (Ireland)
111	Tim Stimpson (England)
110	Neil Jenkins
106	Terry Davies (Wales)

LIONS TOUR CAPTAINS

1997	South Africa	Martin Johnson (England)
1993	New Zealand	Gavin Hastings (Scotland)

1989	Australia	Finlay Calder (Scotland)
1983	New Zealand	Ciaran Fitzgerald (Ireland)
1980	South Africa	Bill Beaumont (England)
1977	New Zealand	Phil Bennett (Wales)
1974	South Africa	Willie John McBride (Ireland)
1971	New Zealand	John Dawes (Wales)
1968	South Africa	Tom Kiernan (Ireland)
1966	New Zealand, Australia	Mike Campbell-Lamerton (Scotland)
1962	South Africa	Arthur Smith (Scotland)
1959	New Zealand, Australia	Ronnie Dawson (Ireland)
1955	South Africa	Robin Thompson (Ireland)
1950	New Zealand, Australia	Karl Mullen (Ireland)
1938	South Africa	Sammy Walker (Ireland)
1930	New Zealand, Australia	Doug Prentice (England)
1924	South Africa	Ronald Cove-Smith (England)

LIONS CAPTAINS IN TESTS

Year	Captain	Played	Won	Drawn	Lost
1997	Martin Johnson	3	2	0	1
1993	Gavin Hastings	3	1	0	2
1989	Finlay Calder	3	2	0	1
1983	Ciaran Fitzgerald	4	0	0	4
1980	Bill Beaumont	4	1	0	3
1977	Phil Bennett	4	1	0	3
1974	Willie John McBride	4	3	1	0
1971	John Dawes	4	2	1	1
1968	Tom Kiernan	4	0	1	3
1966	Mike Campbell-Lamerton	4	2	0	2
	David Watkins	2	0	0	2
1962	Arthur Smith	3	0	1	2
	Dickie Jeeps	1	0	0	1
1959	Ronnie Dawson	6	3	0	3
1955	Robin Thompson	3	1	0	2
	Cliff Morgan (Wales)	1	1	0	0
1950	Karl Mullen	3	1	1	1
	Bleddyn Williams	3	1	0	2
1938	Sammy Walker	3	1	0	2
1930	Doug Prentice	2	0	0	2
	Carl Aarvold	3	1	0	2
1924	Ronald Cove-Smith	4	0	1	3

MOST LIONS IN A TEST TEAM

11   England (2nd and 3rd Tests against New Zealand, 1993)
10   Wales (1st Test against Australia, 1950)

FEWEST LIONS IN A TEST TEAM

0   Scotland   Three times (1st, 2nd and 3rd Tests against New Zealand, 1930)
0   England   Four times (2nd and 4th Tests against New Zealand, 1st and 2nd Tests against Australia, all in 1950)
0   Ireland   Twice (2nd and 3rd Tests against Australia, 1989)
1   Wales   Twice (1st Test against South Africa, 1924, 1st Test against New Zealand, 1993)

LIONS TEST RECORD, SERIES BY SERIES

Year	Tour	Played	Won	Drawn	Lost	For-Against
1924	South Africa	4	0	1	3	15-43
1930	New Zealand	4	1	0	3	34-53
1930	Australia	1	0	0	1	5-6
1938	South Africa	3	1	0	2	36-61
1950	New Zealand	4	0	1	3	20-34
1950	Australia	2	2	0	0	43-9
1955	South Africa	4	2	0	2	49-75
1959	New Zealand	4	1	0	3	42-57
1959	Australia	2	2	0	0	41-9
1962	South Africa	4	0	1	3	20-48
1966	New Zealand	4	0	0	4	32-79
1966	Australia	2	2	0	0	42-8
1968	South Africa	4	0	1	3	38-61
1971	New Zealand	4	2	1	1	48-42
1974	South Africa	4	3	1	0	79-34
1977	New Zealand	4	1	0	3	41-54
1980	South Africa	4	1	0	3	68-77
1983	New Zealand	4	0	0	4	26-78
1989	Australia	3	2	0	1	50-60
1993	New Zealand	3	1	0	2	51-57
1997	South Africa	3	2	0	1	59-66
Totals		**71**	**23**	**6**	**42**	**839-1011**

COUNTRY-BY-COUNTRY BREAKDOWN OF EVERY LIONS TEST TEAM

Year	Test	England	Ireland	Scotland	Wales
1924	SA 1st	5	2	7	1
	SA 2nd	3	1	8	3
	SA 3rd	5	2	6	2
	SA 4th	5	1	7	2
1930	NZ 1st	6	4	0	5
	NZ 2nd	6	4	0	5
	NZ 3rd	6	3	0	6
	NZ 4th	6	4	1	4
1930	Aus 1st	7	4	0	4
1938	SA 1st	5	5	1	4
	SA 2nd	4	5	2	4
	SA 3rd	2	7	3	3
1950	NZ 1st	1	4	3	7
	NZ 2nd	0	3	3	9
	NZ 3rd	1	4	1	9
	NZ 4th	0	3	3	9
1950	Aus 1st	0	3	2	10
	Aus 2nd	0	5	2	8
1955	SA 1st	5	3	2	5
	SA 2nd	4	3	2	6
	SA 3rd	5	2	1	7
	SA 4th	4	3	1	7
1959	NZ 1st	3	5	3	4
	NZ 2nd	5	4	1	5
	NZ 3rd	3	4	3	5
	NZ 4th	2	6	2	5
1959	Aus 1st	4	5	3	3
	Aus 2nd	4	5	3	3
1962	SA 1st	4	3	3	5
	SA 2nd	3	2	3	7
	SA 3rd	3	4	2	6
	SA 4th	5	5	2	3
1966	NZ 1st	1	4	3	7
	NZ 2nd	1	4	4	6
	NZ 3rd	1	5	3	6
	NZ 4th	1	5	3	6
1966	Aus 1st	2	4	2	7
	Aus 2nd	1	4	3	7
1968	SA 1st	3	5	2	5
	SA 2nd	5	4	4	2

Year	Test	England	Ireland	Scotland	Wales
	SA 3rd	5	4	4	2
	SA 4th	4	4	5	2
1971	NZ 1st	2	3	1	9
	NZ 2nd	3	3	1	8
	NZ 3rd	2	3	2	8
	NZ 4th	3	3	2	7
1974	SA 1st	2	3	4	6
	SA 2nd	2	3	4	6
	SA 3rd	2	3	4	6
	SA 4th	3	3	3	6
1977	NZ 1st	1	3	2	9
	NZ 2nd	3	1	3	8
	NZ 3rd	3	1	2	9
	NZ 4th	4	1	4	6
1980	SA 1st	5	4	1	5
	SA 2nd	5	2	2	6
	SA 3rd	5	4	2	4
	SA 4th	5	4	2	4
1983	NZ 1st	2	5	2	6
	NZ 2nd	3	6	3	3
	NZ 3rd	4	3	5	3
	NZ 4th	4	5	3	3
1989	Aus 1st	4	1	5	5
	Aus 2nd	8	0	4	3
	Aus 3rd	8	0	4	3
1993	NZ 1st	9	1	4	1
	NZ 2nd	11	1	1	2
	NZ 3rd	11	1	1	2
1997	SA 1st	6	3	3	3
	SA 2nd	7	3	3	2
	SA 3rd	9	2	2	2
Totals		**276**	**236**	**192**	**361**

Figures exclude replacement/substitute appearances.